# THE TRIAL OF ROCK HUDSON

Other books by the same author

*King of Fools*
*The Princess Royal*
*Five for Hollywood*

# THE TRIAL OF ROCK HUDSON

John Parker

SIDGWICK & JACKSON
LONDON

First published in Great Britain in 1990 by
Sidgwick & Jackson Limited
1 Tavistock Chambers, Bloomsbury Way
London WC1A 2SG

All Photographs courtesy of Associated Press.

ISBN 0 283 99969 1

Typeset by Matrix, 21 Russell Street, London WC2

Printed by Mackays of Chatham Ltd, Kent, England

# CONTENTS

# Author's Note

In the preparation of this book, I was given access to the complete transcripts of the trial of Marc Christian versus the estate of Rock Hudson and Mark Miller at the Los Angeles Superior Court and I am indebted to the assistance of official court reporters Michael W. Pettitt and Benjamin Jensen. The transcript amounted to twenty-five volumes of the daily business of the court and ran to 3300 pages for the first hearing alone. Therefore the evidence and submissions have had to be substantially edited though, I believe, fairly and accurately to present a balanced picture of these legally important proceedings. The transcript also gives verbatim notes of conversations on record in the judge's chambers, outside of the jury's hearing, and in preparing this work I have been able to include a great deal of previously unpublished material which provides a complete account of a highly emotive contemporary drama and also a fascinating insight into the day-to-day work and behind-the-scenes activity of a major American courtroom – with all its pressures, passion and tactical manoeuvres.

I feel obliged to warn that the evidence and additional research incorporated in this book contains detailed description of sexual activity and with it, language which can only be described as akin to barrack-room conversation. However, it would have been wrong and dangerous in regard to accuracy to have edited out such descriptions and only in the most extreme cases have I deleted the more offensive passages.

I should acknowledge the assistance of Professor Ronald L. Davis, head of the Oral History Collection on the Performing Arts of the Southern Methodist University of Dallas, Texas, who tape-recorded the last major interview with Rock Hudson in 1983.

This is now in the archives of the university, along with hundreds of other similarly important tapes in the university's collection. I am grateful to Professor Davis and the SMU for allowing me to use extracts from the interview transcript which provided intriguing personal recollections by Hudson at a time when he almost certainly had the AIDS virus in his body, yet had no way of knowing that within two years he would be dead. In that regard, the interview is ironically frank.

My thanks also to the many friends of Rock, whose interviews (obtained in research for my earlier book *Five For Hollywood*) proved invaluable in writing this work. To Maureen Stapleton, in particular, and Edda Tasiemka at the Tasiemka Archive, I record my appreciation.

*John Parker,*
*Northamptonshire*
*May 1989*

# *Prologue*

Reporters and cameramen surged forward as the tall, blond and handsome young man emerged from the Superior Court of California. He was smiling, beaming. Behind, he left faces of desolation and despair but he strode on ignoring them, out into the sunlight where ten thousand and one residents of his adopted city were manoeuvring their automobiles into the bumper-to-bumper, early-evening crush of the freeways and expressways of Los Angeles to head home. The in-car radios were tuned into local stations for the ever-necessary update on traffic flow. Suddenly the music and the chat was interrupted with a news flash: Marc Christian, former lover of Ruck Hudson has won his case. The jury of twelve – seven women and five men – had awarded him damages that had made him an instant multi-millionaire.

And so had ended one of the most sensational trials involving a Hollywood star in recent memory; a trial which, with its content of detailed sexual description and important implications for AIDS sufferers and their partners, remained in the headlines for seven weeks and provided daily, a highly graphic account of a story that no studio scriptwriter could have imagined or dared to write.

Marc Christian, who had known Hudson for just three years before the star died from AIDS on 2 October 1985, walked from that courtroom with his award for damages in a lawsuit which claimed that Hudson had deliberately and outrageously failed to inform Christian that he had AIDS; that he had encouraged his secretary Mark Miller to join the conspiracy to prevent Christian from finding out; and that he irresponsibly continued to have high-risk sex with his companion, even after AIDS was diagnosed. In a case with unprecedented legal implications, Christian came out to say he had won a battle not just for himself, but for partners of AIDS sufferers (and presumably any other serious disease) the world over.

But it was much more than that. To prove such claims, the evidence to be presented was – by the very nature of Hudson's involvement with Marc Christian and others – at times disturbing and often lurid. From the mouths of the opposing principals and their supporting witnesses came tumbling the stories and allegations which would finally decimate the reputation of one of the most idolized movie stars of the last half-century who, in his day, had risen to number one in the world ratings of male actors. They were allegations that he had himself fought to keep hidden for thirty-five years and now here they were, revealed in a public courtroom: a story of one man's love for another; the reading of intimate letters he had written; and then, descending on into the seedy, there were claims that he regularly attended parties – even when he knew he had AIDS – at which young boys served food wearing only their underwear.

That he was a predatory homosexual was a secret shared and kept by his Hollywood friends; even the local press and showbusiness writers had eventually helped to protect him from the extravagances of some of their mass-market tabloid colleagues who continually sought to expose a true double-life.

It was,therefore, with unspeakable sadness that Elizabeth Taylor, Juliet Prowse, Carol Burnett, Maureen Stapleton, Roddy McDowell, Nancy and Ronald Reagan and so many of his other showbusiness friends viewed the unfolding drama of the trial which opened beneath the glare of television camera lights and a press corps that, in times past, would have welcomed him as he walked the red carpet to some glitzy Hollywood première.

Rock himself had been dead for three years and three months when the squabble over his money and the actions of himself and Mark Miller during those last desperate and traumatic days of his life became a very public and hostile debate over his morality – aired on countless television programmes and in yards of newspaper column inches. The fact that he was no longer there to defend himself hardly seemed to matter as the protagonists lined up for battle. In truth, it was Rock Hudson who was on trial and even Robert Mills, counsel for the defence of the estate of Rock Hudson, ironically kept referring to 'my client' as if he were sitting in the empty chair next to him. In the eyes of some of Rock's friends, it was a blessing that he had not lived to face this ordeal – to witness the clinical dissection of his life and career and to watch it torn to shreds in the application of the due process of law.

They had known the *other* Rock Hudson: caring, gentle and generous to a fault, who would help anyone in distress; a man who had reached the pinnacle of his chosen profession – albeit with ample critics – with sixty-four feature films to his credit; who, because of his sensitivity could be wracked by nerves and insecurity when playing his part; an actor who, like many of his peers, was continually searching for the great role, the one that would make him famous and adored again.

As his friend, actress Maureen Stapleton told me: 'Of course, we all knew he was homosexual and had been for years. Who the hell cares? I didn't. Elizabeth certainly didn't and in this day and age I don't think most of his fans would either. But in Hollywood, these things have to stay hidden and it would have been a disaster for him if it had leaked out when he was making his way along the road; no doubt about that. This is a hard and harsh business and as we all know, there have been many casualties for one reason or another. That apart, we loved him; everybody did. He was a sweet and kind man and he'd give you a party at the drop of a hat. So perhaps he wasn't the greatest actor since sliced bread but he was one hell of a professional.'

Maureen and the rest also knew that he was a very lonely person and that, almost since his arrival in Hollywood, he had maintained a secret private life of dangerous liaisons. To his millions of fans whose devotion had put him on the star pedestal, he was never anything but the all-American, clean-cut he-male who, in his heyday, simply had to smile to make any woman swoon.

For years, the fan mail continued to pour in; sometimes there were 2000 letters or more each week and if any hint of his true sexual preferences did escape, it did not appear to affect his star status. He loved women's company, but not in bed – as Elizabeth Taylor discovered when she first worked with him in *Giant*, and throughout their lifelong friendship. She could easily have had an affair with Rock (at the time her marriage to Michael Wilding was crumbling) and indeed the gossips suggested that a loving relationship had developed between them. But as Elizabeth herself later admitted, she quickly came to the conclusion that no woman could, as she so aptly put it, 'light his fire'. No woman ever did.

Rock's metabolism was that of the true homosexual; from his

early youth he had no serious sexual involvement with a member of the opposite sex, except for one brief and phoney marriage. Yet the handsome, imposing features which made him so alluring to women gave him a double-edged advantage: he could hide behind that mask of machismo to avoid the gossips and conversely, he could use it and his fame to attract a never-ending supply of lovers.

Accepting that homosexuality – and bisexuality, for that matter – is a way of life for so many men, no one in the eighties could attack him for having a preference with which he was presumably born. Homosexuality is as old as mankind and Hudson was a member of a rather large minority: 1988 statistical surveys showed that there were an estimated ten million male gays in America and, like Hudson, most remained in the closet. But he was there at the centre of it when the gay revolution began to take hold in the late 1960s and as it went on to encompass more adventurous sexual activity, he was a frequent, though quiet participant. There was one big difference between Hudson and the gay activists who sought to have their status redefined and be seen as acceptable members of society: he could never be anything other than a covert homosexual because revealing the truth would have ruined him in Hollywood.

He would visit gay areas, like Christopher Street in New York and Castro Street in San Francisco; he would go to gay bars and for years he had companions quietly living at his house. Unfortunately, as with some of the more disreputable areas of heterosexual opportunity, his search for partners and new sexual experiences led him towards the low-life regions and questionable activities as he cruised the gay bars or frequented some of the bath-houses, gyms and massage establishments which were a front for gay pick-ups in many cities of the world. He visited the bath-houses regularly and some were outlandishly open about their purpose. There is no better description of them than in Dennis Altman's book *Homosexual Oppression and Liberation*: 'They resemble nothing so much as giant whorehouses in which everyone is a customer; clad in only white towels men prowl the hallways groping each other in furtive search for instant sex, making it in small, dark cubicles on low, hard, come-stained beds. Disgusting? – yes perhaps. Yet lasting friendships are quite commonplace . . . and to this extent the whorehouse analogy is not fully accurate.'

In an examination of these establishments, they were perhaps no worse – and often a lot better – than some of the brothels and red-light areas in which lonely and lustful heterosexual men, who included some of his famous Hollywood colleagues, sought their pleasures. But even in an alleged liberal society, the revelation of male sexual acts is viewed as intolerable and repugnant because to the heterosexual population the activities of homosexuals still seem unnatural.

The thought of two muscular, strong and totally ineffeminate six-foot males – as were Hudson and Christian – kissing and cuddling and writing down their gentle words expressing love for each other could be abhorrent to 'straights'. To further imagine their indulgence in anal and oral sex would, for many, produce a feeling bordering on revulsion. The arrival of AIDS made the public – primarily the non-homosexual community – even more hostile and critical of these 'unnatural acts' and it was easy to see why so many believed God had displayed his wrath by visiting a plague upon male gays. Hudson came down with the virus at a time when society was casting stones upon the victims. He had unquestionably had many lovers since AIDS first became implanted in his body for he was a vigorous pursuer. When he died, the shock waves of his story would reverberate for many months to come; his female fans cried, their husbands were disgusted, the tabloid voyeurs had a field day, and the extremists who had turned scathingly upon the gay population in the wake of AIDS looked on with glee as each new instalment of the story was revealed. To them, Rock Hudson was a star example of decadence in their persecution of homosexuals.

It was against this background of frenetic concern and massive publicity over AIDS that Marc Christian began his lawsuit to claim damages from Hudson's estate and it was clear from the outset that the trial was not just about money. The gay community was going on trial; the sufferers of AIDS were being challenged over their responsibility to their partners and indeed the rest of the community; anyone of the extreme view that was being canvassed in the early days of AIDS – that those with the virus should be locked away in isolation units – would find ample evidence of support as the actions of Rock Hudson became known.

It was a case, said Christian's lawyer, Harold Rhoden, that would reveal the bigotry against homosexuals in society and he likened his task to representing a Jewish client before a jury in Berlin in 1939. Hudson, Christian and those who would be called to give evidence were members of a group that society referred to variously and insultingly as fags, fairies, fruits and queers; even the selection of a typical jury, picked at random, who did not share this bigotry, was in itself an almost impossible task.

They could not appreciate that a homosexual had the same urges for fulfilment with a man as a heterosexual male had for a woman. That, as Rhoden saw it, was the first hurdle he had to overcome to prove his case. The second was perhaps even more important: how could a man who apparently had not contracted the virus himself claim damages?

In attempting to prove their case, counsel would have to look at the study of AIDS itself and at the 'time bomb' syndrome that still baffles specialists of the disease today. The prospect that the virus could lurk undetected and hidden in bone marrow or bodily cells to become activated at some future date, perhaps seven, ten or even fifteen years hence, was a fear that Christian – and other partners of AIDS sufferers – would have to endure.

The barrage of specialist medical evidence focused not on whether Christian had AIDS but on the fear of whether he would get it. Seven tests since the day it was publicly announced that Hudson was dying had proved negative. Doctors would be called to show that eight years of research since the virus was first identified had still failed to discover the cause of the very reality of the situation: that a man whose tests had proved negative could still have the virus, and die. Quoted cases proved it.

Even as the trial was being arranged, new figures compiled by the office of the US Surgeon-General estimated that by 1991, 270,000 Americans would have full-blown AIDS and almost 200,000 would have died from it. These figures are for America alone and are regardless of the toll in every other country in the world, in particular Africa where it is rampant. Further projections estimated that almost 1,400,000 people in the United States of America were infected with the virus, and did not know it. That was the scale of the AIDS problem – and still is. The time-bomb analogy is a true one, and it is waiting to explode.

Rock Hudson knew that he had AIDS in June 1984. For reasons best known to himself, whether it was because of the fear of blackmail, the exposure of his homosexual life or that his career would finally collapse in ruins, he decided to keep his illness secret and continued to do so for a year. These were the issues that would be at the heart of the trial itself; issues which, because of the mystery of AIDS and the nature of the explicit evidence, would test the jury in a way that no other body of twelve men and women, good and true, had ever been tested in the past.

Christian's counsel would attempt to prove the incredibilities: mainly that by refusing to tell the truth, Hudson could have gone on to infect and contaminate many many more people through the progression of sexual contacts between Hudson and Christian, and Christian with others, or through Hudson's own promiscuity. This type of irresponsibility, as many saw it, was one of the root causes of the spread of AIDS in the early years.

His cold-blooded refusal to tell Christian of his affliction, and his famous love scene with his friend – actress Linda Evans – on the television series, 'Dynasty', in which he proceeded to kiss her on the lips in full knowledge of the fact that he had AIDS and open sores on the inside of his mouth, were the sensational examples of how he put others at risk to save his own embarrassment. These aspects damaged him more than anything else and his reputation was put through the shredding machine by witnesses in the Christian lawsuit and the feverish media reports.

Perhaps, in the final analysis, he had only himself to blame. In the story that emerged from seven weeks of trial evidence, that once-glistening star, whose rise to fame from the obscurity of a mid-western town to movieland greatness – the epitome of the great American dream – had fallen from the heavens, tarnished and blackened. . . .

# CHAPTER ONE

# The Early Years

To understand the reasoning behind Rock Hudson's insistence on keeping his deadly secret from his lover and even his closest friends, we must go back into the past – to the history of his long and hard climb to fame and to the formation of a career which meant so much to him. His career and his image were his life and he was obsessively protective of them. Once tasted, the adulation of millions becomes, to every actor of his kind, an indispensible part of his existence; like an addiction to a deadly drug it is hated and feared on the one hand, yet craved for on the other.

He was forever searching for the next great role and rejection by his public was a constant fear. Certainly, nothing was so clear in his personal reminiscences of his life than the impression of a man continually seeking elusive magic that would project him onto celluloid as a master of his ambition and his art – acting.

It began for him when he was eight years old. He saw a photograph of Jackie Cooper – a child star and also eight years old – with a new bicycle. Roy Sherer Junior, as he was known by his given name, wanted a bicycle so he thought to himself, 'I'm going to become an actor. That way I can get a new bike.' It was a silly childhood dream that remained with him.

Fifty years later on 24 August 1983, Rock Hudson was recalling these memories which flooded back with ease as he lounged in a white sofa in his superb, $5-million home which he called The Castle, on a hill overlooking Beverly Hills – a house which had been his anchor for so many years. He was talking frankly into a tape-recorder microphone for what would be the last major interview of his life and his words would be saved for posterity. (The recording now forms part of the Oral History Collection on

1

the Performing Arts at the Southern Methodist University in Dallas, Texas.)

As he spoke on that glorious summer's day in Los Angeles, with the sunshine beaming through the large, open windows of a house which had seen many happy times and some of the great old-style, star-studded Hollywood parties, Hudson was relaxed and at ease, and the warm smile that had captured a million hearts shone through. He was The Movie Star, which was how his staff referred to him behind his back; faded perhaps, he still had that indefinable aura that took him to the top. On that day, too, he may well have already had the AIDS virus in his body; he did not know then -- no one knew -- that his life was in its final chapter.

Born on 17 November 1925, in Winnetka, Illinois, the boy Rock was brought up in poverty. His father Roy Sherer Senior, had deserted the family, leaving his wife Katherine, a tall, cheerful woman, to bring up their only son, Roy Junior, as best she could. She was the dominant character in his early life, and after the interest he had shown in Jackie Cooper, she encouraged her son's fascination with the movies, even to the point of having him read the dialogue of the latest films printed in the fan magazines to her.

Katherine married Wallace Fitzgerald when the boy was eight, but the relationship with his stepfather was not a happy one. He used to beat Rock and take away all of his toys when he spoke of film stars. So Rock was on his own with his ambitions and by the time he was ten, he was delivering groceries and cleaning chickens for a local butcher to earn money to go to the movies. Rock recalled: 'What I'm saying is that I always wanted to be an actor. It has always hypnotized me. I saw every film I could; when *The Hurricane* came out which was Jon Hall and Dorothy Lamour's first movie, around 1936 – when I'm eleven years old – Jon Hall did a swan dive from a crow's nest into the lagoon and swam to Dorothy Lamour. And as a kid, I was always a diver. So that clinches it, doesn't it. I've got to go to Tahiti . . . I've got to become an actor. The mentality, even at that age, counts. Oddly enough, a few years back we were out skin-diving off Catalina with some friends of mine, a couple of stunt men. And it turns out that this stunt man was the guy who did the dive. It wasn't Jon Hall at all. . . . '

The marriage of Rock's mother to Wallace Fitzgerald was punctuated by unpleasantness and by the time Rock was fifteen, his mother had married, divorced and remarried the same man. During the intervening years, when they were on their own, she took a job as a housekeeper for a wealthy family. She and her son had to share a bed in the servant's quarters. Katherine was, as Rock put it, his mother, his father and his big sister, rolled into one; in other words, she was the major influence on his life. And in those days, he was making no headway at all towards his career goals. He said: 'Back in a small town, I could never freely say, "I'm going to be an actor when I grow up" because that's sissy stuff. You know, they'd say [because of his height], "Don't bother with that; you ought to be a policeman or a fireman." So I never said anything. I just kept my mouth shut. Nor did I enter a drama society or anything like that. I had to work all the time; I had to make a living for myself.'

At eighteen, he joined the Navy for two-and-a-half uneventful years of the war serving as a mechanic. In the Navy he was known as Fitz, because he was then using his stepfather's name. When he came home to be mustered in 1946, he sailed under the Californian Golden Gate Bridge to the strains of Doris Day, singing 'Sentimental Journey'. In a little more than ten years he would be co-starring with her in the film that would make them both a fortune. Back home in Winnetka, life was dull. The only job he could get was that of a piano remover and the call of ambition and a better life forced him to make a decision: it was either New York and the theatre or Los Angeles and films. He chose the latter. There, at least, he knew one person – his father Roy was living in the suburbs and could provide him with a home. He thought he would have greater prospects of making himself 'available for discovery' in Los Angeles.

He also had the initial security of a job: his father got him fixed up as a vacuum-cleaner salesman, although it lasted only three weeks because he failed to sell a single machine. Nor was the reunion with his long-lost father a success; he had to be away and on his own. He tried to get into the University College of Los Angeles but with everyone wanting to enrol after the war, UCLA raised its entrance standards to B+, and most of Rock's fell well short of that requirement; he was a C− or D+ student and no one wanted to know.

At the time, fan magazines – which sold millions of copies a week – were full of stories about young actors who had been snatched off the streets to become instant stars so he began hanging around studio gates, waiting for some producer or director to spot him. It

3

was all 'crap', he admitted, but at the time he was naïve enough to believe that the stories of overnight discoveries were true and while he waited for that moment to arrive, he drove trucks to provide himself with a meagre income.

He found Los Angeles a difficult town. Although it was the mecca for every teenage girl or boy who, likewise, wanted to make it big in the movies, he was shy, awkward, stammered badly, and found it difficult to make friends. Already a year had gone by and he had got nowhere. Rock said: 'I just didn't get to know anybody . . . then I met a guy who was the older brother of a kid I was overseas with. He was a radio producer and I talked to him a little bit and then edged in sneakily that I would like to become an actor. He began inviting me down to his place at Long Beach and we became the best of friends. Anyway, he suggested I get some pictures taken. Now, I'm a mid-western hick, please understand, not knowing anything at all, except to stand up straight, keep your teeth brushed and all that crap. He suggested getting some pictures taken – a little investment – which I did.'

It cost him $65 for 200 prints and he mailed them off to every studio in Hollywood and to as many directors and producers as he could. The response was nil, not a single call. However, he heard that the David O. Selznick studio was casting for a picture and got through the security gates to leave one of his photographs with a reception clerk. It was the turning point, one of those fatalistic moments in life that can mean so much and bring so many repercussions. Rock's portrait and details were picked up by Henry Willson, an agent who once handled Lana Turner and Joan Fontaine, who was currently working as a talent scout for the Selznick studios.

It was a time of great activity in Hollywood. Television was in its infancy and the cinema industry ruled the roost in the provision of entertainment for the burgeoning post-war affluent society. Millions passed through the box offices every week and the big stars could expect thousands of fan letters every single day. The newspapers and magazines were full of film gossip and stories of the stars, churned out by the self-publicising, adulation-inspiring studio system which enveloped the inhabitants of Hollywood in a curious mixture of great success and dismal despair. In the post-war years, as the great male stars of the thirties returned from service with grey-tinged temples, new male leads were in short supply. Rock Hudson was not alone in believing that there

4

might just be a place for him, even a tiny part of what was still the greatest form of mass entertainment available.

Henry Willson, a portly, balding man in his early forties and a rampant homosexual, studied Hudson's photograph and decided he liked the look of him. He called him in for an audition. After the first interview he would say that he saw in Hudson a face that could 'flip a lot of women' (not to mention himself). Yes, the young man was gangly, gawky, could hardly speak through shyness, had a strong mid-western drawl, a twisted tooth and was round-shouldered. 'I knew I could change all of that,' said Willson, 'and I decided to offer him a contract there and then.'

Whether Willson was more attracted to his protégé for his acting possibilities or by the prospect of getting him into bed was never clear, but Rock himself could not have known that he was about to sign with a man who, in this town of casting-couch horror stories, was one of the most infamous exploiters of young talent – a man who lacked any kind of moral code and would stoop to quite despicable deeds in his lust for sex and money. Rock was the young innocent: 'When I went to see him, I was so nervous that I ran into a door. Klutz! I don't exaggerate that. But Henry seemed to like my honesty when I said "I have no training" and he said "You're the only one who's ever told me that" . . . and he took me on as a client. That's how it all started.'

When Selznick closed his studio, Willson resumed his role as an agent and soon acquired a reputation as a star maker who was particularly famous for the names he dreamed up for his stars: Roy Fitzgerald became Rock Hudson; Merle Johnson became Troy Donahue; Francis Durgin became Rory Calhoun; and Art Gelien became Tab Hunter. He was always surrounded by young hopefuls and in one contemporary magazine interview, he boasted that young men and women arriving in Hollywood often sought him out: 'I get thousands of letters and phone calls. I'm what you might call a Salvation Army worker at heart and the kids in this business know it and they come to me.'

Without a doubt, that was something of an insult to the Salvation Army. Willson's claims were as extravagant as they were false. While he did become a star finder and eventually boasted a wall full of portraits of the actors he had helped on the road to fame and fortune, he had a darker side to his apparently successful career as a Hollywood agent. True, he had good contacts and friends in high places, but attractive young men became caught in his web

5

of deceit and were forced into deviant sexual activities which were perhaps best summed up by his secretary and personal assistant Phyllis Gates (who was to become the one and only Mrs Rock Hudson): 'He had an incredible ability to manipulate clients and customers . . . I began to see a pattern in Henry's dealings with his young male hopefuls. When he found a young man who was remarkably handsome though not visibly talented, Henry filled him with dreams of stardom . . . he made furtive attempts for studio auditions but when there was no interest, the young man would become Henry's gofer.' But a worse fate awaited others as Willson pursued his business clients. He used them sexually, providing young men or women for influential producers or young studs for the wives. His pimping spawned blackmail and he would use it to promote Hudson.

Rock himself was seduced by Willson almost immediately; undoubtedly his promise of stardom led Hudson into a dubious relationship. For almost a year, the agent took his new young client around Hollywood, introducing him to important people, and arranging for his name to appear in the influential Louella Parsons column. Rock saw it as a vital preparation period: 'Something within this thick mid-western hick stupidity of mine told me that if you are going to do something, do it. And do it the best you can. I knew that, at least.'

Willson was spending more money and energy preparing Rock for the big break into films than he had ever done for any of his clients, and towards the end of 1948 he managed to persuade Warner Brothers director Raoul Walsh to give him a test. 'I had the interview,' said Rock, 'and Walsh put me in a film (*Fighter Squadron*) in what they call a running bit part. That is to say, an extra who is given lines. And I worked for five weeks. I got $175 a week. Boy, oh boy, was I rich! Rich! Walsh said it would serve as a form of screen test to see what I sounded like, what I looked like, how I carry myself. Which is what happened.'

Unfortunately, Rock was not a smash hit. He had to say one line: 'Pretty soon, you are going to have to get a bigger blackboard,' and he fluffed it thirty-eight times. He did not make another picture for a year, but Walsh put him under personal contract while he and Willson continued to invest their own money on him; they sent him to acting lessons, elocution lessons, dance lessons – tap and ballet – horseback riding, and arranged special tuition to overcome his appalling shyness. He did a few more screen tests but never got a part; one for 20th Century-Fox was so bad that the studio acting school later used the tape to illustrate how *not* to act.

For a time, Walsh had to use Hudson for personal jobs, such as painting his house, chauffeuring and gardening, while continuing to finance Hudson's tuition and give him his own brand of acting lessons. Rock said: 'He took a liking to me for some reason; he was a tough, old timer who had made some wonderful films and he had a terrific way of directing me. I was busy with acting lessons and learning the techniques, which was a lot of junk, and he would say "Don't bother with that, just do it", and his attitude made it all so simple in my head.' The breakthrough came when Rock took a screen test for Universal-International and was offered a five-year contract in 1949. 'It was a working studio,' Rock said. 'They made little pictures with little investment and little profit. It was a fun place.' William Goetz, head of International until it merged with Universal, had taken over as head of the new joint studio and like his father-in-law, Louis B. Mayer, head of Metro-Goldwyn-Mayer, he set out to create a stable of young stars for tomorrow. Willson and Walsh sold him Rock's contract for $9000 which was the amount they calculated they had spent thus far training their boy. Soon Hudson found himself alongside other new Universal names like Jeff Chandler, Tony Curtis, Piper Laurie and Barbara Rush, with a guaranteed salary of $125 a week. 'It was a wonderful studio,' said Rock. 'You knew everybody by their first names; you never locked doors and everybody was a friend. Us kids under contract used to put on a Christmas show for all the employees and their kids and that was great fun. That doesn't happen any more. Now you work until 8 o'clock on Christmas Eve night – you know, the mighty buck. But gradually, Universal became an A studio, they had the mentality of not putting too much money in and not expecting too much profit and then a couple of blockbusters hit and they really went ahead.'

In those early days at Universal, Rock spent long and hard hours in the studio training system, learning to act and being trained in all the other arts that would extend his talents. The studio prepared him for work which would initially be in their renowned, low-budget costume or western movies and Rock would be forever dressing up – a cowboy one day, an Indian or a swashbuckling sword fighter the next. 'It was the best training any actor could have,' said Rock. 'But all that's gone now; goodness knows how the kids today get started.'

The months rolled by and the new Rock Hudson began to evolve, slowly but positively, towards that curious amalgamation of his qualities that turned him into All-American beefcake with an appealing innocence. One Hollywood veteran who saw him described him as: 'a wholesome boy who doesn't perspire, has no pimples, smells of milk and has the appeal of cleanliness and respectability – this boy is pure.'

Off the Universal lot, other aspects of his life were developing which would, in the end, destroy that image and the man himself. Henry Willson had become extremely possessive over his rising young actor and whenever he had free time, he would telephone Rock or visit him at the studio to take him to lunch or to arrange to meet him in the evening. On occasions, Rock even tried to hide from him; he felt Willson was dominating his life and he preferred to spend his off-duty time with his friends, few that they were. To find new friends, he would go into bars alone and it came as a relief to him to find two other like-minded young men on whom he would come to rely heavily. Mark Miller and George Nader were to become his closest friends and confidants. Miller, a year older than Rock, was a singer who lived with Nader, an actor five years his senior, in a house in Studio City. Rock would visit often, and they enjoyed the same recreational pursuits and beliefs, although Miller has always insisted that neither he nor Nader were involved with Rock sexually.

Rock was never short of partners whenever he could spare the time to seek them out and that alone had become a problem: the studio kept him so busy that he hardly had a moment to himself. It was the pattern of life for all young hopefuls contracted into the Hollywood studio system.

They all got their chances to act even if they were only in a one-line part; their turns to bat came frequently, particularly in the smaller studios like Universal whose pool of actors was smaller than most. In a single year from the end of 1949, Hudson was cast in seven films. Among them were: *One Way Street* with James Mason and Dan Duryea (Rock played a truck driver); *Winchester 73* starring James Stewart (Rock was a background Indian; Tony Curtis also had a minor role); *Peggy* starring Diana Lynn and Charles Coburn (Rock in a bit part had to kiss Diana, but was so nervous he missed her mouth at the first attempt); and *Shakedown* with Howard Duff and Brian Donlevy. 'It was good training,' he said, 'but I kept wishing I could get a better part. I was playing chauffeur, doorman, taxi-driver ... whatever. I hated it. One line bits. But the crews [on set] helped you in those days. I remember playing a nightclub doorman to Howard Duff: "Evening Mr So and So" and opened the door and he goes in and that's the end of the scene for me. That was all I had to do. The director told me where to stand and then out came an electrician and he said, "If you stand over six inches to your right, you get a better light." I said, "Will the director let me?" and he said, "Move over there." So I got my spot and a better light. These guys were terrific.'

Gradually, the parts got bigger and in 1952, when he had appeared in fourteen films, he got his name in lights when he was cast alongside James Stewart and Arthur Kennedy in another western, *Bend of the River*. When the film was premièred, a small crowd of fans had gathered outside the cinema shouting 'We want Rock'. Henry Willson had placed some cheerleaders in the audience; the next day Rock was ecstatic. He had made it, he thought, and even wandered by the cinema and stood outside the entrance, next to his picture displayed in the 'stills' gallery, hoping to be recognized. No one gave him a second glance.

His first top-billing role came in a piece of Universal nonsense called *Has Anybody Seen My Gal?*, co-starring Piper Laurie and Charles Coburn. (James Dean had a one-liner bit part.) He was being noticed. Other major roles, albeit in costume dramas and westerns, brought him to the attention of the movie magazines and by 1953 he was beginning to acquire the trappings of minor stardom. He moved into a larger apartment, bought himself a new yellow convertible, in which he was heavily photographed for the movie magazines, and could afford to live in relative comfort. Into his household also, came a young man named Jack whom he had met at a dinner party at Mark and George's house; he became Rock's first live-in male partner who adopted the role of wife. He played housekeeper while Rock went out to work and, like many wives, he got bored and started ringing the studio in the evening to inquire if Rock was coming home yet. The studio people began to get worried – had a hint of gossip leaked out over Rock's home-life arrangement, all that he and the studio had worked for to date would have been for nought. The publicity machine had already swung its weight behind their new star in a major way and, according to them, he was receiving huge quantities of fan mail and 150 proposals of marriage a week.

As his fame grew, he was lined up for endless photographic

sessions which displayed his sexuality as a contender for the Number One Hollywood Beefcake and soon the fan magazines were asking on behalf of their devoted female readers: 'When is bachelor boy Rock going to choose a bride?' Willson and the studio provided him with a stream of attractive young starlets to be displayed and photographed on his arm at parties and Hollywood premières, while at home he and Jack continued their secret co-habitation.

Two pictures released in 1954 put Rock in the major league, and both were brought in by the highly successful Universal partnership of producer Ross Hunter and director Douglas Sirk. In the first, *Taza, Son of Cochise*, Hudson was cast as a young Indian chief and had to overcome some appalling dialogue – with words like Unga bunga wunga – while courting his co-star, the dusky Barbara Bush. The movie was a low-budget Universal 'B' movie posing as a main feature because it was shot in 3-D colour and whilst it did nothing to improve his standing as an actor, his performance as Taza gave him starring-role exposure.

It was a total contrast to his next film, again for the Hunter-Sirk team: he was to play his first romantic lead, and a dramatic role that offered him more scope than anything he had done to date. The film was *Magnificent Obsession*, a remake of the thirties success that made Robert Taylor a star in the role of a playboy who blinds a widow, reforms, goes to medical school, falls in love with her and saves her sight.

It was an unlikely tale, with Ronald Reagan's first wife Jane Wyman co-starring, but Rock was in his element. He explained: 'I'm proud to say that Douglas Sirk took me under his wing. He was like an ol' dad to me and with *Magnificent Obsession* he gave me my first solid dramatic role where I had no physicality to rely on. Now I give the studio credit, they had put me in all those westerns and Indian pictures to get some training, where if my scenes weren't all that good dramatically, it didn't matter that much. And so that was wonderful experience, and by the time *Magnificent Obsession* came around I was ready. In fact, I had been signed for it four years earlier. They were waiting for me to develop. But then two weeks before shooting began, I almost blew it . . . I broke my collarbone.'

That weekend, Rock and Jack had gone surfing at Laguna Beach with an inner tube; Hudson was dashed against some rocks and was knocked unconscious. Jack summoned an ambulance and then telephoned the studio and Willson, and furious words came from both sources. On the way to hospital, Rock was weeping: 'I'm gonna lose the part, I'm gonna lose it.' Rock knew that there were certain people at Universal who wanted him off the picture, but a number of people went in to bat for him. One of them had more than the interests of Universal at heart. Willson knew that Rock had had an affair with the executive, and telephoned him to call in a favour. Rock stayed on *Magnificent Obsession* and began filming with his shoulder still strapped in a figure-eight bandage.

Willson's prophecy that *Magnificent Obsession* would take him into a new arena and higher esteem was undoubtedly true and the film had a strange effect on Hudson when he went to see it in the studio viewing room while the theme music was being set to the movie. 'A full symphony orchestra was playing "Beethoven's Ninth",' he recalled, 'and there I am up on the screen. Well, it was overwhelming. I just couldn't stop crying. Just a blithering idiot, as was everybody else. Ross was crying, everybody was crying, because that's wonderful music. You say a line or two, like "Oh yes, my darling I love you" and when they put music to it, the words become so much more important and stronger. It can be overwhelming, especially the first time of seeing it.'

Rock Hudson had made it and at his first major première they rolled out the red carpet, and trained the arc-lamps upon him as he walked up to the entrance of the cinema surrounded by the cheering crowds, radio microphones and newsreel cameras that were attendant at every major Hollywood première. As he walked through the crowd, someone yelled: 'faggot'. It was an unimportant incident, perhaps, but one which underlined the worry of Hudson, his agent and the studio. Following reviews of *Magnificent Obsession*, he shot to number three in a national magazine ratings poll of top male actors. Universal gave him his own monogrammed dressing room, a new wardrobe of clothes and a salary increase. The publicity people began pumping out fanciful stories about their new macho-man who had the physique and appearance of the total he-man and major magazines featured him in photographic spreads.

Bubbling below the surface, however, was the fear that Rock's private life would be revealed. It was of constant concern to Willson who himself had become wealthy with Rock's success, and he was forever visualizing salacious headlines. He had good reason. The scurrilous scandal sheet, *Confidential*, was already digging into

11

Rock's past. In 1954, *Confidential* was at the peak of its circulation, which had been built up by running sensational stories about the famous. It carried a motto under its title declaring: 'We tell the facts and name the names', and was started in 1952 by its publisher Robert Harrison when he noticed how the public had been riveted by the televised hearings of a Senate committee investigation into vice, prostitution and organized crime. Lurid headlines and current scandals ensured it an avid readership.

Harrison became interested in the Hudson story after one of Universal's executives, who had no time for Rock, leaked news of Jack's presence in the Hudson household. It was a happy coincidence that shortly after the release of *Magnificent Obsession*, Rock was sent away to Europe with his co-star Barbara Rush to begin filming *Captain Lightfoot* and Willson was sure that the absence would quell *Confidential*'s efforts to link Hudson with another man.

While he was away, however, Willson had trouble with Jack. He had thrown a couple of loud parties at Hudson's house and had been seen around Hollywood in the star's highly recognizable yellow convertible. Phyllis Gates was enlisted to keep Jack out of sight by accompanying him on a trip to the mid-west but even she could not handle the situation. Finally Willson called Rock in Europe and said: 'This guy's going to blow it for you. The studio's getting very jumpy.' Hudson telephoned Jack himself and had a blazing row. He called Henry back and said: 'Get him out.' Willson stopped the cheques he was paying to Jack each week and ordered him to leave the house. He threatened violence if Jack did not comply and every trace of Jack's existence was eliminated by the time Rock arrived home. *Confidential*'s interest did not subside.

In Europe Rock had been treated like American movieland royalty; he was surprised at the reception he had received, and enjoyed the fact that his fame had spread worldwide. Louella Parsons, noting that Rock was coming up to thirty, asked, 'Will he put his career ahead of matrimony?' and inferences about his homosexuality were being written. *Confidential* came back to worry them, offering Rock's former lover $10,000 to tell his story. It never appeared. Years later, speculation over how exactly the story was killed suggested that Willson had hired a gangster to threaten *Confidential*'s owner. Anything was possible with Willson but the more likely version was that he eliminated the threat of Rock's exposure by risking the name of another of his clients whose reputation he was apparently willing to jeopardize to save the reputation and career of his biggest name.

As the interest in Hudson of the popular magazines intensified, Willson became increasingly worried that Rock's private involvements – and subsequently his own – might be exposed. It was undoubtedly at this time that Willson turned his devious mind to thoughts of ending the speculation once and for all. The best way, he said, was marriage and thus all the headlines of innuendo about Hudson's bachelor status would cease. In Hollywood at that time marriage also had another big plus: it brought lots of added publicity with the matrimonial bliss of the stars being portrayed in the media. It would also serve the purpose of dispelling the less palatable rumours. Convenience marriages were nothing new in Hollywood but there was simply no one on the horizon as a bride. Hudson had women friends; Betty Abbott, niece of Bud Abbott, was perhaps the closest to him and might well have married him if he had asked. He was also often in the company of other starlets like Marilyn Maxwell and Lori Anderson and there was talk of 'hot romances' in the gossip columns. But nothing came of them: Hudson's women were usually decorative; they were there to be seen on his arm, and to be photographed with at important Hollywood events. In all the speculation surrounding his marital intent, few could have tipped the girl who was to become Mrs Rock Hudson.

She could be found in Willson's own office. She was Phyllis Gates, Willson's secretary and later personal assistant, a hard-working girl who got on with her job, naïvely unaware that her boss had selected her for a very important role. In the beginning, to say that he was arranging a marriage might well have been an overstatement. But as the 'romance' took its course, he appeared to have a hand in each stage of the relationship. They had met fleetingly in the past during Hudson's visits to the office. A more determined liaison came as a result of a dinner date, arranged by Willson himself, at Frascati's, the famed Hollywood restaurant. He invited Phyllis and Rock came too. If Willson was playing cupid, albeit with a poisoned arrow, he would ultimately succeed. Soon, Rock was dating Phyllis regularly and it seems hardly credible that he was not party to Willson's plot to get him married off.

The studio bosses would not be displeased with such a development either. By the end of 1954, Willson's star had risen substantially after the worldwide release of *Magnificent Obsession*. The gamble and expense that had gone into his training and projection, all the years of wearing brown make-up and dressing up in assorted costumes, had paid off. Hudson had become a romantic idol and Universal, who had already increased his lowly salary from $400 a week to $1000, hiked it up again by another $250; in their terms, he was a 'hot property'.

Rock was enjoying life at last. He had become part of Hollywood, a member of the elitist group of stars whose party invitations signalled arrival. He was more confident in his work than he had ever been, encouraged by Willson's continued morale-boosting praise. According to him, Rock had taken over from Clark Gable as Hollywood's most sought-after male lead. Willson was exaggerating as usual but it was a fact that important producers were beginning to cast an eye in Rock's direction. Several approaches were made to Universal for loan-out deals with other studios but they wanted to keep their new star to themselves.

Hudson, meanwhile, wanted to enjoy some of his new-found prosperity. His sexual activities had been low-key after the rumours surrounding Jack and *Confidential*, and the talk of his search for lovers in Europe while making *Captain Lightfoot*. Virtual celibacy and some female company was required to calm the talk and Phyllis had come into his life – with a gentle push from Henry – at exactly the right moment. That Christmas of 1954, they saw a lot of each other and exchanged gifts. Rock was also buying his first house, a two-bedroomed, Dutch-style farmhouse for which he paid $38,000 and he proudly took Phyllis to see it. She noticed he was beginning to talk in collective terms, using 'we' as he discussed his plans for the property and after he had moved in during early 1955, she found herself occasionally staying overnight. She still had her own place – as yet Hudson's intentions towards her were not crystal clear. Henry Willson knew exactly what he wanted from the relationship: marriage, and just as soon as possible. Some time later he admitted: 'I was sure Rock needed to be married for a variety of reasons. And so what if I did play cupid? I gave Phyllis a good build-up to Rock, and him to her and they started dating.'

But career diversions that would force the prospect of marriage to the back of Hudson's mind were at hand. On the horizon was the biggest role of his life and he was terrified.

# CHAPTER TWO

## The Movie Star

It was an ironic and perhaps at times painful situation in which Rock Hudson found himself: romantic idol by day and gay-bar cruiser by night. There was no way that the roles he played could affect his own approach to sex, which remained as pertinent as ever to his way of life. It was dulled only occasionally by fear of exposure and rose again in good times with an unabounding energy for the chase and courtship of the young men who appealed to him. In this, he maintained throughout his life an ageless, even effortless style in which he was neither overpoweringly sexual in his demands, yet enjoyed the pursuit of his lovers. His mentality remained youthful, his humour almost schoolboyish. He was not the suave sophisticated lover in the mould of more famous predatory homosexuals: he was the slightly boisterous 'Hi . . . wanna have some fun, babe' type whose technique remained the same until the year of his death. His masculinity was never in doubt amongst his friends; only in immensely private and jokey situations would he camp up and perhaps mimic some actress friend.

He managed to retain a relative shield of secrecy, in spite of the aspirations of *Confidential* reporters. Yet even though he had now established himself as a romantic lead in his recent successes, it seemed hardly feasible that Rock Hudson could be considered for one of the most prestigious and costly film productions of the fifties. Though popular in Hollywood and with his fans, his dramatic roles had not exactly earned him wide-spread critical acclaim. Suddenly Rock was wanted by one of Hollywood's finest and most influential directors, George Stevens, as he began casting for his film *Giant* in which he personally had much at stake.

Stevens's new film had been the talk of the film community

for months. He and producer Henry Ginsberg, along with author of the epic, Edna Ferber, had formed their own corporation to get the movie into production; many major stars wanted to be in it. No one would have given Hudson much chance against the tough, established competition: Gary Cooper, William Holden, Alan Ladd and Clark Gable, who were all being tipped for the male lead. It was the part of Bick Benedict, the hugely wealthy and bigoted Texas rancher, fighting the dramatic changes in his home state as it switched from cattle to oil. With its undertones of civil rights and a sideswipe at the great American dream of affluence, it was a controversial film and at the time an important one. Today, of course, it is perhaps seen to be no more than a classy soap opera; then, it was a big-budget production and Elizabeth Taylor herself was 'desperate' to play the role of Benedict's wife, a part which seemed destined to go to Grace Kelly.

As casting began, William Holden seemed to have emerged the favourite, but Hudson was aided by some strong lobbying from his friends. Before it went on release, producer Ross Hunter took a print of *Magnificent Obsession*, giving George Stevens a private viewing to demonstrate how Rock's abilities had improved. The director took the bait and offered Rock the contract. He added to the surprise when he signed James Dean, instead of Elizabeth's friend Montgomery Clift, for the part of Jett Rink, the outcast cowhand who inherits ten acres of the Benedict empire and strikes oil.

But even before he had begun shooting, Rock was almost devastated by nerves. He lay awake night after night anguishing over whether he could do it and he was especially worried about the ageing process as the story moves through four decades. Stevens understood and began vitalizing his star. Rock recalled: 'George Stevens . . . he's another I fell in love with. He was like God to me. I mean, I followed him around like a puppy, and his wife, to the point where he got self-conscious. I'd make him blush and he'd say, "Don't do that." He had a richness to him . . . he did all the directing with me before the picture began and hardly a word during shooting.'

Stevens knew he had to build up Hudson's confidence. He took him to the studio carpentry shop where the Benedict film house was being built and allowed Rock to choose the colours of the paintwork. 'He had me so rich and so bigoted,' said Rock. 'I was Bick Benedict before we ever shot frame one. He gave me so much power. But do you see what he was doing? Then Stevens asked me who I'd like as my leading lady . . . Elizabeth Taylor or Grace Kelly. Well, I can work with Elizabeth, I can work with Grace. So I said Elizabeth and he said, "Fine. We'll get Elizabeth." Well I was eighteen-feet tall. What isn't being said here is that they probably had Elizabeth signed. If I'd have said Grace Kelly, he would have found a way to make me think Elizabeth would be better. That was the wonderful way of his direction . . . and I was rich and strong and bigoted and powerful. That's good direction.'

Hudson was right. Taylor had already been signed by Stevens and she invited Rock to dinner at her house since, as she put it, we're going to husband and wife for the next six months. Rock said, 'We had a terrific time. So much so that we'd get smashed and suddenly it's four in the morning. Not two hours later I have to get up and I'm half-drunk and hungover as is Elizabeth. So we arrive on the set . . . and in between shots we're running outside to throw up. We shot that scene and all the women on the set – the seamstresses, wardrobe men, hairdressers, were all sobbing "Oh, what a moving scene" . . . in truth we were so sick, we couldn't move. And that's what made the scene. Everybody loved it, thought it was great. But anyway, Elizabeth and I became great friends. I love her.'

That friendship was noticed on the set and by the time the film unit moved to Marfa, Texas, for location work, the gossips were saying that they had formed a loving attachment, linking stories to Elizabeth's own marriage problems with Michael Wilding. They were then but a few months from separation, a prospect which was fuelled by another 'exposé' in *Confidential* that Wilding had invited strippers to a poolside party while his wife was away.

Phyllis Gates also went down to Texas and heard whispers that something was going on. But many years later, Elizabeth herself admitted that though she was attracted to Rock she soon realized there was no future in any possible romance. If anyone was to have an affair with Hudson during the making of *Giant*, it would have been James Dean with whom he shared a house in Marfa. Dean, a bi-sexual, would mischievously try anything and if speculation that he and Hudson became lovers was true, it was through some ulterior motive of Dean who, in his strange and perverted way, sought to needle his fellow actors. It was part of his technique, particularly when hatred between characters on screen was required. He had certainly made no secret of his contempt for Hudson's style of acting and hated the system that had made Hudson a star.

During filming, Rock became panic-stricken that Dean was stealing the picture from him. Although he was not the central character, Dean's role was a dynamic catalyst to so much of the action. Rock telephoned Willson to pour his heart out. Willson tried to console him and sent Phyllis to Texas to help calm him down. She found Hudson was already being soothed by Elizabeth and did not much care for the rumours that something was going on between them.

After Dean's death, Hudson cried for hours but whatever went on between them at Marfa remained his secret and in his 1983 interview, he gave no hint of pleasant memories: 'I didn't like the fellow too much and I don't know as I should say more.' And, ironically, he added, 'I don't like to talk against the dead . . . so I think I should shut up!'

Hudson did not get the Oscar – which had been predicted by Willson and expected by himself – for his role in *Giant* although both he and Dean were nominated for the award. It was Hudson's one and only Academy Award nomination and, naturally, the performance remained one of his favourites for the rest of his life. He always felt it had been a landmark in his career, the point at which critics began to take him more seriously and the spring-board for the films that would eventually make him a superstar. His fame and status had also taken off and on his return from filming in Texas, *Life* magazine was waiting to see him for an interview and picture feature. In the forties and fifties, this rep-resented a major accolade; for any actor to be featured in *Life* was a signal of acceptance in the higher echelons of Hollywood fame. Although by now, he dreaded giving interviews for fear of the obvious question about his bachelorhood – which even his studio was batting off with an 'official' biographical statement that Rock had decided not to marry until he was thirty or more – Hudson co-operated fully with *Life* whose photographers captured him in the 'handsome male star' poses as well as portraying him as a homely sort of chap who was well used to looking after himself. Hudson and Willson dashed to the bookstalls to get a copy of the issue only to discover that *Life*, too, had angled its story on the lines of 'Rock gets rich alone'.

Coincidentally, *Confidential* were also nosing around again and that month, September 1955, had run a story about another of Henry Willson's clients, Tab Hunter, which claimed some misdemeanour in his youth. Some years later it became a point of speculation that

Willson had once again traded off some information about one of his other clients to get Hudson off the hook. With Louella Parsons, Hedda Hopper and other influential Hollywood writers continually making pointed comments about Rock's lack of endeavour to find a bride, a scenario had been created under which Willson renewed his pleas that Rock should marry as soon as possible. In this he was joined by Rock's employers, the executives at Universal, who also wanted to see the issue settled once and for all. It was not an uncommon situation for studios to suggest marriage to stars whose sexual preferences might be challenged; nor was it unknown for those who ignored their pleas and whose homosexuality became public knowledge to be unceremoniously dumped, never to work in tinsel town again. That was the fact of the situation confronting Hudson: the rumour-mongering could have wrecked his career in an instant.

There were only two women who could be considered contenders for the title of Mrs Rock Hudson: Betty Abbott and Phyllis Gates. Betty was a close friend, too close perhaps, for he seemed to regard her more like a sister than a possible lover. And so his 'romance' with Phyllis intensified. She was naïve enough to believe that Rock Hudson had fallen deeply in love with her when his proposal came out of the blue. At the end of October 1955, he took her for an informal dinner and just said 'Let's get married'. He'd given her a ring some weeks before but had never mentioned engagement . . . or marriage. Only years later did she discover that Henry Willson had already arranged everything: a 'secret' wedding away from the public glare of Hollywood in a small hotel in Santa Barbara where a local Lutheran minister had been hired to perform the ceremony joining Rock and Phyllis in matrimony.

Willson had ordered the cake and the flowers; he had arranged a honeymoon in Jamaica. Rock's best friend from Winnetka, Jim Matteoni, was as surprised as anyone when he was called with the news that Rock was getting married and wanted him as best man. Phyllis was allowed to tell only her best friend, Pat Devlin; she was prevented from telling even her mother until after the ceremony was over and by then, Henry had already 'leaked' news of the marriage to Hedda and Louella. Universal was well aware of the plans for Hudson's marriage and according to Phyllis many years later, had encouraged him all the way; it was also an official Universal photographer who took the wedding photographs which would subsequently be released to world's press with a caption which began 'Rock Hudson elopes with his secret love'.

The honeymoon, Phyllis reported, was idyllic and Rock did not display the slightest hint of homosexuality. He performed his matrimonial task with vigour and, on the surface, was all that Phyllis would have wanted in terms of a sexual relationship. Years later, she admitted bitterly: 'He was a very good actor. When we were together, he did more acting than he did at the studio.' Initially, at least, he put on a very public show of being a happily married man. On their return from honeymoon, they were regulars at Hollywood parties and everyone wanted to know the details: How long had he known her? When did they realize they were in love? Along with others in the elite circle, Elizabeth Taylor invited them up to her house in Beverly Hills (her marriage to Michael Wilding was still intact, but in its final stages of collapse).

Henry also made sure the newspaper columnists and the fan magazines gave his boy a good show. It was a virtual open house for writers and photographers to come in and portray the star's new life as a model of domestic bliss. Rock and Phyllis were heavily photographed in their home, in all the classic poses of homely, cosy togetherness; Rock was playing his part to perfection. On the career front, too, he continued to go forward, first with a highly starred production of *Written on the Wind* with Robert Stack, Lauren Bacall and Dorothy Malone (who won an Oscar for best actress). Then he was teamed up again with the successful Ross Hunter/Douglas Sirk partnership for *Battle Hymn*, with Martha Hyer and Dan Duryea which failed to give Rock the follow-up success he needed.

However, towards the end of 1956 he learned that David O. Selznick wanted him for a new major production, the 20th Century-Fox adaptation of Hemingway's novel *A Farewell to Arms*, to co-star with Selznick's wife, Jennifer Jones. Universal had agreed to a loan-out deal from which they would profit handsomely and Selznick was convinced that the film would recreate his past success of *Gone with the Wind* – talking in terms of Hudson and Jones becoming the new Clark Gable and Vivien Leigh. The renowned John Huston had been hired as director and Rock felt his time had come for another major blockbuster. He recalled: 'David Selznick producing . . . can't go wrong there: Huston directing . . . can't go wrong there . . . a Hemingway novel and a good cast; it all seemed right.' In fact, *A Farewell to Arms* became a nightmare for Hudson, and for Selznick who seemed intent on ignoring the fire of Hemingway's words in favour of a thick overlay of Hollywood gloss. Huston could see what was happening immediately and after some heated exchanges with Selznick over the script, he was fired before shooting even began.

From then on, it was all downhill. Hudson, like most of the cast, was pressurized almost to tears by Selznick and far from presenting him with a huge career boost, the film was a disaster that was all but laughed off the screen. Not the least of Hudson's problems was the state of his marriage, which was in its eighteenth month when he departed from Los Angeles for six months' location work in Italy. Phyllis should have gone with him but the day before he flew out, she was admitted to hospital with hepatitis, a disease which she had undoubtedly picked up through Hudson's continued homosexual encounters.

The sham marriage had run its course; in the past few months Hudson had become almost impossible to live with. Under the shelter of an outwardly respectable marriage, he had returned to his predatory ways and would often go out on his own in search of male lovers, sometimes not returning at nights. His sexual performance had become a nonentity and Phyllis was urging him to seek psychiatric help which he refused to do. And even though Phyllis had become quite ill, his interest in her had waned to the point that two weeks after leaving Italy, one of the gossip columnists took him to task for ignoring her doctor's pleas for him to return home from Italy to visit her. Willson intervened to keep her quiet while Selznick's publicity people in Italy put out fanciful stories about Hudson being desperately worried about his wife but unable to return home because of his filming commitments.

Secretly, Rock was indulging in the company of a new lover, a young Italian actor with whom he had become infatuated, and he spent a great deal of his free time with him, lavishing him with gifts and taking him on romantic trips away from the prying eyes of the studio people and the press. It would all explode in his face a few months later, when the Italian arrived in Hollywood to take up Rock's kind offer of getting him started in America.

By the time he returned home to Los Angeles, the marriage was all but over. Phyllis tried to keep it going as best she could but the rows became more bitter and, according to her, Rock began slapping her in his rages. On 17 October, soon after they had returned from Hawaii where Rock was filming his next picture, *Twilight for the Gods*, and after Phyllis had issued an ultimatum that he change his ways, he packed some things in a suitcase while Phyllis was out and moved into a hotel. He blamed her for the failure of their marriage and said that at the start she was 'unbeatable, she was family and had the greatest sense of humour and we had a ball until we got married. From that day, it was all over. The little piece of white paper changed everything. She became the movie star's wife. She had to have a new dress for everything . . . it just didn't work.' Naturally, Phyllis did not agree. When she filed for divorce the following April, she countered that he had been guilty of extreme mental cruelty, physical violence towards her, and leaving her alone at nights.

Phyllis hired one of Hollywood's most successful lawyers, Jerry Geisler, whose past clients included Marilyn Monroe and Errol Flynn; Hudson and Willson were left shuddering at the renewed prospect of his career being brought down by scandal. Geisler threatened to name the Italian as co-respondent and Willson began his own vindictive campaign to blacken Phyllis by putting it around that the marriage failed because she was a lesbian and a money-grabber which in fact aroused only sympathy for her, and added shame for the Hudson camp. When Geisler announced publicly that Hudson had cancelled all Phyllis's charge accounts, Marlon Brando sent her $1000 and the lawyer knew he had Rock on the run. With the threat of an unseemly public divorce, a quiet settlement of the alimony battle was recommended and Hudson eventually agreed to pay Phyllis $1000 a month, give her the house he had bought for $38,000 just two years earlier and buy her a new car. She would also retain her interest in Hudson's own production company from which she was guaranteed five per cent of the earnings. Later, she returned to the fight when he began to divert his assets into a new company and won a subsidiary payment of $130,000. Hudson's phoney marriage had cost him dear but it had served its purpose and for the moment eliminated embarrassing references to his private life.

The divorce had come at a bad time. Two more low-key pictures which won him no great acclaim pushed Rock further into a deep depression about his life. He became a recluse, hiding away at a house he had rented on the Los Angeles coast where he temporarily re-imposed his celibacy and tried to keep himself out of the limelight. Once again, it was his friend and producer Ross Hunter who would rescue him from a threatening lull in his career with the offer of a new style of picture. Called *Pillow Talk*, it was a sophisticated light comedy that would eventually carry him back to the top of the star ratings. At the time of the offer however he was so down at the mouth, he thought seriously about whether or not to accept.

The film was such a departure from his recent dramatic roles that he felt it could finally ruin him if it did not succeed. He had never played comedy either, and that worried him. But in the end, after a meeting at Hunter's office with Doris, he finally agreed to sign, and as he would later admit, it was the best career move he ever made. Hunter had more problems when Universal expressed reluctance about backing the film, and he even had to fight to get the cinema-chain bookers to take it. Everyone was nervous of what today would be viewed as a fairly innocuous, ordinary sex comedy; but public reactions, when it was released in 1959, took everyone by surprise. It revealed that Ross Hunter was correct in his assessment that cinema audiences had been starved of this type of comedy and they clamoured to see the new starring duo of Hudson and Day.

Rock said: 'Universal just didn't know how to handle it. It was an expensive film to make, in their terms . . . over $1 million which was way above what they normally laid out. In spite of their mentality, they had to think in bigger terms; they were forced to . . . Jesus Christ . . . it made $25 million profit.' And Rock Hudson became the world's number one romantic idol. *Pillow Talk* and the follow-up films that came in its wake would make him a fortune and establish him as the man most female cinema-goers could worship. Through these movies, he displayed a new and forceful appeal; he was cast as the handsome lover and managed to purvey to his audience a sexuality that, beyond doubt, was magnetic. It must have been, for the pictures to become the success that they were; his acting alone was not sufficient in itself to attract the kind of reaction he achieved.

Try as he would, he could never be cast in the same mould as Gable, Cooper, Holden or Grant. The depth of his abilities remained somewhat limited by the fact that he was a manufactured studio product; all the acting lessons in the world could not change that and the critics were usually at one in recording his stiff, placid style and the apparent lack of deep-down emotions and feeling which other male stars of his day brought to their performances. But his approach to the job was enough for him to be regarded by his co-stars as a man who cared. The dedication and effort he put into his work became legend; in the acting sense he was also generous to his colleagues, especially those trying to get a foothold in the business. As Doris Day said: 'I adored Rock Hudson. He was one of the most professional actors I ever worked with. He was one of my best friends, too, by the way. When Rock and I were together, it was just laughter all the way.'

Whatever roles he was playing, the macho-male image of his screen performance never implanted itself on his own personal needs and desires. True, his women friends found him attractive and many would say that they never thought of him as being gay, in spite of the rumours which began to gather momentum in Hollywood at the start of the sixties and beyond. But again, he never formed any kind of heterosexual relationship after the inevitable collapse of his marriage to Phyllis. He had many 'straight' male friends who equally could not envisage him as a homosexual, though most knew that he was. This part of his life seemed to fulfil his earlier adolescent need to be 'one of the boys' and those heterosexual men who became involved with him found him a loyal and supportive friend and a warm, entertaining companion who could drink and curse with the best of them – and better than most. Indeed, his favourite adjectives in conversation were four-letter ones and he liked nothing better than to be sitting around his pool with a gin in one hand and a cigarette in the other, telling some amusing anecdote from the past or listening to ribald stories from his companions.

But then he would wander again. Always, he would return to his pursuits. *Pillow Talk* gave him the confidence and the cash to become a vigorous hunter. There were always men around him, whether heterosexual friends or occasional male pick-ups with whom he would indulge in a brief encounter. He also formed fairly long-term relationships during the next decade and with them came the additional obsession for privacy, for which he required a secure home.

In the early sixties, he bought a small mansion in Beverly Hills from Sam Jaffe, on the market for $167,000 which he felt he could easily afford, given the extent of his recent earnings. However he did not have that kind of cash available and Universal obliged him with a loan on the condition that he sign a new five-year contract.

It was a bitter pill to swallow because, at the time, he had been talking about leaving the studio to branch out into more demanding pictures on offer elsewhere. As a free agent, which many of the established Hollywood stars were becoming by refusing to sign long-term contracts, he could have demanded substantially higher fees. Had not his friend Elizabeth Taylor just asked for and got $1 million to play Cleopatra? It was the first of many millions she would receive and although he did very well in terms of income for the next few years, Rock would certainly have been able to amass a larger fortune. He might also have moved into a higher plane of acting; Universal, he felt, was restricting him in that field, forcing him to turn down several loan-out offers, including *Ben Hur* which did so well for Charlton Heston.

Rows over Rock's financial affairs also brought the parting of the ways between Willson and Hudson. At last, the man who had created him and who had retained such a devilish hold over him for so many years, was ditched. Rock never spoke to his mentor again and when Willson died a few years later, a penniless alcoholic in a home for distressed show-business people, Hudson did not attend the funeral or acknowledge his passing in any way.

With his new permanent base, the home which he called The Castle, Hudson moved on upwards. *Pillow Talk* was followed by a string of films through the sixties, some good, some mediocre and the occasional bad one reaching fiasco proportions. But Rock's years at the top were limited by the demand for his type and style of actor; he knew it himself and that is why he had wanted to branch out to pastures new earlier in his career. The jokes in the sex comedies became stale and his dramatic strengths were not sufficient to sustain him as a character actor. He would have undoubtedly benefitted from a broader scope of picture at an earlier age; now it was too late.

Before the decade of the sixties was out, the calls were becoming fewer and the fan mail had thinned out to a trickle. By 1970, he had made fifty-nine films: in the remaining fifteen years of his life he would make only six more big-screen movies and half a dozen television specials. He was able to identify for himself the moment in his life when his adored screen career reached its lowest ebb, and he had to turn in another direction, television, for employment. He explained frankly: 'I'd come up in the movies and I kept thinking to myself . . . "Shit, it can't be over, it can't be over yet. That can't be all there is." I mean, I was still a comparatively young man . . . When you have been there, at the top of the tree and the number one male actor against people like Cary Grant, it sure isn't easy to accept that people aren't calling any more. I think I did too many comedies and the scripts got repetitive. So there I was doing less and less.'

It was the lack of film offers and the lure of big money that persuaded him to accept his first major television contract for the long-running series, 'McMillan and Wife' with Susan Saint James. It paid him $120,000 an episode but the work was hard, with long, tiring days at the studio. Psychologically, it was also one of the worst periods of his life. 'My drinking got to be a real bad habit,' Rock admitted. 'It went on for a long, long time, too long. I wasn't an alcoholic but pretty damn close. When I was doing 'McMillan', I'd get home at nights after six or seven hours in the studio and all I wanted was a stiff drink. The trouble was, I had another and another. . . . '

Drinking also led Rock into some dangerous flirtations in the gay bars of San Francisco and Los Angeles and his homosexuality had become an 'open' secret. It was towards the end of the sixties that he met MGM publicist Tom Clark who was to become his friend and confidant for the next fifteen years. Hudson had no regular partner and soon the friendship had reached such agreeable proportions that around the time Rock switched to television, Clark moved into his house and initially became a great stabilizing influence on Hudson's life. He organized him, took over the running of his affairs and began injecting a new style of social life at The Castle, with regular formal dinner parties to which he invited some of Rock's most famous friends. Clark was always around and perhaps became too protective and possessive. He also joined Hudson in his drinking bouts and it often became a question which one of them would pass out first.

It was perhaps inevitable with two such masculine, yet volatile, men that Rock's fondness for Clark eventually turned to resentment; he felt Tom had become his keeper and it reminded him too much of the obsessive sway Henry Willson had held over his private life. Hudson and Clark began to row, sometimes violently, and particularly over Rock's promiscuous wanderlust in search of sexual partners. Whatever the relationship was between them, it certainly did not preclude Rock from taking lovers and in spite of his advancing years, his desires and skills in attracting young men into one-night stand arrangements had not diminished. Whether he was in Los Angeles, New York – where he had bought an apartment – or any other city of the world that his work might take him, he would go off in search of good times, new friendships and occasional bedroom partners. He led a very active sex life, though few of his liaisons became serious affairs, nor lengthy ones – until he met Marc Christian. By then, he was entering the final phase of his life. But neither of them knew it. . . .

# CHAPTER THREE

## *The Fallen Idol*

The last three years of Rock Hudson's life began happily and ended in the long and painful illness which stripped the flesh from his bones and left him as skeletal and emaciated as a victim from a wartime concentration camp in the weeks before he passed away. More than that, it also sliced through the aura, for when death came and released him from his agony, it also signalled the onset of a campaign of vilification that dragged his name and reputation into the gutter. In a crescendo of tabloid headlines that shocked even Hollywood, his life was taken apart and past scandals were unearthed.

Until 1982 and the start of his relationship with Marc Christian, his only misdemeanour, if such it was, in his thirty-five years in Hollywood had been that he was a closet homosexual. Yet, as with the comparisons we have already established, his excursions to satisfy these urges were certainly no worse than those of some of his heterosexual colleagues, the one difference being in the sex of the pursued and the providers of their pleasures. Even his marriage and divorce could hardly be viewed as a major scandal; interesting and different perhaps, but certainly no match for some of the more famous matrimonial squabbles within the Hollywood community.

No, homosexuality and his endless battle to hide it, was the only thing the press had on him until he contracted AIDS. Of course, the newspapers and magazines – and the biographers – who chart the activities of the rich and famous would have had a field day in finally exposing the star's double life even without the AIDS element. What made it a sensational story – beyond the normal 'secret, sordid past of a very famous man' headlines – was Rock Hudson's denial to his lover that he had contracted AIDS, a deliberate cover-up of the truth in which he was aided by his secretary and oldest friend, Mark Miller.

Even before Hudson's body had been removed from the house he loved, the battle had commenced. Suddenly, as the reporters and photographers surrounded The Castle, the presence of Marc Christian became known and since he had already consulted one of Hollywood's most flamboyant and publicity-conscious lawyers, Marvin Mitchelson, the young man was certainly not backward in revealing why he lived at The Castle. Typical examples were the *National Enquirer*'s front page which blasted out the story, 'Rock's Boyfriend: Why I'm suing for $10 million', and *People* magazine's, 'Lawsuit over Rock's estate exposes scandal'.

In the weeks and months following Hudson's death, Christian gave repeated and detailed accounts of the relationship and how the truth of his lover's illness had been kept from him. Indeed, Marvin Mitchelson, veteran of such highly publicized legal skirmishes as the Lee Marvin palimony case, Joan Collins's divorce from Peter Holm, and Lesley Ann Downs's divorce and child custody wrangle. Mitchelson took Christian on the talk-show circuit, appearing with heavy-weight hosts like Phil Donahue and Larry King with the sole purpose of giving him media exposure prior to what Mitchelson correctly imagined was going to be a protracted preliminary exchange after he filed a lawsuit claiming $10 million from Hudson's estate. It was, said Mitchelson, a major point of law they were trying to establish on behalf of the partners of AIDS sufferers (and presumably any other fatal disease) who failed to reveal their affliction to their lovers.

In a lengthy plea, Mitchelson charged that Hudson had conspired with Mark Miller to endanger Marc Christian's life by not revealing he was suffering from AIDS for more than a year after it had been diagnosed. In a complicated counter-claim which was eventually dropped, lawyers for Hudson's estate alleged that Christian was aware of his lover's deteriorating condition and assumed risk if he continued to have sex with him, and that if Christian contracted AIDS it was the result of his own promiscuous behaviour and not as a result of sexual contact with Hudson. They also asked for the return of substantial payments made by Hudson's company, Mammoth Films, to Christian. Christian strenuously denied the counter-claims and refused to hand back any money paid to him.

In the middle of this legal activity, Christian lost the services of

Marvin Mitchelson whose thoughts – and press coverage – were suddenly diverted to his own problems. He found himself facing charges of professional malpractice, fraud and misappropriation, a fact that would be kept from the jury of Marc Christian's action, which was taken over by another strong Los Angeles lawyer, Harold Rhoden (who, incidentally, was also hired by Mitchelson to muster his own trial defence).

And so, after lengthy correspondence and pre-trial examination of witnesses, the two sides progressed to the trial itself at which the last three years of the movie star's life would be examined in detail: no stone would be left unturned; no detail, however minute, insignificant or boring would be excluded. The jury had been selected and the trial was to begin on 6 January 1989, listed at the Superior Court of the State of California for the County of Los Angeles before His Honour Judge Bruce R. Geernaert as Marc Christian MacGuinnis, otherwise known as Marc Christian versus the Estate of Rock Hudson and Mark Miller.

An eleventh hour bid to settle – a fact which again would not come within the jury's hearing – was made by Rhoden who indicated that his client would accept $1 million. The estate and Miller refused to budge. As far as they were concerned, Marc Christian was not getting a penny. So the scene was set, and press and television reporters crowded to the courtroom to record the beginnings of what promised to be a fastidious battle.

Even before the trial could begin, Robert Mills, counsel for the Hudson estate, brought the opening shots into the judge's chambers – out of the jury's earshot – to seek a ruling on a key point which would be the thrust of Christian's case. Mills was challenging the opposing side's right to tell the jury that Christian was under a sentence of death as a result of his sexual contact with Hudson. Judge Geernaert agreed with Harold Rhoden: there was no reason why Christian could not testify that he was fearful he was going to die from AIDS, even though all medical tests so far had proved negative. Mills persisted. He did not want Christian saying he might die from AIDS. Overruled. Now, let's get on with the trial, said the judge.

In open court, the jury was assembled. The jury, seven women and five men selected after a lengthy process of presentation and elimination of names, were carefully checked and cross-checked for their possible association or affiliation with any aspect of the trial. Harold Rhoden, the defence lawyer, was particularly keen to see a representative cross-section of black, white, professional or otherwise. He would repeatedly make the point that he sought twelve people who would, as far as possible, attempt to set aside any bias for or against homosexuals, and who had no pre-conceived notions as to the right and wrongs of this extremely well-publicized case. They listened intently as the judge explained that opening statements from counsel were merely an indication of what the evidence might prove, and should be viewed only as a helpful summary of events which occurred prior to the trial. Rhoden, a burly, no-nonsense lawyer wasted no time. Ignoring the chronology of his story, he went straight to the point that Mills had challenged – Christian's fear that he was going to die. . . . .

Christian first learned that Rock Hudson had AIDS when he saw the six o'clock television news on 23 July 1985. Hudson had collapsed in Paris and the news item said he had been diagnosed as having AIDS a year earlier. It came as a devastating shock to Christian because, for the previous two years, he had been Rock Hudson's lover and during that last year when Hudson had developed full-blown AIDS, they had been sexually intimate three to five times a week. Rhoden had to be blunt in his description: it was alternating anal intercourse and neither of them used a condom.

Within hours of this news, Marc Christian received a telephone call from France. It was Hudson's secretary, Mark Miller, and he said: 'I'm sorry, The Movie Star told me not to tell you. I had to lie to cover it up. I know it's not fair, but I was only following orders.'

Christian's immediate reaction to all of this was absolute fear; he felt there was no way he could have avoided contracting AIDS himself because of their relationship, and he felt certain he would die from it. Christian remembered the symptoms and sores he had seen appear on Hudson's body and the dramatic weight loss. This was the man he had been intimate with on at least 160 occasions.

Both Mark Miller and Hudson himself had to know that sooner or later, Christian would find out that he had been misled, and that when he found out he would suffer intense emotional distress and fear that he would die. The motive, said Rhoden, was that Rock Hudson, then fifty-nine years old, wanted to continue to have sexual relations with Marc Christian, then twenty-nine. The motive of Miller was to please his boss, and he conspired to put a young man's life at risk. But his ultimate motive was money (from Hudson's estate).

When Hudson was diagnosed as having AIDS, did he have a duty to warn his sexual partner? That was what the case was about. It was also about fear, an enhanced *fear* of getting AIDS, even if Christian did not actually get it. Doctors had warned that although his tests were negative, they were still unreliable; no guarantees could be offered that he would not develop it. He was also told that the most contagious partners were those who had full-blown AIDS, which is what Hudson's own case had developed into at the time of sexual activity with Christian; the tell-tale signs were already there.

Rhoden looked directly and intensely into the faces of the jury as he pushed the point further: Christian's fear had not been alleviated by what the doctors had told him. It had been advanced because he believed from what he had been told that at any given moment he could begin suffering the same symptoms he knew Rock Hudson had suffered and *that* would mean a diagnosis of AIDS – a sentence of death.

Was that kind of fear something that the law would recognise – that the law would say, yes, there ought to be compensation for? That was what the case was about and it basically stemmed from a point in time when Hudson developed a little sore; a spot appeared on the back of his neck. He took the test. It was affirmative. Hudson had AIDS and he told Miller, 'Don't tell the kid.'

Whenever Christian raised the subject of these symptoms, Hudson gave him some excuse; he was okay. There was nothing wrong. It was something from the sun. It didn't mean a thing. Miller told the same lie. And Christian believed them both; he had no reason not to and their relationship continued as before. The only difference was, Hudson now knew he had AIDS, and he was concealing it. Miller knew the two men were having sexual intercourse, as would be shown by the many comments made by him and to him.

The second lie came in the late summer of 1984, when Hudson said he was going to the Deauville Film Festival in France. In reality, the purpose of the visit was to see Dr Dominique Dormont, a pioneer and one of the world's leading specialists on AIDS, who told him: You have it, and there is no cure. He treated him with a new experimental drug which could arrest the progression. Back in California, where his weight loss was noticed by everyone, he told Christian: 'I'm dieting. I want to look like I did years ago when I did *Pillow Talk* with Doris Day.'

When Christian confronted Hudson in the spring of 1985 with the direct question: Do you have AIDS? he answered, 'No. I've been checked for everything including the plague and I don't have it.' That denial came less than six months before his death and he continued to deny it until July 1985, when the whole world was told. There was no apology. No explanation, except from Miller who said he was under orders and that Rock had told him, 'Look after the kid, I may have killed him.' Even then, Christian did not blast Hudson. He was too ill. But he would not have left him even if he had been told, because he loved him. Neither would he have committed suicide: he would never have engaged in any further sex with Hudson had he known.

Conversely, said Rhoden, the defence would allege that Christian's relationship with Hudson ended before Hudson knew he had AIDS, that Christian was promiscuous and a prostitute. They would also claim blackmail: that Christian threatened to make public the love letters written to him by Hudson and expose him as a homosexual; thus Hudson was forced to allow Christian to continue to live in his house and to pay him money. Rhoden refuted these allegations and would bring evidence that Christian had never had sex with anyone who had AIDS, other than Rock Hudson, in those two years. Was it really feasible, Rhoden asked, that Christian could remain in the Hudson household for thirteen months as some sort of live-in blackmailer?

Returning to the overriding factor in the case – that of fear – Rhoden said that medical opinions had been sought, and these were all basically the same: that the incubation period for AIDS could be as long as ten to fifteen years. One doctor had reported that he knew of a case where all the symptoms were present but tests on the patient had been negative; he died. There was no evidence that Christian had AIDS, there was no evidence that he would definitely get it. He made no such contention.

The issue was *fear* and that alone.


Rhoden thanked the jury for their attention, and handed the platform to Robert Mills, who explained that he was counsel for the estate of Rock Hudson, and that his job would be to defend the estate against whatever the allegations were that Hudson did or did not do.

His contention was that Christian's case was smoke-and-mirrors magic. It was about a will in which Christian was not included; it was about a very large claim against the estate. It was not a case about AIDS, because there was no evidence that he had it *or* the virus in his body. Nor did he believe there would be any evidence which illustrated Christian's increased fear of AIDS when he allegedly found out about Hudson with the rest of the world. Christian's actions after that announcement were not those of a man gripped by terror; other than tests provided for him by Hudson and arranged by Mark Miller, he made no real attempt to seek specialist attention. And while he was awaiting the result of a partial test in Paris taken by Dr Dormont, he went to the south of France for four days and shared a hotel room with another AIDS patient named Steve Del Re who had pussing Kaposi's sarcoma sores all over his body. Was that the action of a frightened man?

Furthermore, how could Christian begin to quantify that fear in relation to his association with Hudson when, as evidence would show, he had sexual relations with between ten and fifteen other men between 1979 and 1982. Even if Hudson had told him in 1984 that he had AIDS, when he learned of it himself, it would not have affected the history of the situation. Mills insisted that Hudson ceased sexual contact with Christian even before he knew he had AIDS. But even if it was accepted – on Christian's sole evidence – that they had intercourse on 160 occasions, after three and a half years, to use the slang: 'He ain't got AIDS.' There were only two people who knew the truth of it and one of them was dead.

What the case was really about came down to one simple fact: Christian claimed that Hudson told him two months after he had moved into his house, 'One day, kid, everything I have is going to be yours. I hope you take good care of it', and before Hudson died Christian hired lawyer Marvin Mitchelson to make sure he got it. Because in fact, Christian was not in the will, and never had been.

Next it was the turn of the third lawyer in the case. Andrew Banks was representing Mark Miller. He explained that Miller had been a close friend of Hudson's for more than thirty-three years and his personal secretary for the last thirteen years of his life. They were not lovers, they were friends. He was a man whom Rock Hudson trusted as close as any man can trust another, closer than a brother. He turned to that close friend, the one man whom he could trust to share his terrible secret and know that it would be safe. The jury, said Banks, would have to compare that bond of friendship with the total lack of any relationship that existed between Christian and Miller. They were not lovers, they were not friends; Miller did not even know him before Hudson brought him to the house. There was no relationship between the two men, and there still wasn't; and when Hudson confided to Miller that he was HIV-positive, he also told him he wanted 'silence'. Miller knew that this meant: 'Please keep my secret.' Miller did so and there was good reason. Hudson feared that Christian and his friend and former lover, Liberty Martin, a woman twice his age, would destroy Hudson's career in five minutes if they got to know, and he did not want that to happen.

At the time Miller also believed there was no sexual relationship between Christian and Hudson; that was an important factor because the allegation was that he conspired with Hudson to do evil things. Banks said Christian had by then moved on to other partners and indulged in love-making with men he brought into Rock Hudson's house. Staff at the Hudson house would testify to their discovery of a blond boy in Christian's bedroom and tell-tale stains on the linen.

Banks also spoke of other blackmail threats which became apparent when Hudson told Miller: 'Give him [Christian] anything he wants; he's got letters.' Miller also came to learn that Christian had threatened to tell the *National Enquirer* that Hudson and his physical fitness instructor, Ron Channell – a young man 'more handsome than Christian' who was at Hudson's side when he collapsed in Paris – were lovers.

Mark Miller had no malice or ill-will towards Christian and intended him no harm. He took no action to induce Christian to continue having sex with Hudson because he did not believe they still had a relationship; what he did do was to ensure that Christian had a complete physical examination after Hudson's plight became publicly known and until that moment he kept Rock Hudson's secret because he knew Rock Hudson expected confidentiality. In the end, it would be a question of credibility: who would the jury believe, Miller or Christian.

Banks was naturally of the opinion that they would come

down in favour of Miller because there were a few other snippets of information he had yet to impart. If Christian was in such mental torment, if he had such a fear that he might have AIDS, why had he not done more to relieve his anguish? It wasn't for the lack of money. Instead, he went with Marvin Mitchelson on America's talk-show circuit and spoke about life with Rock, he gave long interviews with numerous magazines and newspapers, and he posed for many photographs. 'That's how he treated his emotional distress. That's how he got relief from those fears,' said Banks. 'He doesn't have any increased fear of getting AIDS. He doesn't even have a fear he's going to come down with it. What he is interested in is the will, the money and the publicity.'

While he was still living in Rock Hudson's home, still drawing his monthly salary cheque, and while Rock was upstairs dying, he hired Marvin Mitchelson; and when the Rock Hudson gravy train ended, Christian filed his claim because the will had been probated and he was not in it. All Mark Miller did was to keep confidential a very personal secret of a man who was closer to him than a brother. That's all he did; and Marc Christian was not entitled to a penny from him.

And now it was up to the jury to listen to the evidence and decide who was telling the truth. . . .

# CHAPTER FOUR

# Call Marc Christian

Marc Christian is an imposing man with the strong features, and the looks and confidence of someone who, like Hudson, could have made the hearts of women flutter. Indeed, his mannerisms and his walk are similar to his former lover; with the right agent and the skill of studio training that Hudson had received, perhaps, in another era, he would have been 'spotted'. He once had such aspirations; now his mind was set on another course.

He was the star of a different show. It was 11 January 1989, the day that Marc Christian would be called to the witness stand. There was an air of chattering anticipation as lawyers, press and public crowd into the courtroom. But there was a delay. The lawyers were arguing again and they assembled in the chamber of Judge Geernaert to air their views.

Harold Rhoden, for Christian, was protesting that the case was already becoming a trial by television and he was applying for a 'gag' order over counsel for the estate, Robert Mills. All concerned had previously agreed to a voluntary gag but there, on the Channel Nine news after the first day of opening statement, was Mills talking about what the evidence would or would not be; Mills explained to the judge that the television people concerned were not in court for his opening and he was merely restating it for them. He said nothing that he had not already said in court.

The judge took a firm line. Although Rhoden had asked for an instruction to Mills, Geernaert threw a gag over all of them. There was no reason at all, he said, why they should talk to the press. Let that be the end of it.

'All rise please. . . . ' The chattering stopped as the usher called the court to order and Judge Geernaert took his seat.

'Good morning, ladies and gentlemen.' A chorus of 'good mornings' came back in response and it was a polite little scene that would be repeated every morning of the trial for the next seven weeks.

Christian, looking immaculate, clean-cut and six-foot-two, was ready to begin. He was not unduly nervous; the appearances on television talk shows had stood him in good stead and his version of events would not be difficult to bring to mind.

'I call Marc Christian. . . . ' Harold Rhoden rose to face the jury and summoned his client and man of the moment to the witness stand, anxious to clear up immediately some of the points made by opposing counsel in their opening statements which would still be fresh in the jury's minds. First he dealt with the will.

Christian said he had no idea what was in Hudson's will, he had never seen it. Furthermore, the will had nothing to do with his lawsuit. He was suing because Rock Hudson continued to have sex with him after he found out he had AIDS, and Mark Miller lied. Nor had he started the action to get publicity for a career in Hollywood. Anyone who wanted to work in that town could not divulge their homosexuality. He knew of no actor working today who had been able to do that and continue working.

Next, Rhoden wanted to deal with the implication that Christian was a gigolo. No, he certainly was not. Well, yes, he had lived with his friend Liberty Martin before he moved in with Rock Hudson. They had met in 1975 when she was fifty-four and he was twenty-two. It was a good friendship and he was attracted to her intellectually. He rarely related to people of his own age and even to this day, she was still his best friend.

He moved into her one-bedroomed apartment in 1979 and they became sexually involved, though Christian insisted that he normally slept on the couch, while Liberty slept in the bedroom. He had never taken money from her and, in fact, shared the living expenses, paying half of everything. She was not a wealthy woman, and occasionally he lent her money. He had a girlfriend before he met Liberty and also had male partners. He guessed that up to 1982, when he first met Rock Hudson, he had had about twenty sexual partners, evenly split between men and women but none was of a lasting nature, except for his friendship with Liberty.

He met Rock Hudson in October 1982. For the first half of that year, until June, he had worked as a fundraiser for the 'Gore Vidal for Senate' campaign, but salary payments were intermittent so he also worked in a restaurant called the China Club, waiting on tables. He was also working on a personal project called 'Decades', a taped history of popular music since the turn of the century.

It was this topic that interested Hudson when they first met at a political fundraiser. Christian had been there for about half an hour when he heard a voice coming from behind, above his right ear: 'Where the hell's the booze?' He turned around and saw Rock Hudson standing next to him. Rock asked his name and they talked, first about politics, but Hudson said he was not very political, and then about music and films. Christian told him about 'Decades'; Rock showed great interest and said he had some old 78 r.p.m. records he wanted transferred to tapes. He had previously had some done but the tapes sounded just as scratchy as the records. Christian said the filters he used certainly reduced the noise of the scratch marks and he would gladly help if he could.

'Well, thank you,' said Hudson. He made a note of Christian's telephone number and said he would call him and he did, about a week later. [This version of how Hudson and Christian met would later be disputed by Mark Miller who would claim that Hudson told him they had met in a Los Angeles bath-house, establishments which were then a frequent meeting place for gay men in the city.]

Rock said he had a number of records he had sorted through that he wanted transcribed from disc to tape and it was arranged that Hudson should go to Liberty's apartment. He arrived with an armful of records and they sat on the couch for about three hours going through them and listening to other tape recordings.

Counsel Harold Rhoden: 'Did you know at that time Hudson was homosexual?'

Christian: 'Yes. I had heard since I was about fifteen that Rock Hudson may be gay, but I had no direct knowledge. It was something that was known in Los Angeles.'

'Now, before there was any sexual intimacy between you, how many times did you see him socially?'

'Seventy, eighty.'

'How frequently? How many times a week?'

'Nearly every day – every day of the week, except weekends from the time I first met him to well into the next year.'

Christian explained that most weekends he went to see his parents who lived fifty miles away in Orange County. His father was ill, suffering from cancer.

Rhoden: 'Before November 1983 [more than a year after they had first met], how many times did you go to Rock Hudson's house?'

Christian: 'Once, in March 1983. He told me he had been living with a man named Tom Clark for about ten years and they did not get along. He said Tom was an alcoholic and that they often got into fights. He was reluctant to bring anyone new to the house, especially a young man, because he did not want to subject me to any scene with Clark. The day I went, Clark was out of town.'

Christian continued to see Hudson almost daily. Sometimes he would meet him at Liberty's apartment and at other times he would collect him from wherever he was working. In April, they had a discussion about their relationship. Rock asked him if there was anyone else in his life, and Christian said there wasn't. Rock said he thought he was falling in love with him; Christian said he felt the same and they agreed they would spend the night together. It turned into a weekend and it was the first occasion on which they had become sexually intimate. Christian was so happy; he told Liberty Martin what had happened.

At the same time, Rock asked Christian to work for him part-time: transcribing records on to tape, reading scripts, suggesting adaptations of foreign films to American and generally looking out projects for him. He paid him $200 a week, in cash. Christian believed Hudson when he told him the work would be of great value to him.

Liberty Martin was also aware of the arrangement and became a close observer of the developing relationship. Because Hudson did not want to take Christian to his house, her tiny apartment had become the main meeting point between them. Rock often dropped in for coffee, or lunch, and sometimes stayed for dinner and the three of them would play cards. Occasionally, they all went out to a restaurant for dinner. Intimacy between Hudson and Christian also took place in Liberty's apartment when she was not at home; on other occasions they went to motels, but never to Rock's home.

Hudson also joined him on visits to his parents' home in Orange County and from April to November of 1983, they continued to see each other almost every day of the week, sometimes weekends as well. Throughout that time, they were having an active sexual relationship and in late October, Hudson told Christian he was thinking of asking Tom Clark to leave the house. The final split between them came at the end of October: the following week Clark left and on 5 November, Marc Christian took up residence in the Hudson house.

40

Rhoden: 'When you moved in, which room did you occupy?'
Christian: 'Rock Hudson's bedroom, the master bedroom. We called it the Blue Room. I moved in all of my belongings, nothing was left at Liberty's place.'

Soon after he moved in, Rock told Christian that a film project he was working on had been brought forward and he would have to leave for Israel immediately. He was to film location shots for a movie called *The Ambassadors*. [In the late summer of 1983, Rock's whole way of life was changing. In September he had split with his long-time agent, Flo Allen at the William Morris Agency, and had signed with Marty Baum at Creative Artists who almost immediately presented him with an offer he could not refuse. It was a second-billing role to Robert Mitchum in *The Ambassadors*, but it was paying good money: $500,000. But more importantly, it was his first major acting job since he had a heart by-pass operation in 1981, and he was desperate for work. It was also a difficult time emotionally with the arrival of Christian in his life and the departure of Tom Clark, who had moved out to an apartment that Rock owned in New York. When he got to Israel, fellow actors noticed he was edgy; he was also off his food.]

Christian said that almost immediately he began receiving letters, love letters, from Hudson. [Six were produced in evidence for the jury to examine and would form a vital part of Rhoden's submissions later in the trial.] They arrived periodically until Hudson returned home on 4 January. In the meantime, Christian had been working at the Institute of the American Musical, doing filing and catalogue work but Rock suggested that he should discontinue his job.

Rhoden: 'What did you say to him?'
Christian: 'I said I would be uncomfortable not having a job outside of the house. I did not want to be his appendage. Rock replied, "I don't want you to be my appendage. I am offering to help you to finish your project ['Decades'] and you won't be able to find that on the outside." '

Hudson told him he would arrange for him to meet famous singers for his project including Frank Sinatra, Doris Day and Dinah Shore.

The upshot of the conversation was that Hudson offered to pay Marc Christian $400 a month, plus expenses and he began receiving that payment on Rock's return from Israel by way of cheques, issued by Mark Miller and drawn on Rock's company, Mammoth Films, which also provided him with medical insurance.

41

He was also told to save all his receipts, such as restaurant stubs, and purchases of records or tapes which were to be handed to Miller for reimbursement. From the salary he received, he sent $200 a month to his mother.

He denied that he had moved into Rock's house simply for the money; he had done so because he loved him. Miller, he claimed, had once even reprimanded him for not spending enough: 'He asked me why I was going to hamburger joints when I should be going to Chasen's and said, "You are living with a millionaire – spend his money." '

But the new togetherness of the two men was not without its little domestic quarrels. One that came to mind was relayed to the jury by Christian: 'It was over a film we watched in the playroom [the theatre and bar in Rock's house]. Liv Ullman is my favourite actress and she was a friend of Rock's. Halfway through, he said "She is god-awful, isn't she?" and I said "On the contrary, I think it is her best performance. She was nominated for an Oscar." We went back and forth about the quality of the film, but I think he had really become tired of reading the subtitles.'

They made up, and the relationship continued as before. Occasionally, Rock bought him presents. He paid for Christian to have acting lessons, paid for him to have his teeth improved and agreed to pay the bills for the restoration of Christian's 1959 Chevrolet *Nomad* which once belonged to his father, who had bought it from new.

[The restoration of the car became a source of bitter argument between Christian and Hudson, according to Hudson's staff and friends. The car was being worked on by a local garage for more than eighteen months, and was not finished until June 1985. The costs mounted to $20,000 and there were still outstanding payments due when Hudson told Christian: 'That's it. I'm not paying another penny.' The firm doing the repairs would say that this was due to Christian's insistence on replacing even completed work with better second-hand parts as they became available. Christian would say the firm overcharged.]

Rhoden now turned more specifically to the sexual relationship between the two men: 'You testified that your first sexual act with Hudson was in April 1983. From then and up to February 1985, how often did you engage in sexual relations with him?'

'Between three and five times a week.'

'Now, sir, did those acts of sexual intercourse include alternating anal intercourse?'
'Yes, it did.'
'You were sometimes the receiver and he was sometimes the receiver?'
'That is true.'
'Did you ever use a condom?'
'Never.'
Christian explained that he first heard the word AIDS sometime in late 1983; it was called by two different names then: Gay Cancer and GRID, which meant Gay Related Immune Deficiency. But it was not until months later that it became apparent that those who contracted AIDS usually died. It seemed, at the time, to strike young men between the ages of twenty-five and thirty-five who tended to be promiscuous, and it had two predominant centres, San Francisco and New York. There was very sketchy information in those early days.
The point of the question was for Rhoden to establish any previous contact Christian might have had with someone carrying the virus: Christian said that as far as he knew, no one he had previously had sex with suffered from AIDS and from the first moment he met Hudson, his relationship had been monogamous. Hudson also told him that he was not having sex elsewhere. [In fact, after he had been diagnosed as having AIDS, Hudson sent three anonymous letters to men with whom he had had recent sexual activity, including a 22-year-old man in New York. The letter, written in long-hand by George Nader from Rock's draft, read:

> *Hi, This note shall remain anonymous for obvious reasons. Since we have had intimate sexual contact where sperm had passed between us, I feel it only fair to tell you that I have just found out I have AIDS. I am sorry to tell you this. I suggest you have tests made to make sure you are OK. Most sincerely.*]

Rhoden: 'Did it ever occur to you that you might catch AIDS as a result of what you were doing with this man [Hudson]?'
'No.'
Although Christian did not know the cause then, the first signs of AIDS appeared on Hudson's body after his return from Israel. He complained of a growth on the back of his neck, located

43

near the rear portion of the nape of his neck. He thought it was a pimple, or a mole, and that it would show up in photographs. He wanted it removed. He asked Christian to squeeze it for him to see if he could get rid of it, but the growth continued to give him trouble.

The following month Hudson told him he had been to see a doctor about the growth and the diagnosis was that it had been caused by the sun. Mark Miller described it as a 'pre-cancer' caused by the sun. According to Christian, both men told him a similar story about the diagnosis and he had no reason to disbelieve them. [By that May of 1984, Rock was already losing weight. On 15 May, he flew to Washington at the invitation of President Reagan for a celebrity dinner at the White House. He was placed at Nancy Reagan's table and as soon as she saw him she said: 'You're too thin, Rock. You should fatten up a bit.' Rock said he had been dieting and working out. The following week, on 24 May, he went to see a skin specialist about the mole on his neck, on the advice of his own physician, Dr Rex Kennamer. A biopsy was taken, prior to plastic surgery to have the spot removed. Three days later, he took a call from the specialist who gave him the dreadful news. The mole was Kaposi's sarcoma. He had AIDS. Rock went directly to Kennamer for a blood test. He had the mole removed on 5 June and two days later returned to Kennamer's office for a meeting with AIDS pioneer Dr Michael Gottlieb. The diagnosis, tragic and shocking, was confirmed.]

Rhoden: 'Did Rock Hudson or Mark Miller tell you Rock had AIDS at any time in June 1984?'

'No.'

'Did they tell you that the growth on Hudson's neck was Kaposi's sarcoma?'

'No.'

'If you had been told in June 1984, would you have left him?'

'No. I loved him.'

'Would you have continued to have sexual intercourse with him?'

'No.'

'Why not?'

'I don't want to die.'

On to the next crucial issue. Rhoden paused, and cleared his throat, and looked at the jury as he asked the question of his client: 'Did your sex practices with Rock Hudson continue after June 1984?'

'Yes, they did.'
'Same kind of sex?'
'Same kind of sex.'
'Same lack of condom?'
'Same.'

In August 1984, Christian was told that Hudson was planning to go to the Deauville Film Festival in France. He said Hudson had first asked him if he would like to go along but later said perhaps it would not be a good idea. He felt nervous about having his lover – who might be scrutinized by the press – with him. This was not unusual. He had said many times in the past that when they went out publicly together in Hollywood, he felt uncomfortable because he believed others in the restaurant or wherever they were might read his feelings towards Christian; he had difficulty hiding it and felt that all eyes were watching him.

Instead, Hudson decided to take his work-out instructor Ron Channell to Paris; he could see nothing wrong with that. After all, actresses took their beauticians, and in any event, he did not want to miss any of his exercises. Channell [whose evidence would come later in the trial] made the Paris trip with Hudson and they were in Europe for almost six weeks.

Christian understood that Rock would be away for only two weeks, but he was later told by Mark Miller that the trip had been extended because Rock had been approached by various producers about doing films in Europe and he wanted to remain to discuss them. [To some degree, this statement was true. Before he left Los Angeles, Hudson had been discussing with Aaron Spelling, executive producer of the then top-rated television series, 'Dynasty', the prospect of Rock appearing in a short run of episodes. Marty Baum, Rock's agent, was encouraging him to accept because the money was excellent. Rock was demurring, having sworn never to do another long-running television series again. But while he was in Paris, Esther Shapiro who was co-producer of 'Dynasty' with her husband Richard, flew over to try to persuade Rock to finalize the deal. They dined at the Ritz Hotel, where he was staying, and she brought some scripts for him to see. The matter was pressing because Rock's scenes would be shot in October and at the end of the evening he said: 'Oh, what the hell . . . I'll do it.']

When Hudson returned to Los Angeles in late September, Christian was shocked by his appearance and immediately noticed that he had lost a lot of weight. In fact, Rock asked him how he

45

thought he looked, and Christian said, 'You look fine, you look a little thin.' Rock replied, 'Well, I think I look great, don't I look great?'

Again, Hudson never mentioned that he had received any kind of treatment in Paris; neither did Mark Miller. According to Christian, upon his return the sexual activity between them resumed, if anything with more frequency. Other than weight loss, he saw no immediate change in Rock and he seemed quite cheerful. In fact, Hudson was privately elated, though he had no true cause to be. Having undergone an intense course of intravenous treatment by Dr Dormont with his new drug HPA-23, the doctor had told him that the AIDS virus had disappeared from Rock's blood. But Kennamer wanted the treatment to continue; he warned that in no way did that mean he was cured, the virus would almost certainly grow back.

Some weeks passed before Christian began to notice changes in Hudson's physical appearance. His skin became very dry, he had scales and rashes, and was constantly itching. He was also losing more weight, which became visually noticeable, and at nights he was sweating profusely. He began using a skin cream called Tiger Balm and a cortisone cream which Christian helped to rub into parts of the body he could not reach himself. The rashes came and went, but gradually got worse and they were spreading to every part of him.

Christian said he continued to sleep with Hudson although as his physical problems got worse, he moved into another bedroom – the Red Room – initially one night a week, and then later two or three. He could no longer remain in the same bed permanently because he would wake up and find himself drenched by Hudson's sweat.

Rhoden: 'Did you ever discuss this sweating with Hudson?'

'Yes, I did. He told me it was probably from drinking too many scotches and from flu. He told me he had been to Dr Kennamer for a check-up and he had suggested he stopped smoking and cut out drinking. That was it.'

In October, Rock began shooting scenes for 'Dynasty'. He was welcomed to the set by Aaron Spelling and the stars of the show including John Forsyth who played Blake Carrington, and Rock's old friend Linda Evans. They said it was an honour and a privilege to have him working with them; Linda commented that he'd lost some weight since last she saw him.

46

Christian said that he and Rock had had a discussion about his appearance on 'Dynasty', after Hudson had asked his opinion: 'I told him that for someone of his stature to do a show like 'Dynasty' would be demeaning because basically he was still a film star. The plus side was that it was the highest-rated show and he would get a lot of exposure.' Hudson replied, 'Well, regardless of that, they are going to give me $2.5 million and I'm not going to turn that down.'

When the first episode appeared, Christian asked him if he had upset the cameraman because he looked so awful on screen. He looked gaunt – his eyes were vacant – awful. He looked like a walking cadaver. Christian had a passing thought that he was suffering from cancer, just like his own father.

Rhoden now wanted to recap, to make sure the jury had understood the situation: 'Did you have a conversation with Mark Miller regarding your relations with Rock Hudson between June 1984 and January 1985?'

'Yes. He told me Rock had said I was a good lover. He asked me if it was a happy bedroom and I said I believed it was and then he said: "Well, that's what I've heard from Rock, that you are keeping him very happy in these matters and I just love for people to be happy." '

Rhoden: 'Did Miller say anything to you about pretties towards the end of 1984?'

'Yes. He asked me if I had met any pretties lately; he meant young boys, pretty young people and then he said: "I think you should introduce some pretties to Rock to spice up your relationship." I told him I was quite satisfied with Rock without them.'

Christian continued to be concerned about Rock's appearance and his general physical abilities. By February 1985, he was spending most nights in the Red Room and sex between them had virtually ended because Hudson was tired and listless; he had lost interest. Whenever he raised the question of weight loss, Hudson said it was a nagging flu combined with dieting, though other rumours were beginning to circulate. On 24 April, he was called into Mark Miller's office. Miller told him to shut the door behind him, which usually indicated a private conversation. Miller asked him if he had heard the latest rumour going round the Hill, meaning Hollywood. Christian said 'What rumour?' Miller replied, 'There's a rumour going around but first I want to ask you if people are treating you any differently in public; are they avoiding you?'

Christian said he was not aware of it and Miller said, 'Okay, well there's a rumour going around that you have AIDS and you have given it to Rock, and that's why he looks so bad.'

Christian said, 'You're joking.'

Miller said he wasn't; he had heard the rumour but he could not reveal the source.

'Does Rock know?' Christian asked.

'You'll have to ask him that yourself.'

That night Christian confronted Hudson when he saw him in the kitchen, and told him what was being said. Rock replied, 'Well, I don't have it, do you?'

Christian said, 'No I don't' and persisted with his questioning. Rock said everything was fine; he had been checked out by Dr Kennamer and there was nothing wrong apart from the flu.

A month later (when rumours were rife in Hollywood that Hudson was suffering from AIDS) they were both at a dinner party at Liberty Martin's house with two other friends of Christian. One of them, named Bob Dolphi, asked Rock if it was difficult being well-known and reading articles about himself in the *National Enquirer* and magazines of that ilk. Hudson said it was water off a duck's back: 'You should hear what the *Enquirer*'s saying about me now. They're saying I've got AIDS. Well, I hate to disappoint the fucking bastards, but I don't have it.'

There was one more occasion when the subject of AIDS came up, and another denial. According to Christian, he and Hudson were watching the television, and there was an item on the local news about gay bath-houses being closed because of AIDS. Hudson said: 'Fuck 'em. It serves them right. If they go to a place like that they deserve to die.' Turning to Christian, he said: 'What would you do if you got it?'

Christian said: 'I don't know; it's fatal. There's nothing you can do. What would you do?'

Hudson said: 'I'd have one last good fuck and say goodbye cruel world.'

Christian saw the opportunity to question Hudson again and asked him outright: 'Have you been checked for AIDS?'

Christian said Hudson replied: 'How can you ask me that question? I've told you before, I've been checked for everything, including the plague and I don't have it.'

The possibility that Hudson was suffering from anorexia had already been hinted. Christian was with Liberty Martin when she asked Miller the direct question: 'There is obviously something wrong with Rock . . . he can't go on not eating.' Miller replied that he had questioned Dr Kennamer about Rock's condition and had been told he had a form of anorexia. Miller also asked Liberty to cook more dinners for Rock because the cooking of James, the butler, was disgraceful.

The subject was raised again on 14 July, the day before Rock was due to fly to Carmel to film a television special with Doris Day. Christian and Miller were sitting in the kitchen when Rock came downstairs. The three of them sat down to a meal that James had prepared and when Rock got up to get a glass of water – which took him out of earshot – Miller threw his fork down on the table and said, 'This is inedible. How can he eat any food if it's this bad?'

Rock came back to the table and continued with his food. When he had finished, he asked James if he had packed his clothes for the European trip. It was the first time Christian had heard it mentioned and asked Hudson, 'You're going to Europe?'

'Yes,' he said, 'for business.' He seemed disoriented and Christian commented that he did not think Rock was in any condition to travel. Rock did not continue with the conversation; instead he excused himself and went to the bathroom. Christian questioned Miller about the trip and he replied, 'You'd better ask him yourself.'

Christian followed Rock upstairs, but when he got to the bedroom door it was closed. He could hear Rock vomiting in the bathroom. The thought crossed his mind that he was forcing his food back, a symptom of one form of anorexia. When he got back downstairs, Miller beckoned him into the White Room, a large dining room where Rock also had a piano and couches. Miller sat in one couch and Christian in the other. They sat looking at each other for a second or two and Miller took a heavy sigh and, according to Christian, said, 'It's official. Rock has been diagnosed with anorexia . . . it may be too late, he's dying.'

Christian began to cry, and asked Miller why Rock had to go to Europe for treatment. He replied that it was because there was a new experimental drug which was available only from a team of doctors in Zurich, Switzerland. It could not be administered in the United States because it had not been approved by the Federal Drugs Administration. Christian said: 'Rock knows the President, he could cut the red tape and have the drug sent here.' It was impossible, Miller insisted, because the facilities to administer the drug were in Switzerland.

Christian asked to be allowed to accompany Rock to Europe. That too was not possible. There were already too many rumours circulating about Hudson's health and Christian might be discovered as the star's lover. Miller added: 'What I have told you has to remain with you. It's too dangerous If word got out that Rock Hudson had anorexia, people would think he had the same disease as Karen Carpenter [who died from it]. It's a female disease and they would call him a homosexual.'

[In spite of Christian's concern, Hudson prepared that day to fly to Carmel for the Doris Day special. Rock had insisted to Mark Miller and his publicist Dale Olson that he wanted to appear in the show, called 'Doris Day's Best Friends'. He did not want to let her down; he loved her as a friend and since he had been so close at a time when both their careers had hit their highest point, he felt he could not miss attending, especially since this was Doris's first public appearance for many years. When they arrived at Carmel, Olson was expecting a difficult time with the media – he knew that a press conference for Doris and some of her friends had been arranged. Rock arrived late; he looked terrible; tired, dishevelled, and wearing odd, ill-fitting clothes, he could hardly walk without assistance. Everyone was open-mouthed at his appearance and with a far from hostile press, he got nothing but sympathy.

Doris forced a brave smile, kissed him on the lips and said how nice it was to be walking down memory lane; secretly she had considered cancelling the segment in which Rock was to appear, for his own sake. She knew something was desperately wrong and when the famous last picture taken of Hudson with Doris, was flashed around the world, suddenly Olson was confronted with a barrage of telephone calls from a dozen countries, with reporters wanting to know what was wrong with Rock. Still, no public mention of AIDS was made.]

Rock returned from the Carmel on 19 July, and left for Paris the following evening with Ron Channell. The next day, Christian received a telephone call from Miller. He said Rock had collapsed at the Ritz Hotel, in Paris. Christian was surprised. 'Why is he in Paris?' he asked. 'I thought he was going to Switzerland.' Miller told him that the arrangement had been that he would meet doctors in Paris to confer and the whole team would fly to Switzerland. Miller was flying to France immediately, to take care of the press. His passport had expired and Christian said he drove him that morning to get it renewed; then he caught the next plane to Paris.

That afternoon, Christian was back at the Hudson house when Tom Clark came into the patio area; apparently he still had a key to the house. He appeared to have been drinking and was blustering about. Christian asked him what he was doing. He replied, 'That son-of-a-bitch Army Archard . . . how could he do this to me. He's going to say that Rock has AIDS.' Miller phoned Christian upon his arrival in Paris on 22 July; Christian told him about the conversation with Tom Clark. He said Miller replied, 'You can't believe anything Tom Clark says. He's an alcoholic. It's just too ludicrous for Army Archard to pull something like that.'

[Army Archard, a Los Angeles columnist for *Daily Variety*, ran an 'exclusive' story in the 23 July 1988 edition, in which he said: 'Good morning. The whispering campaign against Rock Hudson can – and should – stop. He was flown to Paris for further help. The Institute Pasteur has been very active in research of AIDS. Hudson's dramatic weight loss was made evident to the national press last week when he winged his way to Carmel . . . his illness was no secret to close Hollywood friends, but its true nature was disclosed to very few.' It was a cleverly worded item which did not say that Hudson had AIDS. But the implications were sufficient to cause a furore; later that day, the news became official.]

Meanwhile, in another telephone call from Paris, Christian again asked Miller what was wrong with Rock and was told that doctors now believed that he had something gravely wrong with his liver; either cirrhosis or cancer. Nothing more was said. Then Christian finally learned the truth: 'I was sitting alone in Rock's home that evening when I heard there was going to be an announcement on television, and I turned it on to watch the news broadcast. A French woman, Rock's publicist friend [Yanou Collart] came on and read a statement that Rock Hudson had Acquired Immune Deficiency Syndrome which had been diagnosed in the United States a year earlier.

Rhoden: 'What was your reaction to this news?'

Christian: 'I had several reactions within seconds. First, I did not believe what I was hearing. Then I thought, how could it have been diagnosed a year earlier? And then it sunk in. It was AIDS. I began to sweat and then I blacked out. I just thought "Oh, my god. I'm a dead man." '

'Why did you think you were a dead man?'

'Because I had had sex with him from April 1983 to February 1985. I had had sex with him after it had been diagnosed and at a time when he had full-blown AIDS. That's why I thought I was a dead man.'

Christian said he ran to the bathroom and just vomited, and was scared, extremely depressed. A full day went by before he heard from Miller, who telephoned from Paris. Christian described the conversation to the jury:

Miller asked, 'How are you taking it, kid?'

'I'm not.'

'I'm sorry. But imagine what I've been through; I've lied for thirteen months and I'm sick of it. The Movie Star told me not to tell you. I don't want you to worry. I'm in the captain's seat now and if there's anything wrong you can be taken care of. We want you to come to Paris and be tested by the same doctors that administered this drug to Rock.'

'What drug was that?'

'It's called HPA-23, and if you have it [AIDS] in your system, because you are young and healthy, you can be cured.'

'Miller, there is no cure,' said Christian.

'Well, the only reason Rock got as ill as he did was because he refused to go back for treatment. He was instructed to come back every two months for treatment in Paris and he wouldn't go back . . . you can be cured if you have it in your system.'

Christian asked Miller why he had not been told earlier and Miller replied that he blamed Rock's doctors who had said they had done a study on partners of AIDS victims who often did themselves bodily harm after discovering the truth about their lovers. Miller called back again an hour later and said: 'Rock wants you to come to Paris. He told me "Tell him to come over. Do anything for the kid, I may have killed him. Tell him if he doesn't come over he's an asshole." ' Miller also mentioned that he had a friend called Steve Del Re who had AIDS and was also being treated by Dr Dormont; he was in his late twenties and had shown a marked improvement since he began taking the same drug Dr Dormont had given to Hudson.

After the conversation with Miller, Christian immediately made an appointment with a local physician named Dr Roth but was unable to have a blood test before he flew to Paris for the appointment which Miller had arranged for him with Dr Dormont. He said he bought a plane ticket on his credit card as instructed by Miller and arrived in Paris the following day.

Steve Del Re met him with a taxi and took him to the hotel and then to Dr Dormont's clinic where he gave a blood sample and was interviewed at length by the specialist. Dormont could not understand why Rock had not returned for treatment because it might have prolonged his life; now it was too late. Hudson was near to death. Dormont seemed surprised that Christian had not been told about Hudson's illness and questioned him about their sexual practices. It had been oral and anal, reciprocal.

Christian wanted to know what the chances were of him having contracted AIDS. Dormont, he said, explained that anyone who had had sexual relations with a patient suffering from full-blown AIDS was at far greater risk, and that the incubation period for the virus could be anything from eight to ten years. Dormont took the blood test and asked Christian to return in one week's time.

Earlier, Rhoden had questioned Christian about his contact with Steve Del Re. Miller had suggested that Christian should take Del Re to the south of France for a few days while he was awaiting the results of the test. They were to visit Hudson's writer friend, Lady Vivian Glenavy. Miller told him to pay for the tickets on his American Express card and he would be reimbursed by Mammoth Films.

Rhoden: 'Now, when Miller told you to go to the south of France with Del Re, what did he say to you?'

Christian: 'He told me to "throw a rubber on my dick" and have sex with Del Re. I said he must be insane. Miller then said, "What would it matter? If you got AIDS from Rock, it would not matter if you had sex with Del Re." And he laughed.'

'He did what?'

'He laughed at me.'

When they arrived in Cannes, Christian discovered that Lady Glenavy was unable to accommodate them because she had other house guests. He tried to find hotel rooms but it was high season and could only get one double room which he and Del Re shared for the next two nights.

Rhoden: 'You said this young man had AIDS? Did you see any sign of it?'

Christian: 'Yes, when I arrived in Paris he met me at the airport and as we took a taxi into the city, he rolled up his sleeves and showed me several Kaposi's sarcoma lesions on his arms.'

When he returned to Paris, he went back to see Dr Dormont for the results of the first test. Dormont told him: 'All I can say now is that at this moment you are a very lucky man. I found no trace of AIDS in the first test.' But the doctor warned that he could not say definitely that he was not carrying the virus. The second test which would take a month to culture would be a more definite investigation but even then he should be tested again every two months.

Christian asked Dormont if it were possible for a person with a negative blood test to be infected; he said he had known cases of that to happen. Even in Rock Hudson's case, there were no traces of live virus in his blood after the first treatment with HPA-23.

Rhoden: 'When you returned from Paris, what was your state of mind?'

'I was very confused, panicky. The fact that he had told me a negative test did not mean anything made me totally confused. I was afraid.'

'Afraid of what?'

'Of dying.'

# CHAPTER FIVE

# Calm, Cool and Collected

Much would be made by defending counsel that after the lawsuit was filed, Marc Christian had been ferried around America by his then lawyer Marvin Mitchelson for the appearances on major coast-to-coast television shows and for interviews with big-name writers in mass-circulation magazines and newspapers, sometimes facing hostile and intense questioning. One newspaper interview, for example, had lasted more than four hours.

If Mitchelson's original thought had been to provide his client with a publicity machine, a platform and an image of being a fighter on behalf of other partners of AIDS sufferers, then the rub-off effect had been to rehearse and prepare Christian for what lay ahead in the trial. Christian had become word perfect in his responses; he seldom stammered or stumbled, never appeared nervous or unsure of himself or his answers. As each hour of his appearance on the witness stand passed, he appeared more confident and firm.

He entered the courtroom to begin the second day of his evidence, on 12 January and Harold Rhoden began prompting him towards some of the crucial areas of his story. They related to the period when Christian had returned from Paris after his tests to discover that a huge press corps was camped outside the Hudson house and the University College of Los Angeles Medical Centre to which Rock had been admitted. There now appeared little hope of his survival; Dr Dormont could do no more for him and he was flown home to California on a specially chartered Boeing 747, costing $300,000, with only himself and Mark Miller as passengers. The press coverage of events had reached fever pitch and everyone and anyone who knew Rock found themselves being questioned or having a microphone thrust under their noses for a television interview. At the hospital and Rock's house, sacks full of mail and get-well cards were arriving from around the globe. Hudson himself was unaware of the extent of the activity outside his hospital room; Miller had given strict instructions that it should be kept from him. He even went on television to give a hopeful report that Rock looked fine, very well. Privately, he knew he was dying.

Christian's own role and presence at The Castle had not become public; the press were yet to reveal the involvement of a lover. It had been a daunting scenario in which Christian found himself, and upon his return to the witness stand for the continuation of his evidence, he began recalling the events immediately after his arrival back from Paris.

Miller telephoned him at The Castle, said he wanted to arrange a meeting, and arrived at the appointed time with his friend George Nader. They asked to speak with Christian about the current situation and wanted James Wright, the butler, to sit in on the conversation. Christian agreed and they sat on the couches in the White Room. Christian wondered what they wanted and as Miller stumbled over his words, George Nader interjected and said, 'Just get on with it and tell him why we've come.' Christian relayed his version of the conversation:

Miller told him: 'You have to leave. Rock wants you out of the house.'

Christian replied: 'Why doesn't he tell me himself?'

'He doesn't want to speak with you.'

'How can I believe you. You've lied to me about AIDS. Why should I believe you that Rock has said he wants me out of his house? If he wants me out let him be man enough to call me on the telephone and tell me to leave.'

'I'm only relaying what he told me.'

'I think you're a liar.'

George Nader became angry. 'We don't have to sit here and take these insults,' and they got up and left the house.

The next day, Hudson's business manager, Wallace Sheft, telephoned from New York and repeated the request that Christian leave. He refused and in the meantime had made repeated attempts to speak to Hudson by telephoning the hospital but he was told that on the instructions of Miller, none of his calls were to be put through. By this point he had not seen or spoken to Hudson for more than three weeks since he left for Europe.

He went to the hospital to try to get to see Hudson but a nurse told him that he could not go in. She had a list of people who were allowed to see him, and he was not on the list. The order, she said, came from Mark Miller. [In conversation with Rock's friend, Elizabeth Taylor, Mark Miller had organized a tightly controlled visiting schedule for Rock, and all were forewarned not to reveal what was happening outside. Rock himself was in poor shape; his mind was wandering and on bad days he drifted in and out of a deep, coma-like sleep. He was under constant medical care, with intravenous feeding and blood transfusions. Tight security was in force at the hospital, with specially hired guards on duty to prevent fans or reporters getting through. Outside, a growing group of his fans waited daily for news, carrying a banner which proclaimed: WE LOVE YOU ROCK.]

Christian was arrested for trespassing by two security guards at the hospital and was escorted out of the building, protesting that Rock would have wanted to see him. He saw Miller again and exchanged angry words. Miller relented and gave the hospital instructions to allow him through. He went to UCLA the next day. Christian said that as he walked in, Rock said to him, 'Hiyya, where've you been . . . what took you so long.' He told him he had been trying to see him but Miller would not let him visit. Rock said 'Why would he do that?' He asked about the house and the dogs and then Christian came straight out with it and asked him why he had not told him he had AIDS: 'Didn't you think I had a right to know . . . ?' Hudson replied: 'You're all alone when you've got this.' Christian replied: 'You're not alone. I wouldn't have left you. I would have been there to help you fight.'

Christian mentioned the fact that Miller and Nader wanted him out of the house but Hudson told him, 'Just carry on as usual.' He said he need not leave if he did not want to. Back at the house, Miller had called a meeting of Hudson's staff. George Nader arrived, and they were joined by James Wright, the butler, John Dobbs, the house cleaner, Marty Flaherty, the handyman, and Ron Channell, Rock's aerobics instructor. Miller assembled them in the living room and went through what he called the 'official story' of Rock's illness. James Wright had already been made aware that Hudson had AIDS. He was one of the three people Miller had told at the outset of the virus because doctors had advised him that someone in the household should be aware of the situation to take obvious precautions, prepare the right kind of food and be available if Hudson should collapse. Miller went through the litany of Rock's progression from diagnosis to admission to hospital and concluded: 'I have been lying for thirteen months and that is why I did it.' He said he was under orders from Hudson not to reveal the truth.

The day before Hudson was due to return home from UCLA, Wallace Sheft telephoned Christian and again repeated his request that he should leave the house. Christian said he was told that Rock no longer wanted him there and a moving van had been arranged. Christian said he would not leave. Rock said he could stay. Christian said, 'He may have exposed me to AIDS. I want a chance to talk to Rock when he's home.' Sheft replied, 'Well you might have given him AIDS; we don't know.'

Hudson was brought back to The Castle and in Christian's words, he looked as if he did not have much longer to live. Liberty Martin came over with a pot roast and some lentils, which Rock had asked for. Towards the end of September Christian telephoned Dr Dormont in Paris for the results of the second test. They showed no trace of AIDS but Dormont said he was not out of the woods yet and suggested he should have further tests every two months.

[Hudson was in rapid decline. Only his closest friends were allowed to see him, like Martha Raye, who would sit for hours by his bedside, Roddy McDowall and Elizabeth Taylor. McDowall was deeply affected by the sight of him and Elizabeth Taylor visited often. Rock had been one of her most ardent supporters during her own recent problems and she would sit by his beside, holding back the tears. On better days, his nurses would get him up and he would sit in a chair in his silk robe and pyjamas and she would talk about old times and how they drank chocolate martinis in Marfa, Texas, during filming *Giant*. But the visits became more and more traumatic and though she persisted, she would weep uncontrollably when she left him. At the end of September, she was among those who organized a star-studded gala to launch a fundraising for the new AIDS Foundation at which Burt Lancaster read a message, said to be from Rock, which read: 'People have told me that the disclosure that I have AIDS has helped make this evening an immediate sell-out and it will raise one million dollars in the battle against AIDS . . . I have also been told that media coverage of my own situation has brought enormous international attention to the gravity of this disease . . . if that is helping others, I can at least know my own misfortune has some positive worth.' The audience, which included big names of Hollywood, was in tears. But Rock had not written the message; in fact he was probably unaware of anything. He was now seldom conscious and his weight was down to less than seven stones.]

He died on 2 October 1988 and was cremated. His ashes were scattered secretly at sea. Even at the wake, two weeks after his death, the row over Christian's discussions with Marvin Mitchelson came up again. Christian recalled a conversation he had with Mark Miller. Miller came over to him by the pool and said: 'Are you having a good time?'

'I'm trying to.'

Miller said: 'We can't let this go to court.'

Christian replied he did not want it to go to court either. He just wanted to know what his rights were.

Miller replied: 'If it goes to court, we'll smear you.'

'How will you do that?'

'We are going to call you a male hustler, a street hooker.'

'How can you do that? It isn't true and you can't prove it.'

'We don't have to prove it. If we allege it, it will go all over the world and it will be believed. And if that doesn't work, we'll call you a drug addict.' Christian said there were others present at the wake who witnessed the conversation.

[The funeral was arranged by Mark Miller, in conjunction with Elizabeth Taylor. She suggested a plain Quaker service, chose the flowers and the food, and even checked the suggested guest list, eliminating those she did not want to attend. The service was held in the grounds, and guests were welcomed with Rock's favourites: margueritas and Mexican food. A Mexican band played softly on the terraces. Helicopters flew low overhead, with cameras hanging from the doors. There were eulogies from some of Rock's friends, including Carol Burnett, Tab Hunter, television producer Susan Stafford, and Roddy McDowall. Then Elizabeth said: 'Rock would have wanted us to be happy . . . let's raise our glasses and drink to him.']

At this point in the trial, Rhoden wanted to read from the original statements of defence from Miller and the estate. His opposing counsel objected and once again discussion was taken in the judge's chambers. Rhoden said his point in raising these points now was to challenge allegations they had made against Christian. The judge ruled that it was not unreasonable to conclude that the estate, Miller and George Nader, as primary beneficiaries, were acting in concert in the defence, so the objection was overruled.

In open court, Rhoden began reading from the allegations made by Wallace Sheft in the original pleadings of the defence, which claimed that while Hudson was away in Israel, Christian engaged in sexual activity with one or more men, and one or more women, and had solicited and accepted payment for his sexual favours; that when Hudson returned, he briefly resumed his relationship with Christian until he was told that Christian had been having sex with others while he was away. On learning this, Hudson immediately ended his relationship with Christian and intended to have him removed from the house.

The allegations of Sheft also claimed that Christian, on more than one occasion, threatened to destroy Hudson's reputation and career by publishing the personal and private letters written by Hudson to Christian, which would have exposed him as a homosexual. Because of these threats, Hudson was forced to allow Christian to remain in the house and pay him money.

Now Rhoden wanted to put these allegations to Christian, under oath: 'While Hudson was in Israel, did you engage in sexual activity with any men or women anywhere?'

'No.'

'Did you ever, in your life, solicit money for sex?'

'Never.'

'Did you ever accept money for sex?'

'No.'

'Did you ever say to Rock Hudson that you had engaged in sexual activity and received payment for sexual favours?'

'No, I did not.'

'When Hudson returned from Israel, did he terminate his personal relationship with you, or tell you to leave the house?'

'No.'

'Did you ever threaten to expose Rock Hudson as a homosexual at any time, by any means?'

'No, I did not. Rock was not a wimp. If I had tried anything like that he would have kicked my ass right down the stairs.'

In fact, said Christian, after Rock's death he was offered substantial sums by the *National Enquirer* to tell his story. The first offer was for $250,000, then they increased it to $300,000 and he still refused.

To clear up other allegations which the defence would make against Christian, Rhoden returned to the question of the friends Marc brought into the Hudson household.

Did Hudson ever object to Christian's friends visiting him? No, said Christian, he had never raised any objection and on occasions one or more of his friends had stayed the night. His family also came to the house and Hudson bought Christian's mother several gifts. On 20 May 1984 Hudson threw a surprise party at the house for Christian's parents' 40th wedding anniversary. There were about a hundred people there and he hired a band. When Christian's sister Susan was married in May 1985, the wedding reception was held at The Castle, and Rock also took her and her fiancé out to dinner.

Having established Christian's apparent residency in the Hudson house, Rhoden went on to question him about his reasons for seeking legal advice. Christian said he saw four lawyers and they all recommended that he see Marvin Mitchelson, which he did before Hudson's death. He had done so to establish what his legal rights were: whether or not he could stay in the house, especially since he claimed Hudson had not asked him to leave. He told Mitchelson that he was not seeking palimony (which had become one of Mitchelson's renowned specialities); he was not Liberace's chauffeur! In all, he had four meetings with Mitchelson prior to Hudson's death and finally left the house on the last weekend of October, when he returned to live at Liberty Martin's apartment.

[Rock's house was to be prepared for sale and some of its contents auctioned. The value was set at $5 million but in those days when AIDS scare stories adorned every front page, there was no rush of interest. It stood vacant for eighteen months and made $2.9 million. His other property, an apartment in New York in which Tom Clark had been living, was sold for $2 million.]

Rhoden turned to the medical opinions Christian had sought after Hudson's death. He had been given the all-clear by Dr Dormont and had visited another physician, a Dr Joseph Sonnabend in New York in early December. He had been told Sonnabend was a pioneer of AIDS testing in New York. The tests he took showed no trace of the AIDS virus and he asked Sonnabend if that meant he did not have the disease. He replied, 'I cannot tell you that. I cannot guarantee you do not have it; I can't tell you one way or the other.'

Rhoden was interested in Christian's state of mind after this new test. 'I felt it was like a stay of execution,' he said. 'But I still felt that at any time, I could be given a death warrant.'

He then went to see a Dr Moses Laufer in Los Angeles for a further test. Again, he was told the test was negative and again no guarantees were given. Christian was now totally unsure about his health and worried constantly that he would be struck down.

At the request of the defence, he saw Dr Roth again in December 1986. He said he had heard that the incubation period was even higher than what he had heard a year previously – fifteen years.

Rhoden: 'What did that mean to you?'

'I can't really describe it. It was just like a black cloud. Instead of hearing good news, it was worse. It meant that the virus could be lying dormant or latent in my body for that long before any symptoms, any antibodies, anything would show up.'

His fear of getting AIDS increased. He said his mental state fluctuated. He would get good news about a test and for a few days he might feel a little better; but then, when he would be reminded what the doctors had said regarding those tests, it was a false hope, that really they could not tell him anything.

He was given further cause for concern when he read the report of an international AIDS conference in Stockholm, noting that tests could not always detect the virus in the body, that they were desperately trying to find a better test.

Rhoden had one more question regarding Dr Sonnabend: 'When you saw him in New York, what were you doing there?'

'Marvin Mitchelson took me to appear on the "Phil Donahue Show".'

'And after that you went on other talk shows with Mitchelson, did you not?'

'Yes, I did.'

'Did you want to go on these television talk shows?'

'No.'

'Why did you go?'

'Because Marvin insisted that he knew what he was doing. He said that as long as we didn't talk about the actual particulars of this case, just the reason the lawsuit was filed, I would be doing a public service; that I would be getting the word out that people should disclose to their sexual partners if they have a contagious sexual disease. I was uneasy about doing it, but he said he knew these things. He understood why it should be done.'

'Did you go on the programmes because you wanted personal publicity?'

'No.'

Christian did not receive any payment, nor did he for the newspaper and magazine interviews that Mitchelson set up for him.

Rhoden had exhausted his list of questions, bar one: 'Do you happen to remember the last time you had a discussion with Rock Hudson concerning how he felt about you, the last time?'

'Yes, it was on my birthday, 1985; we were sitting in the Red Room looking at Rock's photographs; he talked about his career. He talked about how we met and he was reminiscing and wished me a happy birthday. He put his arm around me and said, "You know, I love you, and I would never do anything to hurt you." '

'Your witness, Mr Mills.'

Robert Mills, counsel for the estate, rose slowly and deliberately for the cross-examination upsetting the opposition immediately when he asked: 'Mr Mitchelson is no longer your lawyer, is he?'

'No.'

'Decided to take the advice of Mr Rhoden, finally.'

Rhoden: 'Just a moment. The question is argumentative and uncertain as to what advice he is talking about.'

The Judge: 'All right. Sustained.'

Mills: 'You didn't want to go on those talk shows; is that right?'

'Correct.'

'You just acceded to the idea maybe Mr Mitchelson knew what was better than you did as far as going on talk shows or not?'

'I had never been to a lawyer in my life. I had never been on a talk show in my life. I had no experience in those matters and I just deferred to Mr Mitchelson.'

'Okay. That is fine. And you deferred to him for the "Donahue Show", right?'

'Correct.'

'And you deferred to him for the "Larry King Show", right? – And you deferred to him for the "Good Morning San Francisco Show"?'

'For every show.'

'Well, I will go through every show: 'P.M. Magazine", right? – "Good Morning Australia" – *New York Native* Interview – *Penthouse* Interview. That didn't bother you emotionally, getting up and going on national television to explain what your feelings were with regard to this lawsuit or with respect to Rock Hudson?'

'Yes, it did. I threw up on several occasions before I went on.'

'You forged ahead and did it anyway, didn't you? The *New York*

*Native* interview that you gave, you actually did talk about your feelings – you talked about your relationship with Mr Hudson, and you did the same thing in the *Penthouse* magazine article. You said around October of 1984 Mr Hudson had this skin rash disease called Impetigo? That you put balms over his body?'

Mills next pressured Christian on his claim that they had sex three to five times a week from April 1983, until Hudson became so sick that he was not interested in sex. He wanted to know where these encounters took place before Tom Clark moved out of The Castle. There were numerous places, said Christian: a North Hollywood motel, a motel on Ventura, Mark Miller and George Nader's house at Palm Springs, Liberty Martin's place and a house he used in Santa Barbara.

Turning to the question of Rock Hudson's will, Mills wanted Christian to re-affirm his pre-trial deposition which was read to the jury: 'Rock Hudson told me he was going to put me in his Will, at least a half a dozen times. First when I moved into the house and ending the last time, I would say, in January of 1985; most specifically in August of 1984 when he told me he was going to take Tom Clark out of his will. He told this to me in private and with witnesses, much to my embarrassment. When he returned home from Paris initially for the AIDS treatment, I assumed it was a stop in New York to change the will. He never mentioned it again and I never brought it up. But in the following January, in 1985, he did, again, in a very warm state, say, "You know, I hope you take care of this place and love it as much as I did." ' Christian was adamant. Yes, Hudson had said all of those things.

Now Mills turned to the question of what Hudson had paid him: 'Do you have any idea just how much you expensed into Mammoth Film Company during the time that you were able to expense items through that film company?'

'I don't know the exact amount, because often Mr Miller would give me a cheque over the amount of what I would turn in in receipts, because he needed cash himself. So he might write me a cheque for $500 and I might keep $200 of it and he might have needed the $300 for spending money for the house. So, broken down, I don't know exactly what my personal expenses were.'

'If I told you that over this period of time from 4 November of 1983, until you moved out sometime in December of 1985, about two years, that you expensed over $70,000; would that figure be too inaccurate for you to accept?'

'I can't imagine it being that high because my expenses basically were for record albums, books, and meals outside of the home. But then I often ran errands for Rock and turned in receipts for him. I don't know; and it might very well be $70,000 and it might be $10,000, I have no idea.'

'Did you and Mr Hudson ever have an argument oveer you having the 1959 Chevrolet *Nomad* that he apparently paid $20,000 for restoration and which was parked on his premises?'

'An argument? We had a very heated discussion about it, yes.'

'You didn't threaten him at all?'

'No.'

Mills returned once again to the question of sexual relations and asked Christian to confirm that they had never used a condom. Christian said he never had, nor with other males before Hudson. He could not recall ever having known a homosexual male to wear a condom with another man in 1980, 1981, or even in 1984; possibly 1985. There was no fear of pregnancy, so, no, he did not wear a condom with Rock Hudson or anyone else.

Mills's cross-examination moved to an area of questioning in which the clear implication was that Christian could have given Hudson AIDS. Christian agreed that the disease had an incubation period as long as ten years, perhaps even fifteen. Mills asked: 'Technically it could have been back fifteen years ago that you were carrying this disease?' Christian said it was possible, but unlikely. He agreed that of the ten or fifteen people with whom he had had sex between 1979 and 1982, he had never asked if any one of them had developed AIDS. Some he had never seen since, some had moved. The rest knew who he was and he assumed they would have told him.

Mills: 'Does that cause you any concern, as you sit here today, that maybe you could be getting AIDS from somebody else, let alone Mr Hudson?'

Christian: 'To be honest with you, it has crossed my mind. I'm sure that anybody in the gay community would be wondering if they got it, who they might get it from, but with those particular individuals, I can't remember the kind of sex I had with them. I do not remember whether it was a particular kind of high-risk and I would certainly hope that if any of them came down with AIDS that they would tell all of their sexual partners, myself included. And then if that were to happen, yes, I would have greater concern.'

65

'Do you have any concern that maybe you gave Mr Hudson AIDS?'

'I did until what I learned recently and that was from the Stockholm Conference, and that was that someone who has antibodies is probably not very infectious, but once the disease enters into full-blown AIDS, then they become very infectious. So I tend to doubt now that I could have passed it onto Rock. But I'm not a medical expert, I don't know.'

Mills, however, got a surprising response when he persisted that Christian could produce no evidence of sex between them after Hudson had been told he had AIDS.

Christian replied: 'That's not correct.'

Mills: 'All of a sudden, somebody has come up and told you that they happened to see you?'

'Unfortunately, yes.'

'Well, didn't you know they were there? Were they looking through a peephole? Where were they?'

'This is very embarrassing.'

'Well, I hope so.'

'No, the other person was not there with me or Rock, to my knowledge, and I'm certain Rock did not know about it or he might have been a bit upset.'

'Give me the person's name.'

'Wayne Bernhard.'

Rhoden interjected: 'Just a moment, Your Honour. The snickers still from Mr Miller ought to be ordered stopped. Because what he's doing is trying to make an argument before this jury. He's going to hear the testimony in a few minutes, and he'll know what it's all about. But this habit that the man has of snickering before the jurors is something I ask that Your Honour put a stop to now, and that also goes to snickers in a lesser extent from Mr Mills.'

The Judge: 'Okay. Well, ladies and gentlemen, I have noticed that occasionally there have been smiles or condescending expressions and in this case there definitely was a snicker or laugh, and you must just disregard that. I mean, that could be for a variety of reasons. That could be true feeling or attempting to influence you. So I can't be watching all the time to see if somebody is smiling at the time testimony is given; and I suggest that you pay no attention to that at all and to assess the testimony as it comes on, without regard to what somebody in the audience or somebody sitting at Counsel table may indicate by way of expression.'

Mills resumed: 'So from 1983 in April up until three days ago, did you know that somebody was watching you and Mr Hudson have sex?'
'No, I didn't.'
'Wayne Bernhard is a friend of yours; you met him from Greg Rice?'
'I met him about twelve years ago.'
'He's homosexual, correct?'
'Yes, he is.'
'Now, did you ever hear Wayne Bernhard ever say before three days ago that he saw you and Mr Hudson having some kind of sexual contact?'
'No, he did not. He never volunteered the information to me until three days ago when I made a comment.'
'Okay. Where was he when he was looking at you and Mr Hudson?'
'On the patio, the night of my birthday party: 23 June 1984. I was on the side of the jacuzzi, with Rock after the birthday party was finished and everyone went home. Mr Bernhard spent the night because it was a long drive to Orange County. He had had a bit to drink and I wouldn't let him drive home. I asked him if he saw what he really saw, and he said, "You were not playing Scrabble." Those were his exact words.'

Mills now turned to the question of why Hudson had never taken Christian on any trips outside of the State of California, attempting to illustrate that Hudson was already losing interest in Christian before AIDS was diagnosed.

Mills: 'He didn't take you on the times he went to Hawaii, both in 1984 and 1985, right?'
'He begged me to go with him. But I couldn't because my father was dying, and I spent Easter with my family, and he understood that and apologized. He thought it was insensitive to have forgotten.'
'So he took Ron Channell instead, right?'
'I have no idea.'
'He didn't take you to Washington, DC, to the State dinner?'
'I don't know what you're talking about.'
'Were you ever taken to Washington, DC, and to meet President Reagan and Nancy Reagan at that State dinner with Mr Hudson?'
'No, no. He told me the reason for that.'
'Oh, of course. Let's hear the reason. I want to hear all your reasons. What was the reason he didn't take you to the State dinner?'

'Because he said that Nancy Reagan would figure out our relationship because she was a very bright woman, and he was embarrassed.'

'You didn't go to New York with him when he flew there in August of 1984, right?'

'He went on business,I believe . . . No. Actually, he went to go get treated for AIDS. So, no, he did not take me.'

'He took Ron Channell, right?'

'Yes. He took Channell because he wanted his work-out partner to be with him, and well, there was a reason why he took Channell, according to Mark Miller.'

Mills: 'It's your testimony that you had sex with Mr Hudson approximately 160 times between June of 1984 and 5 February of 1985?'

'Yeah. I'm not adding it up right now, but that sounds about right.' Some weeks there would be no sex, he said, sometimes maybe twice a day; it wasn't clockwork.

It seemed a lot of sex, said Mills, considering Hudson was away: at the Deauville Film Festival approximately six weeks; at the Presidential dinner; in Las Vegas from approximately 9 July of 1984 to 10 August of 1984; for four days in December when he took Ron Channell to Disneyworld; and for ten days in February when they went to Hawaii.

Christian replied: 'Yes, but I also recall that whenever he would return from a trip, especially the one in Paris he wanted me to make up for lost time.'

Returning to the question of Christian's trip to the south of France with Steve Del Re, Mills wanted to know if he was worried about being in contact with a man who had pussing Kaposi's sarcoma? Didn't it cause him concern that he might get the infection into his own blood stream?

Christian said he had already been reassured that AIDS was transmitted only through blood or semen and since he was not about to exchange anything of that kind with that person, he was not panicky about it. He was extra careful, though, and checked his entire body daily for any cuts or spots. He also carried a can of Lysol disinfectant with him. He had talked specifically to Dr Dormont about it. He had over thirty patients in Del Re's condition at the time. As a doctor he did not feel any unreasonable concern that he would get AIDS through his patients which put Christian's mind at rest.

The cross-examination by Mr Mills continued for another day, taking Christian through every step of his earlier evidence, picking up points which the defence challenged, thus to engender doubt in the jury's mind as to the total credibility of the young man's claims. But Christian had become well-versed in the process of law and the tactics of lawyers; he was even employing his own diversions, such as giving opposing counsel a fuller answer than they had expected – and for which they would constantly ask for the judge's reprimand.

In a court of law, the insistence upon a 'simple yes or no' can often mean that a lawyer is fearful that a more expansive reply might introduce previously unheard facts, or specific detail that counsel had not bargained on being revealed. This happened more than once and left counsel, who had been trying to score a point, with egg on his face.

In the case of Christian's testimony over his sexual acts with Hudson, for example, Mills had re-iterated the point that no one could corroborate Christian's claims because the only other person who knew what had happened was Hudson and he was dead.

'Wrong,' said Christian, and before Mills had a chance to limit the reply, Christian had told of the occasion when Wayne Bernhard saw them together beside the jacuzzi. Why, asked Mills, had Christian never mentioned this before? There had been other opportunities during his evidence to have stated this new fact. The reason, said Christian, was that Bernhard did not mention it to him until during the weekend recess from the trial.

Mills, and soon Mr Banks on behalf of Mark Miller during his cross-examination, delved deeply into the facts surrounding the rebuilding of 1959 Chevrolet, which Christian himself had admitted was a 'rip-off' at $20,000 [the final amount which Hudson paid]. Wasn't it true, asked counsel, that at the time the work was being carried out, Christian's friend and former lover Liberty Martin was working at the firm called Image Makers that did the work, albeit in a part-time capacity? And wasn't Christian's friend Bob Dolphi also employed in a senior position by the same company for a time? True, admitted Christian, and his explanations were lost by counsel's insistence on a straight answer.

Both Mills and Banks dwelt heavily on Christian's apparent lack of concern that he might have AIDS, insisting that the majority of the tests conducted upon him after Hudson's death were at the instigation of the defence. The reason for this lack of concern, the defence would infer, was that Christian knew full well that his relationship with Hudson had broken down: wasn't Hudson absent from the party given at the house for Christian's mother and father? Wasn't he also absent at the reception given at the house on the occasion of Marc's sister's wedding? That was true, Christian explained, but Hudson was working at the time.

Mills questioned another example which he believed indicated that Hudson and Christian were no longer talking to each other by the spring. It was the night of the Oscar presentations and Governor's Ball for the Academy of Motion Picture Arts and Sciences of which Hudson was a member. Wasn't it correct that although Hudson acquired tickets for Christian and Liberty Martin, he went to the event alone? Yes, said Christian, but he had originally intended to sit with them until a few days beforehand when he was asked to be a presenter with Liza Minnelli; he could not then sit in the audience because he would be required backstage. Christian sat next to Meryl Streep. Afterwards, Hudson went on to four or five parties and made a brief appearance at the Governor's Ball. They departed in separate cars.

Mills laboured the point: Did Christian and Liberty go with Hudson to the Governor's Ball? He received the same response, 'No, but . . . .' until finally Mills protested to the judge: 'The answers are calling for a "yes" or "no" and I am tired of these narratives.' Rhoden interjected to defend his client against 'ambiguous questioning'. The judge became rattled and ordered counsel to proceed. By that time, whatever point Mills had been attempting to make seemed lost on the jury.

Christian was equally adamant that the affair continued actively, well into 1985 – didn't Rock himself throw a birthday party for him, at which Hudson himself cooked chickens over a barbecue (much to the distress of some of the guests when they later discovered that Hudson was already suffering from AIDS, that he had actually cut himself and had perhaps bled over the food)?

Christian said he had to be satisfied with the medical opinions he had sought, starting with Dr Dormont in Paris, that he had no resources of his own to fund expensive tests other than the $5000 in his savings account, which he said had been given to him by his mother. He did not feel able to go more extensively into medical opinion or psychiatric treatment which he felt he needed because of the intense worry he suffered from the fear that he might have

AIDS; nor did he want to endure the embarrassment of group therapy at free clinics.

It was during the questioning of Christian's medical research in the possibility that he might have AIDS that Mills, perhaps inadvertently, introduced another potentially damaging aspect against Rock Hudson's already tarnished image. Wasn't it true, he asked, that Christian had Herpes?

Christian was shocked. He had never been aware that he had Herpes. But there it was, said Mills, in a medical report prepared by one of the doctors who examined Christian for the defence: blood tests revealed that he had antibodies of Herpes in his system. Christian said he had never been aware of that; he had never had any symptoms, nor had he ever consulted a doctor for Herpes.

But the question begged others and it led back to Rock Hudson, who had been treated for the disease after a nasty anal rash occurred soon after his return from filming in Israel. Realizing that the answers to his questions were already pointing the finger at Hudson, and that it was possible that he had passed on the disease to Christian, the defence counsel finally managed to get Christian to admit that he could have picked it up from encounters before his involvement with Hudson began. 'I am not saying I got Herpes from Rock,' said Christian, 'what I am saying is that if he lied to me over AIDS, he was capable of lying over Herpes.'

As he was answering the point, he made a half-heard reference to 'Dynasty' star Linda Evans. Christian said he had been told by Marvin Mitchelson that at the time Hudson did the 'Dynasty' love scene with Miss Evans, he had open, Herpes-like sores on the inside of his mouth.

[Hudson's role in 'Dynasty' was to play the part of Daniel Reece, a millionaire equestrian stud farmer who was supposed to be a former lover of Krystle Carrington, played by Miss Evans. Their reunion in the script called for a passionate scene where Rock and Linda are locked in heavy embrace. He was, of course, well aware then that he had AIDS and had apparently questioned his doctors before doing the scene whether it could be transmitted by kissing; he was told it was unlikely and went ahead. Whether he also mentioned that he had open sores on the inside of his mouth is not known but after the announcement of his affliction eight months later, newspapers and television reports focused heavily on the scene; clips of it were repeated in television newscasts.

71

The Linda Evans story became a worldwide topic for columnists, medical writers and even comedians, like Joan Rivers, who used Hudson as a target for sharp criticism. Miss Evans herself put on a brave face and showed only sympathy for her friend Rock; she was not worried by it, she said. Nonetheless, the Screen Actors Guild later introduced guidelines for its actors and, temporarily, open-mouthed kissing on screen became very definitely taboo.]

Christian's mention of Evans sent counsel for both sides into a huddle which led eventually to a hasty conference in the judge's chambers out of the jury's hearing. Miss Evans had been subpoenaed by the defence to make a statement, with her own lawyers present; Christian's lawyer had not been present when Miss Evans gave the statement and he cited the defence for misconduct.

It was irrelevant, ruled the judge. Miss Evans's statement had no bearing on the case and it would not be admitted into evidence. But in open court, he allowed further questions on Rock Hudson's apparent knowledge that he suffered from Herpes – as well as AIDS – and the jury was left to draw its own conclusions.

The cross-examination by Andrew Banks extracted from Christian a further insight into life at the Hudson household both before and after Christian moved in. Christian claimed that Hudson had told him he hated Tom Clark because he was a 'horrible person, a user, a son-of-a-bitch' and he had thrown Hudson out of his own bedroom which Clark then continued to use as his own, leaving Hudson to take one of the other rooms. Christian asked him why he had not asked him to leave. Hudson replied: 'I just haven't got the heart to do that. He had nowhere to go.' He did take Clark out of his will in 1985 thus leaving only George Nader and Mark Miller as the eventual beneficiaries.

According to Christian, Hudson didn't much care for his butler, Englishman James Wright, or his part-time handyman and occasional actor, John Dobbs, but they amused him and kept their mouths shut. He thought Wright's cooking was appalling which was why he often cooked for himself or went out. Rock had talked of firing them, and Mark Miller too. He was tiring of having Miller around the house, not because he did not like him but because he felt he no longer needed him; he was fed up with the trappings of being a movie star and felt he had no need for a press secretary or a personal secretary. He even talked once of selling The Castle and buying a smaller house on the coast to get away from Hollywood.

Then he could dispose of his staff, including Miller, and live a more relaxed life. He made that statement soon after completing the episodes of 'Dynasty' which had left him in a bad state; he said he never wanted to do anything like it again.

Banks questioned Christian on his earlier observation that no one who wanted to work in Hollywood could reveal themselves as homosexual. It was true, said Christian, and he knew that from his own experience and observations of others. If Hudson had come out earlier on in his life and announced he was gay, there would have been no career.

Marc Christian's evidence was concluded. He had remained cool and calm throughout the days of his recollections of his life with Rock Hudson and the trauma that the association had brought him. Under intense questioning from counsel for the estate and Miller, he had remained unswerving in his answers which, in essence, came down to one thing: that he had suffered incredible mental strain from the fact that his relationship with Hudson had continued – with Mark Miller's knowledge – long after the star had been diagnosed as having AIDS. It would be for the defence to prove otherwise.

# CHAPTER SIX

# The Lonely King in his Castle

The activities inside Rock Hudson's house would increasingly become the focal point of the trial. It was like a huge imaginary film set and the jury was shown photographs of the property, taken both inside and out, with each room carefully described on the back. Situated at 9402 Beverly Crest Drive, high on a hill overlooking Beverly Hills, The Castle was a stylish mansion of Mexican influence and Rock was immensely proud of it; he had spent almost fifteen years remodelling the property since he bought it and would often say that it was his retreat from the pressures of being a movie star. There, he could relax. Play around. Swim in the pool. Have parties and enjoy, behind the large security gates, the privacy which he so earnestly required in his private life.

The main part of the house was on two floors, in an 'L' shape butting on to an additional single storey 'L', the whole set around a terrace and the vast pool and patios. It was surrounded by wooded grounds and mature trees which provided a seclusion that could only be intruded upon from the air, although from the balconies of the upper floors, Rock could look out across the city to the Pacific on a clear day, or to the mountains in the east. Inside, there were two large living rooms, a kitchen which he used frequently for informal meals; there was a sauna room and a gymnasium; a theatre with stage and footlights and cine-equipment to show movies; and additional sleeping facilities which were required because the house only had two bedrooms. These were situated on the upper floor of the main building, the Red Room and the Blue Room, reached by a grand staircase leading from the hall. The grounds were rich in plant life and immaculately tended by Hudson's Japanese gardener who came with the house when he bought it. Hudson also had his dogs – seven at one time – which he loved.

The house had seen some great Hollywood parties in its day and many famous names had passed through the heavy timber front doors. In the early days of Tom Clark's arrival at the house, particularly, Rock gave fashionable dinner parties for the elite of his profession but in later years, these had dwindled. Not the least of the reasons was his strained and, at times, bitter relationship with Clark, who he thought had become too possessive of him. They had violent, drunken rows and the homely atmosphere that The Castle had once known descended into an unhappiness that became so bad, Hudson decided to eliminate Clark from his will. Rock himself became a lonely, almost isolated man whose reunions with his star friends became fewer. Because of it, he went again in search of the day-to-day companionship that he needed so badly.

As the trial progressed, the jury was provided with further vignettes of his own life and life at The Castle, which gave a poignant insight to the last years of Hudson's strange existence in a world dominated by male companions. It also showed the extent to which he had given over the use of his house to Marc Christian and his friends and relatives. This would become clear as Harold Rhoden proceeded with his case.

By 20 January 1989 Rhoden had completed the smooth extraction of his client's evidence. He appeared satisfied that Marc Christian had dealt confidently and adequately with the heavy cross-examination of the two opposing counsel and now he would move towards questioning witnesses who could back up some of the claims Christian had made, and confirm conversations overheard or deeds observed. To achieve this, he would call some of Christian's friends, his mother, a middle-aged belly dancer who performed at his birthday party, and, surprisingly, Rock Hudson's secretary Mark Miller who would be classed as an adverse witness.

But the first supporting voice Rhoden called to the stand to corroborate the story so far was Liberty Martin, Christian's friend and former lover. Now sixty-six years old, she was a frail but exceedingly polite witness who, like the lawyers, insisted on being precise, but whose powers of recall tested all three counsel to the limit.

In an American courtroom, as in Britain, counsel presenting the case is not allowed to 'lead' his witness into making statements he knows have already been made in pre-trial depositions; he must confine his questions to a gentle factless prodding, designed solely to elicit the witness's testimony and direct it towards his own line of inquiry. As soon as a question moves into the area of 'leading' the witness, counsel can expect to receive an instant interruption from the opposing side – a shout of 'Objection'.

With Liberty Martin, that proved difficult for Rhoden, Mills and Banks alike during their examination and cross-examination. The problem was Mrs Martin's difficulty with dates, and in any trial – and particularly this one – dates, times and places were vital. She kept apologizing and the lawyers kept their cool as they meticulously took her through the events of her life since she first met Rock Hudson in November 1982, when he came to visit her apartment to call for Marc. It was the first of many visits.

Sometimes, she would cook a meal for all three of them, and she and Rock would play cards. On other occasions, they would go out to a restaurant. Initially, before Christian moved out of her apartment and into Hudson's house, Rock came around five or six times a week, every week. 1982 was the first year that she exchanged Christmas gifts with Rock – he gave her some books and an autographed photograph of himself.

They became very good friends, and Rock would often call around just before lunch time, but one day he telephoned her at midnight. He wanted Marc but he wasn't in. She said, 'Rock sounded distraught and then he said to me: "I have to get out of this house Liberty. I know it's late and forgive me for calling at this hour, but would it be possible to come down and see you?" '

Liberty said that would be all right and he arrived about half an hour later, apologizing for the late hour and thanking her once again for making him welcome at her apartment. He was feeling guilty about seeing Marc, who had been her lover, but Liberty reassured him there was no reason for that; they were both adults and everyone was friends so there was nothing to worry about.

Rock then explained his need to visit her at such a late hour: 'I just had to get out of the house. I was afraid I would do something drastic. I was ready to throw Tom Clark against the wall, I was so angry.'

Liberty inquired: 'You are miserable in your own house?'

Rock said: 'Yes, frequently. You know I love Marc very much and with all this going on at the house, I need him more than ever now.'

Liberty told him he could come around any time, and the

visits became more frequent as he escaped what she described as 'the harassment that was going on at that house'. On one other occasion, she had another heart-to-heart with him; Rock was concerned about the intensity of his feelings for Marc, and about his jealousy. 'It's an illness,' he told her. 'I get so jealous that I vomit.' She said he suffered 'horribly' through his jealousies and had sought help to try and rid himself of them, but nothing could be done.

The picture she was painting was one of a pathetic, lonely man who frequently needed someone to confide in, or simply talk to. She said that he occasionally spoke of past relationships – one in particular, with a business manager who had ripped him off, had virtually destroyed him. He told how the same thing had happened to Doris Day.

[Hudson was referring to his relationship with Henry Willson who had handled his business for sixteen years, and systematically robbed him. The same had happened to his friend, Doris Day, only she was married to her manager, Marty Melcher. When Rock and Doris first met to co-star in *Pillow Talk*, Marty invited Rock to dinner and offered to invest Hudson's earnings and double his money, just as he was doing for Doris. Rock correctly declined his kind offer and was glad he did: when Melcher died, Doris discovered that after a lifetime's work, and seventeen years of marriage to him, he had left her half a million dollars in debt.]

Liberty asked Rock if he liked his current manager (Wallace Sheft) and Rock replied: 'I don't have to like him . . . let me put it this way: he can take a dollar and stretch it around the block. He's very good with money.'

Rhoden asked Liberty if she recalled the night of the Oscar presentation in April 1984. She did: Rock gave her and Marc tickets to attend the ceremony. She also remembered the birthday party for Marc, when Rock had burned his arm while cooking chickens on the barbecue, and other of Marc's family occasions which she attended at Rock's house; she remembered that around the time he was appearing in 'Dynasty' she had commented to Mark Miller that Rock looked ill, and Miller told her Hudson was anorexic. She told the court that in the late summer of 1985, Rock had paid for a surprise event in her life – by flying her daughter Juana from Madrid, where she lived, to Los Angeles and to a party which had been specially arranged at the Hudson house.

Liberty gave a graphic description of the day they learned

77

from the television news broadcast that Rock had AIDS. She was alone in her house, and sitting watching the news. Shortly after the announcement, Marc telephoned her and said, 'My god, did you hear that?' She replied, 'Marc is your life in jeopardy? Are you going to be all right?'

He replied: 'Am I going to be all right? I'm a dead man.' Then he lost control of himself, he fell apart. Later, he came over to her apartment, where they talked until he had regained his composure.

At this point, her evidence was interrupted. Earlier, defending counsel had complained that Christian, from his position at the front of the court, had been nodding or shaking his head during her recollections of events. It had happened again. She apologized. 'I don't do it voluntarily. It's so easy for me to glance at him from here.' Rhoden told the judge that was understandable, because Christian was the most familiar face in the courtroom.

The Judge: 'You are not prohibited from looking at him. He is directed not to give you any signal of any kind. Would you prefer not to have Mr Christian in the courtroom?'

Rhoden: 'I think he has a right to hear what's going on, but I've warned him at this time not even to shake his head accidentally.'

Christian moved to another seat in the audience. Mrs Martin said that was an improvement but she could still see him.

Rhoden: 'Would you like to get under your chair?' (Laughter ensued.)

Returning to the questioning, Rhoden became stern and deliberate: Did she ever threaten Rock Hudson with exposing him as a homosexual if he did not allow Marc Christian to live at his house.

Mrs Martin said she had never done that and in fact she had been offered between $100,000 and $200,000 by the *National Enquirer* to tell what she knew about Rock Hudson, but had turned them down.

Returning to the time when it was confirmed in Paris that Hudson had AIDS, Rhoden asked Mrs Martin if she had spoken to Mark Miller at any time.

She had. He telephoned her from Paris to enlist her aid in getting Christian to go there for an AIDS test. She asked him why it could not be done in America, and Miller, she said, told her about Hudson's instruction: 'Bring him over as soon as possible . . . I may have killed the kid.'

She asked him why he had not told Christian earlier that Hudson had AIDS. Didn't he realize how devastating it could be? Miller replied, 'Now look, don't blow up. This is a time to be calm. We'll take Marc to Paris. There's a Dr Dormont here who has been treating Rock and if Marc has AIDS, don't worry about it. He can put him into remission.'

She repeated conversations with Miller that were similar to those relayed to the court by Christian himself: that Miller said he had been lying for thirteen months, and was sick of it; that he was only taking orders, and that he was in the captain's seat now and everything would be all right.

Under cross-examination by Miller and Banks, Mrs Martin agreed that Christian had moved back into her apartment for a time after Hudson's death, and yes, after the lawsuit had been filed she did have about eight conferences and five personal meetings with Marvin Mitchelson who was then Christian's lawyer. And yes, she was still a very close friend of Christian.

Gregory Dale Rice, also in his early thirties, was the second of Rhoden's supporting witnesses. He had been a friend of Christian's for fifteen years and was a teacher in special education units for the autistic and mentally handicapped. He first met Rock Hudson in October 1983, when he drove with Christian to the star's house to pick up some records. Marc buzzed at the security gate and the car proceeded through to drive to the house; at the front entrance, Marc went in through the garage door directly into the playroom.

Rice followed shortly afterwards, and when he got into the house found Rock Hudson relaxing in the playroom. It was the first of many meetings, he said, over the next couple of years. Once, at a party at Rock's house in December 1984, he was left alone with Rock while Christian drove Liberty Martin home. Rock began to talk about his feelings for Marc. Rice said, 'He was looking a little sad and I asked him if anything was wrong. He replied, "You know, I just love the kid so much that it sometimes hurts, but it's a good kind of hurt. Greg, I've been so lonely all of my life; people wouldn't understand how lonely I have been . . . I've no family really, until Marc." Then he just began to cry and I reached down and touched his head, like you would a small child . . . and he began to calm down. Then Marc came back and they went upstairs.'

Rhoden's questioning moved his witness quickly to April 1985,

79

when he was at Hudson's house with Christian and some others. He had overheard a conversation between Christian and Hudson about the rumour going around that Christian had AIDS. He repeated the same allegation that Christian had made earlier: 'Rock said, "Well do you?" Christian said "No, no. Do you?" and Hudson replied, "No, I'm fine. I've been tested for everything. Everything . . . ".'

Two months later, in June, he was again at the house with Christian and Mrs Martin when there was another discussion, this time with Mark Miller. Rock was now looking very poorly and everyone was concerned about him but no one, he said, would say exactly what was going on. Liberty, fed up, decided to confront Miller and asked flat out what was wrong with Rock. Miller replied: 'Nothing really. He's dieting. He wants to be slim. He's exercising and has anorexia . . . it's all in his head.'

After news of Hudson's illness became public, he was at Hudson's house with Christian, Wayne Bernhard and another man, Mark Parker. They were all in the playroom and everyone was being fairly pleasant, including Mark Miller when he came into the room. But Rice got irritated and asked Miller why he hadn't told Christian about the AIDS earlier and, according to Rice, Miller repeated what he had already told Christian and Liberty Martin: that he was under orders, that's what he was being paid for.

He was also at the wake for Hudson and heard Miller threaten to smear Christian if he went public. He heard Miller say that they would call him a male hustler, or even a drug addict to which Christian had responded contemptuously: 'At least don't tell them I voted Republican.'

The cross-examination by Banks had an edge to it; he began with a line of questioning which could lead members of the jury towards the supposition that Rice had discussed what he would say in evidence with Marc Christian – he noted that there were remarkable similarities in their recall of events.

Banks asked him when he had last seen Christian. They had met for lunch on the Saturday of the weekend that had just passed; no, he had not discussed his evidence with Christian nor had he asked Christian what he had said in court. He had been able to read that for himself in the newspapers.


Sondra Dokan came next. She was the belly dancer who had performed at Marc's birthday party. She met Christian through her old friend Liberty Martin whom she had known for twenty-five years; their children were in kindergarten together. On the night of the party, she felt delighted and honoured when Rock thanked her for her performance and she said it had been a pleasure, because she really liked Marc. Rock replied that he liked him a lot, too.

She had met Hudson once previously, in the spring of 1984 when she was visiting Liberty Martin in hospital. While she was there Rock turned up for a visit, bringing gifts of a plant and a needlework kit. Liberty was not very good at sewing and Rock showed her how to use the kit. [In fact Rock found needlework a way of relaxing. He took it up while briefly in hospital in 1975 for a leg injury and when Paul Callan of the London *Daily Mirror* interviewed him in 1981, Hudson proudly displayed his latest piece of embroidery. He told Callan: 'It's a card-table cover, very delicate work, I can tell you. Why did I take it up? I got tired of watching television in the afternoons, and someone said "Hey Rock, what about embroidery?" and that's when it started. I've done some lovely bedcovers since.' To see the six-foot hulk sewing gave an opportunity for further questioning in this interview – Hudson was challenged publicly for the first time about his homosexuality. In a bassoon voice, he growled: 'Bullshit, I've heard that rumour for years and I just don't care about it. Look, I know lots of gays in Hollywood and most of them are nice guys. Some have tried it on with me but I've always said, "Come on, you've got the wrong guy" and as soon as they know that, it's all okay.']

The belly dancer could add little further to the testimony already heard, other than to pass on a few relatively unimportant snippets of conversation she had had with Christian over his fear of having AIDS. Mr Banks began to cross-examine. She had last seen Marc Christian the previous Saturday, in Mr Rhoden's office. And then let it rest when he elicited more information about her presence at Marc's birthday party: 'Who invited you to the party?' he asked.

'Mrs Martin.'

'No further questions, Your Honour.'


Mrs Jeanne MacGuinnis, Christian's mother, arrived at the witness stand, apprehensive and timid. Marc was a good son; since leaving home, he visited her almost every other weekend and they spoke almost daily on the telephone. She also had fond memories of Rock Hudson whom she thought, initially, was an absolute gentleman.

They first spoke on the telephone when Rock called her home from Israel to speak to Marc early in 1984. When he returned to America, Rock came with Marc to visit their home in Orange County. They all went out to dinner: herself, her husband, Rock and Marc. She found Hudson 'lovely', very friendly – as if they'd known each other for years – just delightful.

She understood that Marc's role was to house-sit for Hudson and he began sending her $200 a month from his salary; he had done it previously for other people. No, she had never been invited to any previous employer's home but she did go to Hudson's. The most memorable visit was on 20 May 1984, the occasion of her 40th wedding anniversary. She and her husband arrived at the house expecting simply to go out to dinner with Marc. But, surprise, surprise, there was a party: about thirty-five people were there, and a band. She was also handed a note which instructed her to be close to a telephone at 5 p.m. At that time, Rock called from New York and wished them a happy anniversary. Rock later sent them a signed photograph bearing the inscription: *'To Jeanne and Miles* [her husband] *with love, Rock.'*

A year later, Rock insisted that her daughter's wedding reception should be held at his home. Rock himself could not be present, but he sent a gift and the bridal couple had their photographs taken on the rear terrace of Rock's home, beside the fountain. Earlier she had had a conversation with Rock after she had seen him on 'Dynasty'. She told him she thought he had lost too much weight and did not look well. He replied that since returning from Israel, he had not been able to retain food. She gave him some motherly advice about vitamins and suggested he should take an appetite stimulant. Marc told her he thought Rock had anorexia.

Recalling the day of the public announcement, Mrs MacGuinnis said Marc telephoned her at home: 'He was terribly worried as was I. It was almost more than Marc could bear . . . the depression and sorrow over the two men he loved very much, first his father [who had died of cancer a few weeks earlier, in May 1985] and now Rock.'

The cross-examination was brief. Mrs MacGuinnis's testimony had provided no vital or controversial aspects. She told Mr Mills that in December 1985 she had given her son $5000 as a Christmas gift, with no strings attached. He could use the money however he wished. No, Marc had never discussed with her the prospect of him going to see a psychiatrist. But she knew he had been to see a number of doctors for tests and it was necessary for him to continue seeing them every four months; he had told her so. She, like her son, was constantly worried. But Mr Banks would not leave the witness on a note of advantage to the other side.

He asked: 'What has he [Marc] told you about the results of the tests?'

Mrs MacGuinnis: 'That they are negative.'

Banks: 'No further questions Your Honour.'


At this point in the trial, Harold Rhoden, counsel for Christian, explained that he wanted to call Hudson's secretary Mark Miller as an 'adverse witness'. At a later stage in the trial Miller would have the opportunity to give his evidence in full, but there were matters in his pre-trial depositions which Mr Rhoden felt compelled to bring in as part of his case. After a brief conference in the judge's chambers, Mark Miller was called to the stand and the judge explained to the jury the Code of Civil Procedure which allowed Rhoden to question him directly. As Rhoden began his questioning, the jury would note that Miller looked uncomfortable and his responses were tense, almost pedantic. Clearly, he was not going to make it easy for Rhoden to extract from him any support for his cause.

Once again, the story reverted to the time of Christian's arrival in the Hudson household and Miller immediately disputed Rhoden's claim that Marc moved straight into the master bedroom with Rock. He said Christian was given the Red Room, and all his clothes were put in there; if they ever occupied the Blue Room together, he never saw it.

Rhoden reminded Miller that in his original deposition made in 1986, he was asked the same question and replied: 'From 4 January 1984 to approximately the last week of March '84.'

Rhoden: 'Now,let me ask you again, did those two men occupy the same room?'

'Under those circumstances, yes.'

'What circumstances?' ·

'When he moved in, all of his things were moved into the Red Room and he may have slept in the Blue Room.'

'All right. Now, when you said they occupied the same room during those three months, was your answer truthful?'

'Yes, it was.'

'Would you like to change it now?'

'No. No.'

Rhoden moved to his crucial question: 'At the time that Rock Hudson told you he had AIDS, did you say something like this, "Are you going to tell the kid?" '

'Not those words, no.'

'What?'

'Hudson replied, "Absolutely not, because he will destroy me." '

Rhoden: 'I didn't ask you why. Did he say "absolutely not"?'

'He said, "Absolutely not, because he's –" '

Rhoden: 'I'm not asking for anything more at the moment . . . When Rock Hudson told you he had AIDS, did he say to you "Under no circumstances are you to tell him I have AIDS"?'

'No.'

'I am going to read an extract from your deposition:

'When you said to Rock Hudson, "You might have exposed him to AIDS", did it occur to you to warn Christian that he might be exposed to AIDS? Answer: Of course. But I was being told, under no circumstances'. Hudson pointed his finger like this "Are you to tell him that I have AIDS? Absolutely not. I have the disease. It is my disease. Let me handle it my way." '

Miller: 'That is true.'

Rhoden: 'A minute ago I asked you if he said to you, "Under no circumstances are you to tell him I have AIDS" and you said, "No, he didn't say it like that". But I was reading from your answer in the deposition, and he did say it like that, didn't he? Again, in that conversation when Rock Hudson told you he had AIDS, did you say to him, "There is a possibility you have exposed Christian to AIDS"?'

'Yes.'

'Sir, did you receive a direct order from Rock Hudson to not tell Christian that Hudson had AIDS?'

'Well, it wasn't a direct order. It was a discussion between the two of us, and I said –'

'Just a moment. I am not asking you what you said. I am asking you if an order was given. We will work it out. In this conversation when Hudson told you he had AIDS and you were discussing Christian, did Hudson say to you that "Marc Christian is not to know I have AIDS under any circumstances"?'

'Yes.'

'What I want to know, sir, is this: Did you receive an order

from Rock Hudson to not tell Christian that Hudson had AIDS?'
'Well, "order" is a strong word.'
'Did you?'
'No, not an order. We discussed it.'
'From page twenty-four of your deposition, you were asked: "Did you receive any orders from anyone not to tell Marc Christian that Hudson had AIDS?" Answer: "Yes. Rock Hudson." Your answers were truthful, weren't they?'
'Yes.'
'As a matter of fact, didn't Rock Hudson make you keep secret from Christian the fact that Hudson had AIDS?'
'Yes.'
'And you agreed to do this, didn't you?'
'Yes. I did.'
'Now, the time, sir, when Hudson told you this tragic news was June of 1984, correct?'
'Correct.'
'Sir, isn't it true that in June of 1984 you knew that there was no cure for AIDS?'
'That's correct.'
'And you knew it was a disease such that once somebody got it, it meant they would die?'
'That's correct.'
'Death and no cure?'
'I knew both of those things.'
'At the time Hudson told you this, gave you this order and you agreed to it, did it occur to you, Mr Miller, that not knowing anything about Hudson's condition or his own, Marc Christian might infect others with AIDS and kill them unknowingly?'
'From what I knew about AIDS, after speaking with the experts from UCLA, I knew Mr Christian would not infect others.'
'I am talking about the time when Hudson told you he had AIDS. He told you not to tell Christian. You agreed on the spot, didn't you?'
'Yes.'
'That is the moment I am talking about, that moment. Did it occur to you that if Christian didn't know about the fact that Hudson had AIDS, that Christian, since he could have it and you said he could have it, might go out and infect other people and they could infect other people and it could mean the death of thousands?'

'No, I did not know that. I knew Christian's sexual habits. I knew that he did not do anal sex. He had told me so. I knew from Mr Hudson he did not do anal sex. And I knew that it was anally transmitted. That is all I knew.'

Rhoden: 'You say Rock Hudson told you he did not engage in anal sex with Marc Christian?'

'That is correct.'

'Did you ask him?'

'Yes, I did.'

'And that was when he told you he had AIDS?'

'Two days later.'

Rock Hudson gave him an instruction to say to people who asked about his health to pose the question 'Do you suppose he has anorexia?'. He was intentionally creating a false impression on Hudson's orders. On the question of sexual relations, he said he knew they were not intimate at the time of the diagnosis and hadn't been for months.

Rhoden was challenging again. He pointed to Miller's original deposition in which he had said he had 'no knowledge' of sexual activity. Now that had changed to a definite knowledge that they were not intimate.

He asked: 'Were you lying?'

'Well, I had knowledge that there was no sex after February of 1984.'

'Why did you say when I asked you in the deposition –'

'I don't know. I don't know. I did have knowledge, so there you are.'

'Is this answer: "I have no knowledge" a false answer?'

'Yes.'

'Why did you want to give a false answer.'

'I don't know. I didn't understand your question, maybe.'

He agreed that after the public announcement in June 1985, at some time later, he said to Marc Christian: 'Look, kid, I'm sorry, I know it doesn't seem fair.' He was sorry that it had all turned out the way it had turned out.

Rhoden: 'If you thought that there was no sex between Christian and Hudson after Hudson had AIDS, what were you sorry about?'

'I was concerned about Marc Christian, and he knows this, that he was exposed; he was exposed to AIDS back in 1983 and early 1984. There, I was sorry for him. I still am.'

He agreed he told Christian: 'If you think it has been easy for me, I've been up all night wondering what I would say to you. You know The Movie Star. He made me keep a secret.' When Christian asked, 'Well if Rock is so concerned about me, why didn't he tell me a year ago?' Miller replied, 'You know The Movie Star. He's got that stubborn head of his?'

Under further questioning, Miller continued to insist that at the end of February 1984 Rock Hudson told him that his affair with Christian was over. Hudson told him, 'The affair is over. I'm moving on to Ron Channell.'

Rhoden: (*with surprise*) 'He said I'm moving on to what?'

'Ron Channell, the work-out man.'

'Ron Channell?'

'Yes.'

'Ron Channell is a heterosexual, isn't he?'

'That's what my understanding is, yes.'

Soon afterwards, said Miller, Hudson came to him and said: 'He [Christian] has letters; give him anything he wants.' Hudson feared that Christian would take the letters to the press, and reveal that he was a homosexual.

Later, Hudson told him: 'Christian stays in the house or he and Liberty will destroy me in five minutes, so give him what he wants.' Give him anything he wants which Miller took to mean money. In essence Hudson was saying, 'I'm going to submit to this blackmail and just pay him money to keep his mouth shut.' Miller also claimed that Hudson later said: 'I'd like to throw him out' to which Miller replied: 'No, don't do that, Rock. First because it's morally wrong, second you may have exposed him to AIDS.'

Rhoden snapped up the point: 'What took Hudson so long to get this blackmailer out of his bedroom? After Hudson told you "I want this blackmailer, this guy is threatening to blackmail me, he's got letters, our affair is over", he told you that. But a month later Christian is still in the bedroom sleeping in the same bedroom with Rock Hudson. Did you say to Mr Hudson: "How come you are letting that conniving blackmailer still sleep in your bed for a month after you said the affair was over?" Did you say anything like that to him?'

'No.'

'Isn't the truth that you just don't have any idea at all why Christian remained in that bedroom after Hudson said the affair was over?'

'I also don't know that he did.'

Rhoden: 'But did Hudson ever explain to you why he tolerated the presence of a despised blackmailer in his own bed for weeks after he decided the affair was over?'

'I don't know that he did. But Hudson thereafter stopped speaking to Christian although Christian lived in the same house.'

Rhoden grasped his opportunity: 'Do you know if Hudson spoke to Marc Christian in April 1984, the evening of the Academy Awards celebration?'

'No, I don't.'

'You weren't there, were you?'

'No, I was not.'

'Do you know if Rock Hudson spoke to Marc Christian any time during the birthday party he gave for him on 23 June 1984, at his house?'

'I do not.'

'You weren't there, were you?'

'I was not.'

'Do you know if Rock Hudson spoke to Marc Christian at the time that Rock Hudson had Liberty Martin's daughter flown in from Spain as a surprise for Liberty Martin?'

'No, I don't.'

'Do you know if Rock Hudson spoke at all to his live-in blackmailer in 1984 when Rock Hudson had a surprise anniversary party for Christian's mother and father?'

'I do not.'

'You weren't there, were you?'

'No, I was not.'

'Did you ever see Marc Christian face-to-face with Rock Hudson when Marc Christian made a threat to Rock Hudson to ruin his career? Yes or no?'

'I have the right to think, I believe.'

'Did you hear such a thing?'

'No.'

'Sir, you very much want the estate to win this action, don't you?'

'Yes.'

Miller agreed he was beneficiary under a trust which itself is named as a beneficiary in Hudson's will. George Nader, his companion, was the first beneficiary to take an annuity for life. After his death, Miller would also begin to take a certain amount for life.

Rhoden concluded his examination and Andrew Banks said he would reserve his questioning for later in the trial.

# CHAPTER SEVEN

*Hostilities and a Caring Friend*

As they listened to the stream of witnesses, the jury would identify with ease the point at which the evidence and questioning began to take on a different tone as it moved from the case in support of Christian's claim towards the two-pronged attack of the defence. The defence would aim to prove alleged blackmailing infidelities of Christian and the fact that far from remaining Hudson's lover well into 1985, the relationship was all but over a year earlier. In the latter, their case would rest heavily upon the account of Ron Channell, the actor, singer and physical training instructor in whose company Hudson spent many hours during his last year alive.

But first Christian's lawyer had one more surprise up his sleeve and before the public hearings began on 24 January, Harold Rhoden had requested a private talk in the chambers of Judge Geernaert where he would make an unexpected application.

After much heart searching which had kept him up until 3 a.m. that morning, he had decided to call a witness under subpoena, who was 'very hostile'. His name was Tony Rocco, an actor and acquaintance of Marc Christian whose pre-trial deposition was taken by lawyers for the estate and, regardless of what the reasons were, they did not intend to call him and it might be thought that he was now out of the case.

'Not quite,' said Rhoden. He himself now wanted him to testify to the jury but first he sought the approval of Judge Geernaert for what he planned. Rhoden said: 'I want to ask him one question: "Did someone representing the estate offer you money to commit perjury?" I have had no communication with Rocco, I don't know what his answer is going to be.'

The judge: 'Let's do it outside the presence of the jury. If it is "no", the jury should not hear it.'

Rhoden challenged the judge's ruling. He intended to call a back-up witness named Kevin Lee Short, who was sitting outside, and who would say that Rocco admitted to him that he had been offered a bribe. If Rocco said he was not offered a bribe, Rhoden would call Short. If Rocco said 'yes' he would ask for details of what he was offered; he believed it to be in the form of a percentage of whatever the estate did not have to pay Christian. Counsel said he understood that the man Rocco dealt with was Paul Cohen, an investigator. Rhoden's statement to the judge sparked off an angry exchange.

His opponent for the estate, Robert Mills, said: 'Are you asserting that I am bribing this witness?'

Rhoden: 'Oh, shut up.'

The judge: 'Sit down, Mr Rhoden.'

Rhoden: 'Listen, you fat pig. Don't pull any more of that crap on me.'

Mills: 'Well, you did say –'

The judge: 'That was totally uncalled for.'

Rhoden: 'Well, this loud mouth –'

The judge: 'You are the loud mouth. There is no reason for you to be that upset.'

Rhoden complained that Mills had earlier accused him of lying; he kept on doing that and there was a real problem. 'I didn't say a word about Mills,' he said. 'He will get his later.'

The judge smoothed the row between counsel and listened to their legal arguments over whether or not Rocco should be called. Eventually, it was agreed that Rocco should be taken through his evidence without the jury being present so that the judge could assess the position. This was done, and then finally Rocco was called to the stand to make his testimony before the jury.

Tony Rocco, a fast-talking yet well-dressed young man in a three-piece suit, could hardly have been viewed as an exemplary witness and as he began to give evidence, it became clear that he was going to deny most of the allegations Rhoden put to him. In the end, the jury might well have been left wondering why he had been called at all. Counsel for the opposing side could have had little doubt in their minds that it was a tactic to implant in the jury's mind a hint of impropriety in the case for the defence.

Rhoden's strict questioning of Rocco brought quick-fire answers.

Yes, he did know Kevin Short: they had 'dated on three occasions'. No, he had not told Short that an investigator from Rock Hudson's estate wanted him to testify that Marc Christian knew that Hudson had AIDS before the public announcement. No, he did not tell Short that the investigator wanted him to say that Christian had been sleeping around. No, he did not tell Short that the investigator had offered him money and he was going to tell the story they wanted to get it.

What he did tell Short was that a lawyer friend had advised him that if he did make a statement about his knowledge of Marc Christian, he should ask for 'a piece of the action', perhaps $250,000, but he did not have the nerve to do it.

Mr Mills, anxious to ensure that the jury was clear on the position, obtained from Rocco, under cross-examination, further denials that he [Mills] had ever offered him money on behalf of the estate, and that no one had offered him a car in return for giving a deposition. 'No to all three,' said Rocco.

Rhoden now kept his promise and brought Kevin Lee Short to the stand. Short agreed he first met Rocco three months earlier, in September 1988. They were at a gym together and Rocco had invited him home for a meal. He said he made the best chilli on earth and wanted some company. He was feeling low, so he went. While they were in the kitchen, Rocco began to talk about the Rock Hudson case and said that someone from the estate had asked him whether Christian knew that Hudson had AIDS and that Christian had been sleeping around.

A week later, he saw Rocco again; he appeared very happy and said he was going to say 'yes' to both questions the estate investigator had asked him, and he was going to get some money and buy a car. He said the estate was going to pay him a percentage of what they would not have to pay Christian. Later, Rocco pointed to a sports car parked in the road, and said he was going to get a car like that one.

Short said it seemed to him that Rocco was going to give false evidence and by chance, about six weeks later, he saw Marc Christian having lunch in the International House of Pancakes. He did not know Christian, had never met him before, but recognized him from television. He reported to Christian what Rocco had said, and Christian said he was very grateful and would tell his lawyers.

Short, under cross-examination, repeated his allegation that from their very first meeting, Rocco began talking to him about being contacted by an investigator but he did not know what Rocco eventually said in his deposition because he had not seen him since.

Mills: 'You are absolutely positive he said he was going to get a car?'

'He said he was going to get money and that would help him to buy a car that he liked.'

'He didn't say he was going to get a boat, did he?'

'No.'

'He didn't say he was going to be taken to Acapulco after this trial was over did he?'

Rhoden interjected: 'Just a moment sir. Counsel is being flippant and argumentative.'

Judge: 'Sustained.'

Mills: 'I intend to tie this up, Your Honour.'

Short: 'No he did not.'

Mills: 'And the first, or second time, you ever met this man, he told you he was going to commit a crime, to commit perjury by giving false testimony for taking money.'

'Yes.'

The cross-examination by Mr Banks, who had no interest in this exchange other than to score points for his client, Miller, took a more pointed line. Hadn't Mr Short been talking with Marc Christian in the hall during recess, for about ten minutes.

'Yes,' said Short. But they had not discussed the evidence; Marc just mentioned Kevin's smile. That was it, really. He had spoken to Marc on the telephone on a number of occasions previously, but the only other time they met after their first encounter in the pancake house was when they went together to Christian's lawyer where Short gave a statement on what he knew.

Rhoden's insistence on calling Rocco as a hostile witness left Mills, for the estate, little alternative. Although he had not planned to do so previously, he now recalled him to the stand as an official witness for the defence which would allow further questioning to the estate's advantage, without him being classed as hostile. Mills went straight to the contentious issues: Did you have a homosexual relationship with Kevin Short? Yes, said Rocco, on all three times they met. [Short himself had denied this suggestion.]

He had first met Marc Christian and Liberty Martin around 1980 when they were spectators at a Gay Softball League; he noticed

Marc because of his attractive, sensitive features. They continued to socialize from time to time, meeting either at the gay ballgame or in a gay bar. Liberty and Marc were always together. He moved to Long Beach and did not see them again until 1984, when he saw Marc driving a Mercedes Convertible and said: 'You're moving up in class.' Marc said he was just house-sitting for a friend, but didn't say who.

In September 1984, when he was appearing in a play at the Gardner Theater he saw Liberty and Marc again; they came to watch him, and afterwards he joined them at Rock Hudson's house. Liberty, Marc and Greg Rice were in the party. Rock was not at home when they arrived and Marc took Rocco on a tour of the house. 'We walked through a room that was like a theatre with a stage and a bar; and there was a kitchen with lots of butcher's blocks. And he showed me his bedroom and said, "I sleep here" and then he pointed to a stairwell and said "Rock sleeps up there". Later, we talked, and Liberty said something about how wonderful Rock was and how good he had been to Marc – how he took care of Marc's sister's wedding, helped him with his teeth, refurbished his car, and refurbished Liberty's couch. I mean, they praised him, they talked very highly of him.'

Rocco said Marc then brought out some movie tapes. 'We watched a movie of Marc doing Doris Day, lip-synching to "My Secret Love", and another movie with Liberty and a bunch of other people.'

Mills: 'Was Christian a person in the movie?'

Rocco: 'Yes, he was singing with a blond wig on and lip-synching.'

'Did you ever have any conversation where you asked Mr Christian, in effect, whether or not he was sleeping with Mr Hudson?'

'I didn't ask Marc that. When he pointed that out, I just looked at him with a strange look. And he looked at me and said: "Could you get it up for that old fart?" and started to laugh. I don't know why he said it. He could have been embarrassed in front of me; I'm not a mind-reader. That's what he said.'

'How did this come about?'

'Well, he'd just got through showing me where he slept and pointed to the stairs where Rock slept. I just looked at him curiously and he started smirking and said "Could you get it up for that old fart?" '

Rocco stayed in the house until a very inebriated Rock came home quite late. Liberty and Marc talked him into playing re-runs of his TV series 'McMillan and Wife', but Rocco fell asleep and, according to Liberty, started to snore. They woke him up and he left.

He met Rock again a few days later on the set of 'Dynasty'; Rocco had been given work as an extra. Rocco said that apart from that incident, he knew nothing of Christian's sex life and he had no knowledge of whether Marc had slept around. However, he was with Marc on one occasion in 1987 when a mutual friend, Diana Livingston, asked Marc if he had ever loved Rock. He said Christian replied: 'No, I never loved that asshole. I'm glad he died. Everybody else was getting a piece of the action, why shouldn't I?' Before the trial began, he received two phone calls from Christian and in one of them Christian apologized to Rocco because he had been subpoenaed to appear at the trial.

Counsel Banks continued to remain aloof from this testimony and raised no cross-examination. Rhoden came back with one single question: 'Mr Rocco, did you tell Marc Christian last September that in 1981 you were diagnosed as having AIDS but that you cured yourself by willpower?'

'Yes.'

'No further questions.'

The exchange on the allegations and dispute surrounding Rocco's earlier evidence was completed by the testimony of Paul Cohen, a licensed self-employed private investigator, who denied that he ever attempted to elicit false testimony from Rocco or offer him money.

Mr Rhoden's case was concluded.

Mr Banks, for Miller, moved to have the case against his client dismissed; he claimed there was insufficient evidence against Mark Miller for it to proceed. The judge disagreed and the motion was rejected.


25 January 1989: The day's hearing once again was delayed by a conference in the judge's chambers. Someone had noticed that two of the jurors were in possession of tape machines. The need for light relief during this intense often dramatic hearing was perhaps understandable. Members of the jury were often left for long periods of inactivity while counsel argued a point in the

privacy of the judge's chambers, or where the jury were evacuated from the courtroom while assessments of evidence to be presented were made to avoid crossing into legally fraught areas. It was during these periods that the two members of the jury with personal stereos were playing tapes to themselves; they assured the judge that they were not recording any part of the trial. Other than these instances, the jury sat without many signs of emotion or shock at what they heard throughout the trial. Eyebrows were raised occasionally, especially as some of the cross-examination became heated in the early stages of the hearing. Their attention would often be drawn by the tactics of lawyers so that they sat, bolt upright, listening and attentive. But once the initial shock of the descriptive detail of the evidence had been overcome, few showed any special indication of their feelings, one way or the other, as the trial progressed. With that minor problem resolved, Mills proceeded with the presentation of his defence.

Ron Channell is a handsome, muscular and heterosexual thirty-two-year-old from Tampa, Florida; a rather naïve country boy who became a central figure in the last months of Rock Hudson's life, his evidence would show that at the very time when Hudson was courting Christian, the new young man in his life had not entirely overwhelmed other friendships.

In between acting and singing engagements, Channell was also an experienced instructor in physical fitness. In fact, he first met Rock Hudson at the Sports Connection health club which had many gay members. Rock had come in for a tour and some advice on getting himself fit but he was embarrassed about working out in front of other people. Had he thought about private instruction? Channell told him there were a number of instructors who would be interested, himself included. Rock took his card and called him a month later. He wanted to arrange private work-out sessions at his home and would be happy to hire Channell to help him. He explained that he had had heart surgery in 1981 and Channell should call his doctor first.

Channell said Hudson was really out of shape, and the doctor told him that they should not do anything strenuous. He worked out a basic fitness programme and in July 1983 – when Hudson's friendship with Christian had also become intense – Channell went to Rock's house. They sat by the pool and Rock showed him around the house and the playroom where they would do the exercise routines. He began going to the house five or six days a week, depending on Rock's work schedule. To begin with, Channell would be there for half an hour or so each day but gradually the visits became longer. By October 1983, he regularly stayed for lunch; sometimes he would be there for the entire day.

Rock would have his butler James Wright prepare a meal for them and Mark Miller often joined them. Channell said: 'We were fast becoming friends and after lunch, we would go to other parts of the house . . . in his bedroom he has a collection of plays, bookshelves with lots of plays. We would go through them, and talk. One of my most cherished possessions is his original *Camelot* script which he gave me after a while. It was his favourite.'

[Rock became fascinated by doing stage plays and musicals in the mid-seventies when his film work began to subside and he became increasingly disillusioned by the daily drudge of television production work. Although nerve-wracked at the prospect of playing in front of a live audience after his twenty-five years in front of the silent camera, he pushed himself into singing lessons and with his old friend Carol Burnett at his side, went on tour with the musical *I Do, I Do* in 1974 and eventually took the show to London with Juliet Prowse. The critics were not rapturous about his wooden acting, neither were they especially unkind. He went into *Camelot* in 1977 and did a third musical, *20th Century*, in 1979. Though he thoroughly enjoyed himself, he faced the problem of stage fright almost every night, and on occasions beads of perspiration flicked off his face into the front row.]

Channell said Hudson's knowledge and eager conversation on anything to do with acting captivated him. If Channell had an interview for an acting job, Hudson would rehearse him before he went. Once, they made a film at the house. Hudson had told him to go to the vault where he kept all of his tapes and find one from his short-lived television series, 'The Devlin Connection', which he was doing when he had his heart attack. Hudson told him to find one that he liked, pick out a couple of scenes and he would arrange for a film crew to come up to the house and shoot the scenes, with the two of them playing roles. It was a great experience, said Channell, and he still possessed the ten-minute tape of himself working with Hudson on film.

Throughout that time, from July to November, when Hudson left to go to Israel to film *The Ambassadors*, he never once saw Marc Christian. In January 1984, when Hudson returned, they resumed the five-day-a-week fitness regime and Channell soon realized that it was no longer an employee-employer situation; they had become close and devoted friends and he began to spend more and more time at the house.

He first saw Marc Christian in February when he walked through the playroom where they were exercising, on his way to the garage. He thought Marc was an employee; there were always people working round the house or in the gardens and he asked Hudson, 'Who's he?' Rock replied, 'He's just staying here until he gets on his feet.' There was no other conversation between them, about him and Hudson seldom mentioned Christian.

As their friendship grew during the first half of 1984, so did Channell's knowledge of Hudson's professional life. In the Red Room, he kept photographs and mementoes from the various roles he had played; they would spend hours going through them and Rock would talk of the film stars he had worked with. He would screen his old movies in the theatre and they would sit and discuss them and analyse them, or read the original scripts together.

Channell said he christened Rock with the nick-name 'Speed' after watching his 1951 movie, *Iron Man*, which starred Jeff Chandler. Rock played an up-and-coming heavy-weight boxer and in one scene Hudson had to say 'Call me Speed'. Channell thought it was the funniest thing he had ever seen and was rolling on the floor laughing. He said to Hudson, 'That's it man, from now on, I'm going to call you Speed.' Hudson loved it and would leave messages on Channell's answering machine just to say 'Hey, it's me, Speed. Call me.' They also wrote music together and they played it back on the piano: 'Rock would play boogie-boogie which he said was the thing in his day and he'd show me how to do it. We did lots of things together and sometimes we would go out to dinner. That was his big thing; dinner was his big outing and he loved it.' Sometimes they would go to the house of one of his friends, like Dean Dittman, who was one of the closest of Rock's confidants and the only other person outside the Hudson household who was to be told he had AIDS; other times they went to restaurants.

For the evening, Hudson would put on more formal clothes. Channell noticed that all of the cupboards were full of clothes, literally dozens of suits, jackets, trousers and shirts, which Channell found ironic; Hudson invariably wore the same thing: a casual shirt, khaki pants and moccasins. He was a very casual, relaxed person.

Mills: 'Was Christian ever party to any of these events?'

'No sir.'

'During that period from January to June 1984, did Christian ever go to lunch with you and Mr Hudson?'

'No sir.'

'How about dinners, when you went out with Mr Hudson, was Christian ever there?'

'No sir. There were others there on occasions, male and female, but never Christian.'

Towards the end of July 1984, Hudson told Channell he was planning to go to France in August for the Deauville Film Festival and would be away for about six weeks; he asked if Channell would like to go with him. [When Rock was first given the news of his illness, he was warned by Dr Rex Kennamer and the AIDS specialist Dr Michael Gottlieb – as they discussed the implications and developing symptoms – that he should not travel long distances alone. Advanced sufferers of AIDS had a tendency towards fainting, or other attacks of disorientation and whenever possible, he should have someone available to watch over him.]

Channell said: 'Rock knew I had never travelled much outside of the United States. He wanted to show me around; he had been everywhere himself and loved geography. Before we left, he bought four books on Paris, to read about the history of it, the language, places to eat, just to prepare me. He also got me a huge Atlas.' They flew from Los Angeles by Concorde on 21 August.

Although he was now aware that he had AIDS, Rock gave a relaxed view of his life in an interview with the *Los Angeles Times* before he left, revealing no hint of his hidden terror. He told the reporter he was very contented, had no burning desires, burning revenges or burning loathings. In truth, he must have been burning with anguish over what awaited him in Paris, where it had already been arranged that he would meet with Dr Dominique Dormont immediately upon his arrival so that Dormont could explain the intensive, and at times uncomfortable, nature of his treatment.

In Paris, they checked into a suite at the Ritz Hotel and an early pattern was established, where Hudson would go out very early in the morning and would be away for several hours. He told Channell he was going to discuss film business, or was working on scripts and he had no reason to disbelieve him. Rock's true daily routine would be revealed later; each morning for almost five weeks, he took a taxi from the hotel, or occasionally would be collected and taken to the Percy Clinic by Dr Dormont personally. There, he would spend three hours lying on a bed with an intravenous needle and tube attached to his arm through which Dormont pumped his new drug, HPA-23. He would do this for four consecutive days, and then rest for two or three days. Dormont wanted Hudson to continue the treatment for six months; he felt Hudson was in the middle stages of AIDS progression and told his patient that long-term treatment would possibly extend his life. Hudson refused; he told the doctor he had pressing work in Los Angeles but, in reality, he feared that such a long stay in Paris would soon be noticed and his reason for being there revealed.

While Rock was away each morning, Channell would wander around Paris on his own; when he returned they did some light exercises together. Rock attended the Deauville Film Festival alone, although he was joined there by Dale Olson who had flown in from Los Angeles to set up media interviews at which Rock appeared calm and relaxed.

For the rest of the time, Hudson and Channell were seeing the sights of Paris. They took photographs of each other at some of the famous Paris landmarks, like the Eiffel Tower and Arc de Triomphe. Rock fooled around and some of the photographs produced in evidence showed jokey poses of him partially hiding behind a pillar with just part of his head showing. Jurors examining them would perhaps muse on the fact that Hudson was apparently doing a good acting job, covering his inner torment. During weekends and rest days from treatment, Hudson took Channell on trips to Rome, the south of France and Barcelona.

[His old friend, the French publicist, Yanou Collart, whom he had met eight years earlier at the home of Danny Kaye, was totally unaware of Rock's ulterior motive for being in Paris, and in conjunction with Rock's personal publicist, Dale Olson, had arranged media events for him. She had also planned his trip to Rome and secured a television interview for him in Barcelona. She made the arrangements for his visit to the south of France where Rock's friend – Vivian Glenavy – lived, and then for him to go to London. In between she gave a dinner party for Hudson, also attended by Ron Channell, at which he proudly announced to the guests that he had just signed a lucrative contract to appear in 'Dynasty'.]

When they flew to London, Ron Channell found himself in the luxurious surroundings of Rock's favourite hotel, The Savoy. It was around the time of Channell's birthday, 20 September, and

Hudson played another of his boyish jokes on his companion. On the morning of Ron's birthday, he hid a note in the hotel suite and Channell had to hunt for it; he found it in an envelope which bore the words: '*Ron, September 20th 1984: Signed Your Friend Speed*'. Inside was a note telling Channell that when they returned to Los Angeles there would be a video-tape recorder waiting for him.

Mills: 'While you were away, in any of these locations, France, Spain, Italy, England, did you ever observe Mr Hudson write any letters to Marc Christian?'

'No sir.'

'Did you ever see him make any telephone calls to Marc Christian?'

'No sir.'

'Did he ever tell you he was purchasing any gifts for Marc Christian?'

'No sir.'

'Did he ever mention Marc Christian's name?'

'No sir.'

They returned to Los Angeles on 4 October 1988, and Rock appeared in good spirits. [After his last consultation with Dr Dormont in Paris, he was told that the AIDS virus appeared to have been eliminated from his blood. But Dormont warned Hudson that he should not take this as meaning he was cured; it was very likely that the virus would grow back, as indeed it did rapidly. Rock remained elated, however, and appeared to be rejecting the truth and seriousness of the situation, despite Dormont's warnings and those of his doctors when he arrived back in Los Angeles.]

Channell said Rock never appeared depressed in any way, and they resumed the work-out regime at the house immediately and continued to go through the exercises every morning, just as they had done before, except that now, Hudson appeared to want to spend more time in his company. They would hang out together, sometimes going to Channell's house or his brother's. They went out to dinner often. Hudson would pay for the expensive meals, but Channell said he insisted on paying sometimes: 'I would say "Okay, I'm buying so we'll go to a Whopper Burger" and he loved it. He liked going to those places. He had no problem with being a star and never baulked at going to a drive-in for take-away food. He liked it. He liked it when I took the initiative and said I was going to pay. I think he felt that I wasn't trying to take advantage of him.'

100

Mills: 'How often did you have lunch with him, or go out to lunch with him after work-outs?'
'Every day.'
'Did Mr Christian ever eat lunch with the two of you?'
'No.'
'What about dinner engagements . . . did Mr Christian ever go along with either of you?'
'No.'
Channell said that if there were days when he did not go to the house, Hudson would telephone him, sometimes four or five times. He would just say 'Hi, it's me. Whattaya doing?' or he would tell Channell about his plans. The relationship, said Channell, was one of 'best friends'.

Marc Christian, he said, was never involved with any of their activities. He continued to see him around the house, occasionally he would wander into the playroom and work on some tapes but there was never any extended conversation, nor did there appear to be any rapport between Hudson and Christian; in fact, Hudson's general attitude towards Christian was developing a more negative tone, said Channell. Hudson would be sharp with him.

In the early part of December 1984, Hudson was booked to narrate a nativity scene at a Christmas pageant in Orlando, Florida. He suggested to Channell that he might like to go along and bring his parents over from Tampa, which was an hour's drive away. Ron said that would be a great idea, and Hudson arranged it all. He booked two suites at the hotel in Orlando for Channell's parents and his sister and her three children who lived with them. He got them all tickets to see the pageant, took them all out to dinner and to Disneyworld. Channell said: 'It was terrific, probably one of the greatest trips they had ever had in their lives; he spoiled them rotten.'

Christian's counsel, Rhoden interjected: 'Objection, Your Honour, the witness is going beyond . . .'
The judge (*to witness*): 'Okay. This is not a social conversation where one subject leads to another. Just answer the questions.'
Mills (*returning to his witness*): 'Was there ever any mention of Marc Christian during this trip?'
'No sir.'
That Christmas of 1984, when Rock was working on 'Dynasty', Channell spent a lot of time at Hudson's house and Rock bought

101

him several Christmas presents: two suitcases, a suede coat, two cashmere scarves, two flannel shirts and two regular shirts. He also gave him a host of cooking utensils, a crockpot and some other pots and pans; that was a joke between the two of them because unlike Hudson, Channell was not a very good cook.

It was around the turn of the year that Channell began to have suspicions about Rock's health. He was insistent on carrying on with the work-out exercises, but Channell said he did not appear to be responding in a positive way and they had to cut back some of the more strenuous activity. He was itching a lot and constantly kept scratching himself; his weight loss was also becoming increasingly apparent.

[Rock's Hollywood friends were also beginning to notice his dramatic weight-loss. There was a birthday party for him at The Castle towards the end of November and some of his friends had not seen him since his return from Europe; they were shocked by his gaunt appearance, and protruding eyes, but rather than display their concern, one or two complimented him on managing to lose so much weight. Roddy McDowall who was among them, commented on his slim-line figure and Rock made an excuse about getting fit and watching his diet.]

Channell said he became so concerned that he asked Hudson if there was anything wrong. He said there wasn't. Channell suggested he should go to another doctor and get a second opinion, and even suggested the name of a specialist if nothing else but to see about the itching. Hudson agreed and Channell went with him on several occasions but at no time did Hudson ever mention AIDS.

[By the turn of the year in the gossipy world outside, rumours about the true nature of Hudson's illness were already rife. His name was being openly linked with AIDS; people talked in whispers at parties for, like Hudson himself, it was not something they would have liked to have seen in the newspapers. Even close members of the Hudson entourage, like Wallace Sheft and Rock's former live-in friend Tom Clark, were beginning to pressure Mark Miller for answers; they received no confirmation from him.]

Channell said that the way Rock's friendship and generosity towards him had developed was illustrated in early 1985, when his sister was having divorce problems and was moving to California. Ron's mother and father were helping her move and Channell also went to Florida to lend a hand and return with them on the drive back. They stopped off in Arizona so that his sister's husband could see the children but there was a bad scene when the husband tried to obtain possession of them. When they finally got back to California, Channell said his sister was a nervous wreck and so he booked her and the children into a local motel. She was still afraid her husband might catch up with them. He rang Rock to tell him he had arrived back.

Hudson asked, 'Where are you?' Channell told him, and related what had happened. Thirty minutes later, Rock arrived at the motel with armfuls of food and soon turned the tense and tearful scene into a more relaxed one, by bouncing the children on his knee and telling jokes. Then he turned to Channell's sister and said: 'I know you are afraid so if you and the kids want to come to my house, you can stay as long as you like. No one will get to you behind those gates.' The Channell family thanked him, but did not take up his offer.

In February, Hudson took Ron Channell on another trip to Hawaii. It was to be purely vacational said Channell, and they lay in the sun for a week – which seemed to improve Hudson's rashes, if only temporarily. He would soon be seen scratching again and Channell became increasingly concerned about him. He talked to Mark Miller about it; he was worried too, and talked of anorexia. Hudson's decline continued to the point that he was virtually unable to continue the work-outs; he had become very slow in his movements. By July, said Channell, he had become very, very weak; his mental state had also deteriorated and he would 'talk out of his head sometimes'. He would be talking about one thing, and then abruptly change the subject. He was tired all of the time, and would fall into a couch and go into a deep sleep.

On the weekend of 14 July, Channell said Mark Miller asked him if he would go back to Paris with Rock. Channell believed Hudson was to receive treatment for anorexia. [During the following week, the whole of Hollywood was discussing the rumours about Rock, which were heightened by the publication of a photograph in *USA Today* of Hudson and Doris Day taken at Carmel when Hudson arrived to appear on her television special and Dale Olson, Rock's publicist, was suddenly faced with a barrage of questions from newspaper reporters from around the globe. Olson batted them off with excuses about Rock having a severe bout of flu.]

When Hudson returned from his trip to Carmel for his appearance with Doris Day, Channell was ready for the journey to Paris which he viewed with some apprehension.

Mills: 'Did Mark Miller ever tell you he had asked Marc Christian to go with Rock to Paris?'

'No. He said there was only one way Rock would go, and that was if I went with him.'

'Can you describe the way Rock was moving at that point in time?'

Channell said Rock was taking baby steps, very slow, and by the time they arrived in Paris he was extremely tired and could hardly move. They were supposed to have been met by a representative from the hotel to help Channell get Rock off the plane, but no one turned up and he had to manage alone. Rock could hardly stand up, and his mind was wandering. On the flight over, he thought they were going to Hawaii; when they arrived in Paris, he had no idea where they were. Channell tactfully suggested that he order a wheelchair but Rock showed a dogged determination to walk; it took what seemed ages to get him from the aircraft through the airport to a taxi and on to the hotel. He went directly to the hotel suite that Mark Miller had reserved; he walked through the sitting room and into the bedroom and lay down.

Channell's account moved to its dramatic conclusion: 'I remained in the sitting room, trying to get my composure from the trip ordeal when I heard him breathing strangely, in short gasps. I got up and just stood at the bedroom door watching him breathe. I was frightened and I just got on the telephone to Mark Miller.'

Miller told Channell to ring the house doctor at The Ritz and get him up to the room immediately. He thought he should go to hospital; he should go to the American Hospital. He was also to call Dr Dormont and tell him what had happened. Dormont subsequently arrived at the hotel, and assisted with Rock's removal to hospital. Channell said Mark Miller came immediately to Paris, and the following day, he himself returned to Los Angeles.

With his evidence concluded, Harold Rhoden rose to cross-examine: 'Before you left Paris, did Mr Miller buy you a Rolex watch costing $2000.'

'He bought me a watch.'

'Was it a Rolex?'

'Yes. But I don't know what it cost.'

Channell also agreed that for a time after Hudson's death he had worked for Miller and the Rock Hudson estate, assisting with correspondence and the maintenance of the house. Rhoden challenged him over his lunch arrangements with Hudson, and again Channell denied he had ever been to lunch with Hudson when Marc Christian was also present.

One final question from Mills after Rhoden had queried the relationship between Hudson and Channell: 'Did you ever have a homosexual relationship with the late Rock Hudson?'

'No sir.'

# CHAPTER EIGHT

# The Faithful Retainers

Rock Hudson's household management and chores were in the hands of a rather unorthodox band of people. Marc Christian called it a 'gay house'. There was the English butler, James Wright – whose accent remained typically British even after so long in America but whose cooking was apparently not quite so precise – against whom allegations would be made that he brought boys off the street to The Castle; a houseman named John Dobbs who doubled as a Shakespearean actor; a young part-time gardener named Marty Flaherty who, it would be said, was also very close to Mark Miller and had been going to Hudson's house since he was a teenager; an ageing Japanese gardener named Clarence Morimito who observed all comings and goings and said little; plus Miller himself, the retired opera singer and dancer turned real estate agent and then secretary. They would all be called to the stand to deliver their recollections of the events leading up to the star's death and, more importantly, the activities of Marc Christian and his friends, which counsel would claim revealed an insight into the relationship that existed between Hudson and Christian at the time.

Indeed, the whole thrust of the defence case would revolve around efforts to disprove Christian's insistence that he had had no sexual activity other than with Hudson. But counsel must also have been aware that in producing some dirty linen, literally, they would risk the presentation of accusations of an unseemly nature against both Miller and James Wright. In that aspect, Harold Rhoden let no opportunity slip and as these new additions to the story unfolded, it would become clear that while the defence would do its best (or worst) to discredit Christian, he would match them in attempting to demolish the credibility of the opposing witnesses.

The first hint of what was in store arrived when defence counsel Robert Mills called the gardener, eighty-four-year-old Clarence Yoshimitsu Morimoto to the stand. The wiry old man had been working at The Castle for almost thirty-five years: first in the employ of the previous owner, Sam Jaffe, then for Hudson when he bought the property, and now for the new owners. He generally tended the gardens – filled with shrubs and trees – and it was also part of his duty to water and care for Hudson's collection of house-plants, scattered through the interior rooms. In this work, he naturally had to go inside the house frequently.

Mills was interested in one question: In the spring of 1984, when Hudson was away from the house, did Clarence have occasion to go into the upstairs rooms? Yes, replied the gardener. With watering can in hand he was going through the bedrooms when he noticed the door to Hudson's room was slightly open, about eight-inches ajar; he did not expect anyone to be inside and went in. As he turned the corner from the entrance lobby of the room, he saw Marc Christian and a blond boy sitting on the corner of the bed. Both were stripped, as far as he could see, and the boy was stroking Christian's back.

Clarence stood there for between twenty and thirty seconds and then he left without saying a word; apparently his presence had gone unnoticed. Mills had no further questions but Rhoden challenged the witness's memory of who and what he actually saw.

Was he sure it was Christian? Clarence said there was no doubt in his mind that it was. Rhoden reminded him that in his pre-trial deposition he had recalled, 'Marc Christian . . . I presume was sitting on the bed and his blond partner was probably kneeling and they were embracing'. Did that mean he merely presumed it was Christian? Clarence said it did not mean that; he saw Christian's face which was half-turned towards him and he used the word 'presumed' because he was not sure whether he was kneeling or sitting, nor could he see what they were doing.

Clarence agreed that in April 1988, he had a conversation with Christian who came to the house while he was working there but he did not remember saying anything about money. Rhoden pressed him on the subject: Did not Christian ask him if he was expecting money, and that he replied: 'Yes, when the estate is free.'? No, said Clarence, he did not remember saying such a thing.

At this point, Rhoden was able to introduce the name of Martin Flaherty, a tall, blond twenty-nine-year-old whose name would crop up more pointedly later in the trial. Clarence said Marty had been working at the Hudson house for about five years on a part-time basis. He was a friend of Mark Miller and was a very youthful, boyish young man who assisted him occasionally in the gardens. That was all he could say about him and there were no further questions.

Clarence was followed to the witness stand by James Oswald Wright, Hudson's live-in butler since 1978 and a man who perhaps knew more about the activities within the household than anyone. His duties were wide-ranging: to take care of the star's clothes, answer the telephone, make the beds, change the sheets, do the shopping, cooking and some cleaning. He himself had quarters there, a small apartment attached to the house to which he retired whenever his duties were concluded.

He first saw Marc Christian when Hudson brought him to the house in the summer of 1983 and he did not see him again until November, shortly after Tom Clark had moved out. Hudson knocked on the door of his apartment and asked him to come into the kitchen because he wanted to talk to him.

Hudson said to him: 'My friend Marc has nowhere to live. Is it all right with you if he moves in here while I am away in Israel?'

Wright said: 'Certainly', and Christian began moving in his belongings that day. It was 5 November and Hudson was to be away until 4 January 1984. Christian moved into the master bedroom where he also hung some of his clothes and slept in Hudson's bed.

Mills: 'During that period Hudson was away did Christian have any friends to the house?'

Wright: 'Yes, he brought two friends who introduced themselves to me – Wayne and Craig. I didn't know their surnames, but I always thought that one of them looked like Barry Manilow. When they came over, Marc stayed in the master bedroom; the other two slept in the Red Room and the theatre.'

'Later, were you introduced to others?'

'Yes, we were in the kitchen and there were one or two other people there, and Marc introduced me to a young man. He said, "This is Kevin, my friend Kevin" but did not give a last name.'

'Part of your function at the Hudson residence was to clean or wash the bedding, sheets, and pillow cases?'

'Yes.'

'Between November and January, before Hudson returned, did you observe anything on the sheets?'

'Yes. I saw some grease stains and empty yellow packages – I think people call them poppers* – in the bed and a towel on the floor. I think they call the towel a trick towel. There were "skid" marks from sex grease on the sheets and other brown stains.'

When Hudson came back from Israel, there was a fond reunion between himself and Christian. Marc surprised him with a special Christmas tree which contained notes and presents from many of Rock's friends who had come around to decorate the tree while he was away. Later that day as he was passing the kitchen on his way to take a jacuzzi on the patio, Wright happened to glance to his right, and saw Hudson and Marc embracing and kissing; that night they shared the master bedroom which Christian had used since he moved in and they continued to sleep together for some time.

However, in February, a month or so after his return from Israel, Hudson took Christian away for the weekend to stay at the home of Mark Miller and George Nader in Palm Springs. It was the first time he noticed a change in the relationship. When they came back, he asked Rock if they had had a pleasant weekend, and he replied, 'It was the worst weekend I've ever spent in my entire life', but did not elaborate on the reasons for his displeasure.

There were other examples which indicated all was not well between the two men. One morning, he went upstairs and found the mattress to the bed laying on the floor and he asked Hudson: 'What's this?'

Hudson replied: 'Marc had had problems with his back; he's been sleeping on the floor.' Then, in early March, Wright said he noticed that Christian had begun to sleep in the Tijuana Room, the Red Room, opposite the master bedroom. As far as he knew, Christian did not move back into Rock's bedroom after March. At the same time, he noticed a friendship developing between Hudson and Ron Channell; a very nice friendship, he called it. They got on very well, and Hudson was

---

* 'Poppers' is a term used for phials of the drug amyl nitrate which is sniffed to heighten sexual satisfaction.

always giggling and laughing and enjoying himself. He was like a new man.

Christian continued to sleep in the Red Room. The relationship between him and Hudson appeared to have become somewhat strained and he reckoned that Hudson never slept with Christian after March of 1984, which was also around the time that Hudson began spending more time with Ron Channell. Further, while Hudson was away in New York, Wright found similar evidence of stains on the bedclothes in the Tijuana Room as he had earlier found in the master bedroom and he once discovered Christian in bed with a dark-haired young man.

Wright then went on to describe the moment he learned that Hudson had AIDS: he was in the kitchen doing his cooking when the phone rang. Mark Miller took the call; it was Rock calling from Paris. 'Tell Mr Hudson Hello from me,' said the butler, and carried on with his work. Miller looked stern when he put the receiver back on the hook.

Wright asked: 'What's the matter?'

'James, I have something to tell you . . . something very bad. Mr Hudson is dying of AIDS . . . that's why he is in Paris, to be treated.' Wright said he could not believe it at first, but Miller said it was undoubtedly true. At the time, he did not think Hudson was aware that Mark Miller had told him, but later Wright found he had to tell him he knew, to save embarrassment.

When Hudson returned from Paris, he immediately began preparing for rehearsals for 'Dynasty' and he was working on the show throughout Christmas of that year. Aaron Spelling, executive producer of the show, sent Rock a Christmas present of a bed tray with all the accessories. Throughout that time, he said, Christian continued to sleep in the Red Room and remained in that room until Hudson returned from the UCLA hospital in the summer of 1985, when Marc moved into the playroom because Hudson's nurses required the other bedroom.

Christian continued to have friends visit him at the house from October 1984 through to the point where he began sleeping in the playroom, after the public revelation of Hudson's illness. They were usually male friends and the same evidence of sexual activity was present in the laundry. The atmosphere between Hudson and Christian had become more difficult and occasionally there were rows. Once, Rock blew up when Christian wanted to bring the refurbished Chevrolet to the house and park it in the driveway.

110

[At the time, there was still a large unsettled account for which the firm employed on the renovations were seeking payment; Christian had secured the car but Hudson had refused to pay out any further cash.]

Wright witnessed the scene, Hudson shouted: 'I do not want that car on my property. I do not want those people coming up here after that car . . . '.

Christian replied: 'Well, I live here as well . . . this is my house too.'

Hudson was adamant; the car could not be brought to the house and Christian furiously turned away, picked up a chair and flung it across to the other side of the room. As Hudson left with Ron Channell, Christian said, 'I'll see those two in the papers' which Wright and Miller, who was also present in the room at the time, took to be a threat.

Counsel Banks, for Miller, in his cross-examination of the butler, was interested in Christian's claims that Hudson burned himself while cooking chicken on the barbecue. Wright could not remember such an incident and said he had never seen the barbecue used to cook chicken for forty people; the only time he saw it in use around that time was a 4 July party in 1984, when Hudson wanted to cook a turkey on it. The whole thing went up in smoke and the fire department was called.

During the last months of Hudson's life, Wright said he and his employer were often alone together; he seldom saw Christian during the day. He would return home at night for a meal and then usually went out again in the evening. Just before Hudson died, Wright received a cheque for $50,000 severance pay from Hudson. When Mark Miller handed it to him, he said Rock wanted to show his appreciation for the care he had given him and for staying with him until the end.

Banks: 'Let me ask you this. Since you received this money, sir, do you feel . . . has your testimony here been the truth, Mr Wright?'

Rhoden: 'Objection. Argumentative and calls for a conclusion on the part of this witness. The jury will determine if he's telling the truth.'

The judge: 'Sustained.'

Banks rephrased his question: 'Just because you received that money, Mr Wright, do you feel obligated to say anything other than the truth in your testimony?'

111

'No.'

'And after you received that money, did you have to lend some of it back to pay for Rock Hudson's funeral?'

'Yes. To the estate.' [At the time of Hudson's death, his estate was temporarily frozen because of his state of mind at the time of his death and following the commencement of legal proceedings by Marc Christian, neither Miller nor the main beneficiary George Nader were able to draw on Hudson's funds.]

Harold Rhoden, in his cross-examination of the butler, returned to the question of Christian's alleged sleeping partners. Wasn't it a fact, he asked, that Wright had told John Dobbs that he had never seen Christian sleeping with anyone? Wright said he may have said that but he did not believe he had.

And did he not say in his pre-trial deposition, under oath and with penalty of perjury, that he had not seen Marc Christian sleeping with anyone?

Yes, said Wright, but he remembered the incident later, after he had signed the deposition.

Rhoden: 'Isn't it true that you hate Marc Christian?'

'No, sir. I don't hate him. I don't hate anybody.'

'Isn't it true that you despise Marc Christian?'

'I didn't like him too much.'

Wright agreed that for eighteen months after Hudson's death, he continued his employment at the house at the same salary of $2000 a month, paid by the estate.

Rhoden: 'But a few minutes ago, you said you received $50,000 severance pay. Was your employment severed or not?'

'Well, in a sense it was, because he wasn't there and there was no one there for me to buttle, but the estate asked me to stay on while the house was being sold.'

'But the $50,000 you got wasn't for severance pay, was it? You got it for something else?'

'I would think it was for severance pay.'

'But since your employment was not severed, it was not severance pay, was it?'

'Well, I think it was. Mr Hudson had demised; he was my boss and I got a severance cheque. The estate asked me to stay on to take care of the house while it was being sold and to show people around. I had to be there all of the time to keep it in good order, and for the prospective buyers.'

Rhoden became more assertive in his quest for answers: 'Isn't

A famous kiss and Rock Hudson's female fans everywhere quivered. The epitome of the archetypal, macho male, Rock Hudson was never suspected of being gay. *Pillow Talk*, the first of his films with Doris Day, established Rock Hudson as a screen lover in the mould of Cary Grant and Clark Gable and sent him to the top in a poll of male stars.

*Above* Rock and Elizabeth Taylor became life-
friends after starring together in the film *G*
with James Dean. Elizabeth led the servic
remembrance after Rock's death and organize
AIDS benefit in his name. They are pictured
at Grauman's Chinese Theatre in Hollywood be
the release of *Giant*. *Left* Rock in a $7000 n
coat wearing only swimming trunks underne
He had to wear the coat — a film prop — w
Doris Day was alleged to have stormed off the
of *Lover Come Back* in 1961. It was a publi
stunt.

*e* Rock Hudson and Phyllis Gates were ~~ied~~ in November 1955. Secretary and ~~o~~ Hudson's agent, Phyllis didn't realize ~~~~ marriage was a sham to put off the ~~dal~~ sheets who suspected Rock's double ~~~~ They were soon divorced. *Right* When ~~~~et Christian, Rock had just come ~~~~gh a traumatic time. He had bypass ~~~~ry in 1981 after a heart attack while ~~~~ing the T V series 'The Devlin ~~~~ection' for which this picture was ~~~~. The series flopped and Hudson took ~~~~avy smoking and drinking.

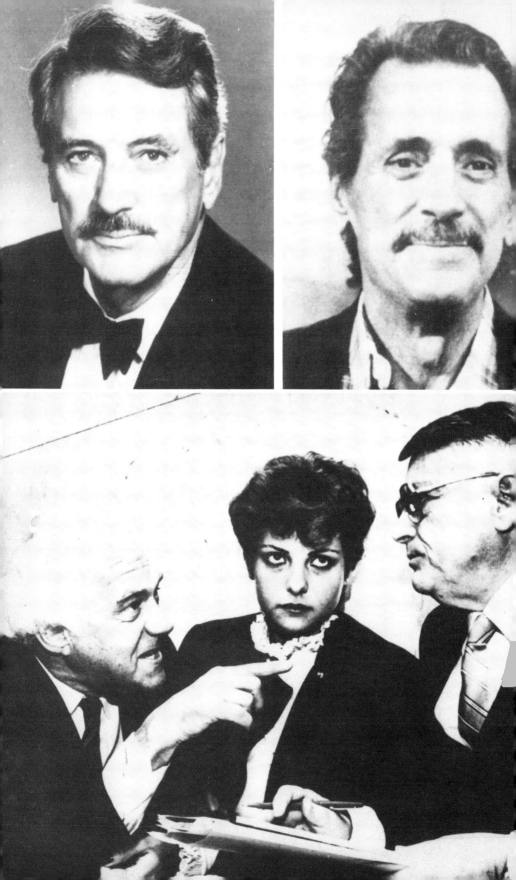

Opposite page, top The contrasting faces of Hudson made the front pages of newspapers worldwide when it was disclosed he had AIDS. In 1982 (left), he was still the handsome star. By July 1985 (right), the ravages of his illness are evident. Opposite page, bottom The lawyers in Christian's case were stars of earlier famous Hollywood courtroom battles. Harold Rhoden (right) took over the case when Marvin Mitchelson (left) dropped out to concentrate on his own problems. Left Marc Christian, lover and friend of the late Rock Hudson, emerges from the trial of his action against the estate. Below Rock Hudson, two years before his death, in the garden of his home — The Castle — which he shared with Christian.

Opposite page, top In 1984 with Linda Evans of 'Dynasty'. He caused an uproar by giving her a screen kiss at a time when he knew he was suffering from AIDS. Opposite page, bottom Marc Christian pores over legal documents at the commencement of his trial. Left Rock the TV star first achieved success on the small screen with Susan Saint James in 'McMillan and Wife' in 1972. Below February 1989 and Marc Christian was the man of the moment as he received news of a further settlement of $7.25 million to top the $14.5 million awarded previously. He remained cool throughout seven weeks of high drama as his life with Rock was revealed in sensational detail.

Ironically, the last picture of Rock Hudson depicted Rock with the co-star of his heyday, his beloved Doris. Taken three days before he left for Paris to be told by his doctors: 'There is no hope', this photograph was flashed around the world, shocking fans everywhere. Said Doris Day after his death, 'I knew he was dying; I thought he had cancer'.

it a false statement that you received $50,000 for severance?'

'No, I don't think it is.'

'Is it a true statement that when Marc Christian was in the house, there were young boys also there? Is that true?'

'Yes.'

'Sir, isn't it true that throughout 1984 and 1985 there were a lot of teenage boys brought into the house because you have a practice of picking up teenage boys and bringing them to the house for your own pleasure?'

'No. Certainly not.'

'Did you ever, during these times, pick up teenage boys in Hollywood, homeless boys, and bring them back to Rock Hudson's house for any purpose?'

'No.'

'Did you ever make a statement to Marc Christian like this: "Look, you're a nice guy but you're dealing with a lot of sick people. If I were you, I'd get out while I could"?'

'I don't remember saying that.'

Rhoden once again pointed Wright to his earlier depositions, in which he admitted he might have made that statement, and pressed again with the question: 'If you might have said it, might you have been telling the truth that he was around a lot of sick people?'

'I don't remember saying it.'

There was a similar exchange over whether or not Wright had warned Christian not to trust anyone, especially Miller and once again Rhoden read into court the butler's previous statement agreeing that he probably did say that to Christian.

'No further questions,' said Rhoden.

Susan Stafford had been a close friend of Rock's for more than fifteen years; she was among his inner circle of showbusiness friends who were aware of his sexual preferences but never betrayed them. She, too, was a well-known face in Los Angeles, stemming largely from her appearances on the game show 'Wheel of Fortune' on which she preceded Vanna White as hostess for seven and a half years. When she left that show, Susan went into documentary work and produced a health programme called 'Alive' for the Christian Broadcasting Network. She also made three documentaries with the American surgeon-general, C. Everett

113

Koop, for the American Leprosy Ministries and progressed into social work and psychology. Through this she became a chaplain intern and rover at hospitals, paying special attention to helping AIDS patients even before she was aware that her beloved friend was suffering from it.

She first met Marc Christian while Rock was filming in Israel. Mark Miller and George Nader had given a party at their home to which several of Hudson's close friends were invited. Several of them had heard about Christian, but few had met him. [When Christian was first introduced to Ross Hunter, the producer who brought Hudson and Doris Day together for *Pillow Talk* and who had remained one of Rock's most devoted friends, Hunter threw his arms around him and said, 'So you're the one we've all been waiting to see.' Christian said later that he felt like a 'mail-order bride'.]

Susan said that on that Christmas in 1983, she went over to Rock's house to help decorate the Christmas tree. Afterwards Christian drove her home and on the way, he made a pass at her which surprised her in view of his relationship with Hudson. She laughed it off but then on the day Rock died, she met him for lunch at Butterfield's restaurant. They had made the appointment some time earlier and she was somewhat surprised that he still wanted to keep the date, even though Rock had died only that morning.

During the meal, she said Christian spoke of Hudson's will and mentioned that Tom Clark had been taken out of it and he [Christian] had been put in. He also mentioned that he had been to see Marvin Mitchelson and planned to get lots of money, enough for them both to fly away together to Mexico or somewhere.

Christian showed no outward signs of grief although he did say he was scared that he might get AIDS. Later when they went back to Rock's house, she thought it strange when he changed his clothing two or three times for the benefit of the press who were gathered outside the house. She did not see him cry or appear in any way affected by grief, nor was he crying at the memorial service or the scattering of Hudson's ashes into the sea.

[Susan read a eulogy at the service; she is a Born Again Christian and Mark Miller, who had also been her friend for many years, turned to her for advice when it became clear in September 1985 that Hudson could not be expected to live much longer. She contacted a showbusiness priest, Father Tom Sweeney, who had produced many television religious programmes and was an advisor on the television mini-series of 'The Thorn Birds'. Though Rock had never been a religious man in any way, he allowed Sweeney to visit him frequently in his last days, though increasingly the priest found him incoherent and often unable to respond to his offers of sacrament. He administered confession and absolution but was never sure whether Hudson knew what was going on. He was also joined by a group of other Born Again Christians, including Pat Boone and his fervently religious wife Shirley, who visited and prayed at his bedside. She would sit and hold Hudson's hands and at one stage believed the force of prayer and a fast by herself and others in prayer meetings was beginning to have good effect; she, more than anyone in her group, was deeply affected by Hudson's death.]

Miss Stafford's beliefs and conversations with Marc Christian prompted unusual cross-examination from Harold Rhoden who appeared to want to demonstrate that she was somewhat eccentric in her attitudes to religion.

Did she ever say that Rock Hudson was still her friend a couple of years after he had died, and would remain her friend? And even now, as they sat there, Rock Hudson was her friend?

Yes, said Susan, the spirit continued to live and the memories of that person could not be taken away simply because he had died. He continued to be her friend, even now and in answer to further prompting from Rhoden she agreed that it was quite likely she had said to Christian, on the day of the funeral, that Rock was watching them.

Rhoden: 'And did you say to Christian, "Now that dear Rock has departed I don't think he would mind if we had a little bit of an affair together"?'

'You want an answer to that question?'

'Of course I want an answer. That's why I asked you, ma'am.'

'I came down here to testify the truth . . . '

'I don't want a speech. Just yes or no.'

'The answer is no. And I'm insulted.'

'I'm sorry about that.'

'I doubt that you are, sir.'

'Well, I won't argue, I'm not allowed to do that. Did you ever make a statement to Marc Christian that you have made a pass at the Pope because he was a very attractive man?'

'No. I might have said the Pope was a very attractive man. I like people who have, shall I say, high character. I think what I

115

said to Marc was a little joke and he has misunderstood it.'
'Did you say to Christian "The good Lord has a plan for us all . . . let's go away together"?'
'No sir, not at all.'
Mr Banks interjected, protesting to the judge: 'Your Honour, I am going to object to Mr Christian sitting here giggling and shaking his head up and down or sideways and otherwise engaging in activities. I think it is improper and I ask he be instructed to discontinue it.'
The judge: 'It applies to all parties and counsel. Mr Christian you will refrain from any expressions during testimony.'
Rhoden came back with his last questions: Did Susan ever suggest to Christian, 'We can go away to India. I have a Swami who can do you some good'?
She doubted that she had ever said such a thing, being a follower of Christ.
'Did you ever attend parties given by Rock Hudson for lawyers at his house?'
'Yes.'
'And did you tell Marc Christian that at one of these parties you stripped naked and walked around?'
'No. It never happened.'
'It did not happen or you did not tell it to Marc Christian?'
'Absolutely. It did not happen and I did not tell it to Marc Christian.'
Miss Stafford added 'Oy!' and laughed, and in this she was joined by members of the gallery, ever anxious for a moment of light relief.
Rhoden waited for the giggles to subside and pressed on: 'Did you ever tell Christian that Miller had arranged for you to get a loan of several thousand dollars from Rock Hudson?'
'Never. I never borrowed a dime and never arranged anything, ever.'
'Did you ever tell Marc Christian you had been to bed with two men who had AIDS but you were okay because a priest had performed exorcism and drove out the virus?'
'No.'
Rhoden's examination was complete, but Mills appeared anxious to clear up the question of Miss Stafford's alleged pass at the Pope. How had that conversation arisen?
Stafford: 'Do I have to? This was a story, a joke. I'm sorry I ever

told it. Okay – there are these 3909 nuns on the way to Rome. And there are three hot tamales – chicks – dolls on the way to Rome. Who's going to have the most fun – and this is the joke – the 3909 nuns or the three hot tamales?'

Banks: 'I give up. Who?'

'The Pope.'

Harold Rhoden could not understand what the joke had to do with making a pass at the Pope. Susan replied that she did not know one was related to the other; all she did was tell the joke and perhaps Christian had misunderstood that she was referring to the Pope's sexuality.

Rhoden: 'Oh, I understand it now. All you did was tell this joke and you think that because Christian thought you were saying the Pope was an attractive man, you would have made a pass at him?'

'I don't think it's too rude to think that a person with charisma and of high character is attractive.'

'No further questions, Your Honour.'

Mr Mills had, though. He wanted to clear up this seemingly unimportant piece of banter which had kept the court rivetted for some eight or nine minutes: 'Did you ever make a pass at the Pope?'

'No. I have never even met the Pope.'

'Next witness.'


Richard Glenn Lovell, aged fifty-eight, earned his living as a theatrical agent whose extensive client list included Hudson's close friend of many years and fellow-homosexual, Dean Dittman, who invited him one evening in the spring of 1984 to a dinner party at the Hudson house. It was an informal gathering, originally intended for just the three of them and Rock himself had prepared the meal for which he had set the table in the kitchen.

Later, Lovell saw that a fourth place had been set and learned that they were to be joined by Marc Christian who arrived after they'd sat down to eat their salad and drink their aperitifs. Suddenly, he appeared and sat at the table but did not stay long. He listened to the conversation for a short time and then got up and left. Hudson commented, 'Oh, he has to make a phone call. He's probably going out drinking with his buddies tonight.' Christian returned briefly and then excused himself. As he left Hudson said, 'See, no class.'

117

Lovell thought he detected an atmosphere between them.

However, they continued their meal and drinks and Christian was not mentioned again until three days later, when Rock telephoned Lovell at his office and asked: 'Would you please interview Marc? He may be a prospective actor. He is interested and I would like to find something for him to do in order to get him out of here.' Lovell subsequently interviewed Christian at his office.

Mills: 'What did you do in terms of the interview?'

Rhoden interrupted: 'Object. Irrelevant.'

Judge: 'Sustained.'

Mills ascertained from one further question that Lovell had not met Mark Miller previous to the time he was invited to dinner at Hudson's, and he was dismissed from the witness stand. As Lovell walked from the courtroom, however, Harold Rhoden rose quickly after a consultation with his client and requested his recall.

Back on the witness stand, Lovell was questioned by Rhoden on what happened at the interview in his office with Marc Christian: 'Isn't it true that when he came to your office, you asked Marc Christian to have sex with you?'

Lovell: 'I won't even acknowledge that. How degrading.'

Rhoden: 'Yeah? Now answer it.'

'No, sir.'

# CHAPTER NINE

# The Loyal Secretary

Mark Miller first met Rock Hudson in 1951 when he and George Nader were sharing a small house in Studio City. Miller and Nader had been together since 1947 when they met while appearing at the Pasadena Playhouse in *Oh Susannah!* and had seldom been apart since. Rock was brought to a foursome dinner party at their house by an agent and they all got on so well, they invited him back to visit any time he was at a loose end. Like them, he was trying to make his way in the Hollywood jungle; he was lonely, virtually penniless and with few friends. They were also like-minded in their sexuality which in the fifties meant that they were firmly in the closet and no external hint of their relationships could get out. George Nader knew it would have finished their careers before they even started.

Behind the closed doors of home, they could talk openly and act the way they wanted without being branded 'fairies'. Certainly, none of them possessed the more effeminate, lisping traits that identified showbusiness homosexuals. They all looked and appeared every inch the athletic, handsome, young he-men, archetypal of the age of fan magazines and adoration from movie-goers. While George pursued his ambitions, Mark took on other work outside of his professional role as a singer and dancer to help with the household expenses and eventually took a job in real estate so that George could continue his acting (in which he achieved moderate fame). He also helped Rock in many ways with his career and both he and Nader were always on hand, whether Rock wanted advice or just companionship. They spent many hours in each other's company, with Rock joining Mark and George on trips to secluded beaches where they could swim and play around. Thirty-two years later, Rock said of Mark Miller: 'He runs my life . . . he's my man Friday; he makes me laugh. He's my best friend, drunk or sober. I couldn't exist without Mark Miller . . . and George Nader. I can trust him to tell me the truth. People have tried to break us up but it never worked.' Rock would reward their life-long friendship in his will.

Next, Mark Miller, sixty-two years old and a thick-set, even tough-looking man, almost six-feet tall with brown hair and moustache, took the witness stand to begin his evidence and tell of his life as Hudson's personal organizer.

His defending counsel, Andrew Banks, led him into his story: He had been Hudson's secretary since 9 August 1972. He managed the payroll for the house, paid all Hudson's personal bills, his credit cards and accounts; he kept the cars up to date, arranged for them to be repaired, filled with petrol, and valeted. He supervised the staff and handled all of Hudson's fan mail. He had an office in Hudson's house and worked from nine to five each day, five days a week, although in the last two or three years of Hudson's life this had been cut to four days a week.

[Since the late seventies, Rock Hudson's career had been in decline and fan mail became sparse. Although Rock had said he would never appear in another television series after his long-running 'McMillan and Wife', he signed for 'The Devlin Connection' in 1980 on the basis that his own company, Mammoth Films, would share in the profits. He was to play a CIA agent named Brian Devlin and was instrumental in casting his friend and protégé Jack Scalia to play the role of his son. But he had completed only four episodes when he suffered a heart attack and was out of action for a year after by-pass surgery. When 'The Devlin Connection' was finally shown in 1982, reviews were so bad that it did not return for a second series. And apart from a couple of mediocre television films, Rock did not work again until Menahem Golan offered him the role in *The Ambassadors*. Again, the film was not met with acclaim, and after a short provincial cinema-run, it disappeared until it was released on video in 1986.]

Miller first met Christian in October 1983 when Hudson introduced them and said that Marc was going to house-sit. Later Hudson told him they had met at the Brook Street Baths in Los Angeles. Hudson had been there many times for a massage, as had Miller himself.

While Hudson was away, Miller saw Christian on many occasions and had various conversations, and it was Christian, he said, who met Hudson on his return. The star appeared happy and cheerful and he was obviously pleased to be back home with Christian. However, his mood changed a day or two later when Hudson came to Miller looking miserable and relayed a conversation that he had had with Christian. He said Christian had come to him the night before with something to tell him, something he ought to know: 'Before you hear it from any of your rich friends, I want you to know that I have taken money for sex from people, from men, but only when I was down and out, only when I did not have a bartending . . . '. Miller said Christian had made the same confession to him.

Also, while Rock was away, Miller had seen Christian in bed with another young man, named Kevin Johnson, one morning when a publicist called for a photograph of Hudson and Mae West, taken in 1958. He had gone upstairs to get the photograph from the Red Room and discovered the two of them asleep in the same bed.

Hudson was clearly worried about the relationship and said to Miller, 'I will take him [Christian] nowhere. I cannot be seen in public with him.' Later, around 16 January, there was another conversation. Miller had arrived at his office around nine o'clock and found Hudson waiting for him.

'Why are you here?' Miller asked, since it was unusual to find Hudson in the office. Normally they met later in the kitchen for coffee.

'He didn't come home last night,' said Hudson, referring to Christian.

'The plot thickens,' Miller replied. Then Hudson explained what had happened the night before. He had taken Marc to dinner at Dean Dittman's house.

Dittman gave 'mixed' parties – with heterosexual and homosexual people – and when Hudson and Christian arrived, Dittman said, 'There's a straight man present' and pointed out who he was so that everyone was aware of the situation. Hudson complained that Christian 'zeroed in' on the straight man and spent the entire evening talking to him. They had gone to the party in separate cars – Christian in one of Rock's which he regularly used, the Cadillac *Seville*, and Hudson in another – and at the end of the party they left separately. Christian did not return home and Rock was upset, said Miller.

By the end of February, in Miller's view, the affair between Hudson and Christian was over. They had gone to spend the weekend with Miller and Nader at their house in Palm Springs. It was a lousy weekend; Hudson and Christian hardly spoke and there was obviously something wrong between them. Miller asked Hudson what was going on and he said their affair was over, adding: 'He has letters. Give him anything he wants. Money.'

By March, Hudson had begun to spend more time in the company of Ron Channell. On one occasion Christian came home at lunchtime to watch the soap opera, 'Days of our Lives', which he viewed every day, and asked, 'Where are they?' Miller told him that they had put on their suits and ties and had gone for lunch to a restaurant.

Christian, he said, was angry and replied, 'I'll see them in the *National Enquirer* as lovers and don't think I don't know the press because I do' and stormed out of the room. It was Miller's belief that the relationship between Hudson and Christian had ended. His attempt to testify that Christian and Hudson no longer had sex together brought swift objections from Harold Rhoden who submitted that because of the hours Miller worked at the house, he was in no position to give evidence on this issue. Rhoden's objection was sustained.

However, Miller was able to show that during the first half of 1984, Hudson went on several trips but did not take Marc Christian with him. First, he went to Hawaii at Easter with a companion named Gunther Goloff and later travelled to New York for 'The Night of a Thousand Stars'. Christian stayed in Los Angeles on both occasions.

[Unbeknown to Miller, Hudson also went to Mexico for a weekend with a young man he met at a gay bar in Long Beach, California. They saw each other again at a Dean Dittman party on the night of the Academy Awards in April. A week later, he flew down to Mexico and stayed at the home of the young man's father.]

In May 1984, Hudson had the mole on the back of his neck removed by plastic surgery. It was the second time he had had the operation. The first time was in January but it had reappeared quickly. This time, he came back to the house, said Miller, with a bandage across his head and around his neck. He explained it to Miller by saying it was a skin cancer which had been removed, although at the time of this operation, Hudson was already aware from a biopsy on the mole that he had the AIDS virus; he kept it to himself for more than a week.

Miller's story now moved to the day Hudson told him he had AIDS. It was two o'clock in the afternoon of 5 June 1984. Rock had been taking a nap. He came downstairs, sat down and said: 'I've got AIDS. I've been crying for a week. I don't want anybody to know it. Not even George Nader.' Miller could not think of anything to say except that he was sorry.

They talked more and Hudson was obviously extremely embarrassed about his situation. 'It seems so filthy', Hudson kept saying. He was very low. Miller asked Hudson to allow him to tell Nader and eventually he agreed, and then told Miller: 'I have an appointment with a specialist from the UCLA in Dr Kennamer's office on Thursday, the 7th. You have to go with me and I want you at all future doctor's appointments that you can possibly be at because I have that white-coat syndrome. I don't hear what a doctor says and I want you to hear it.'

Two days later, Miller went with Rock to Dr Kennamer's office for a meeting with Dr Michael Gottlieb from UCLA, for what would be a two-hour consultation. [Kennamer was one of Hollywood's best-known and respected physicians and had many famous clients, including Elizabeth Taylor. Gottlieb was already one of the top American specialists on AIDS. As an immunologist, he was among those who were present at what was considered to be the start of the AIDS story. In 1980, Gottlieb was called in by another doctor at the UCLA School of Medicine to examine a thirty-one-year-old Los Angeles homosexual artist who had an abnormal fluffy white growth in his throat that was choking him. Gottlieb, with the latest technology available, carried out tests which indicated a major attack on the man's immune system. The artist soon developed pneumonia and died. As Gottlieb continued his work, other cases became known and specifically, the medical reports of five young homosexuals proved similarly worrying. By June 1981, he and the other colleagues he had contacted were so concerned that they published their findings in the 5 June issue of the 'Morbidity and Mortality Weekly Report', brought out by the Centre of Disease Control in Atlanta, Georgia. And suddenly the homosexual communities of American cities, and soon the world, began to get frightened.]

Miller sat beside Hudson as Gottlieb explained the origin: 'It is transmitted anally and the anal receptor, up to this point in time

123

we think, is the one that comes down with it. It is also passed by IV needles. The anal intruder to our knowledge [in 1984] does not come down with it. Therefore, we are assuming that it is in the semen and the AIDS virus goes into the blood when there is bleeding in the anal tract.' Gottlieb took further blood samples for testing. It was a long discussion, with the specialist attempting to place before Hudson, in the simplest terms, all that the medical profession then knew about AIDS. He talked of the progression of the illness and its various stages (which would encompass emotions of fear, denial, anger and finally acceptance). He outlined the future that lay ahead.

Hudson asked him: 'Is it definitely fatal?'

Gottlieb paused too long, and finally said, 'I would get my affairs in order if I were you.'

Gottlieb also warned Hudson against having sex of any kind. He knew it was difficult to repress the urges and said that if he did have sex, he should certainly wear a condom. Miller said he was still in the room when Gottlieb asked Hudson if he had a lover, and he replied 'No, not now. I did have and he lives in the house but we have not had a sexual relationship for some months.'

Gottlieb replied: 'Some lovers freak out and depart, abandoning the mate. Others stay to the end. Since you've told me that you no longer have a lover, that you are a very famous person and that this news will be headlines when it is announced, I'm going to leave it up to you to decide how to handle telling your former lover [Marc Christian].'

The consultation was concluded and as they left Dr Kennamer's office, Miller's first question to Hudson was: 'Is Marc Christian exposed?'

Miller claimed that Hudson replied, 'I could have gotten it from him. I want him out of the house by five o'clock this afternoon.'

Miller replied: 'That is morally wrong. From what Dr Gottlieb told us, he could be exposed.'

Hudson said: 'Marc Christian and Liberty Martin will destroy me in five minutes if they have this news.'

As they drove back to the house, Hudson was agonizing over his future and his career which he thought would be ruined if the news leaked out. They discussed again the exposure of Christian and others to AIDS. Miller said he asked Hudson specifically if he had had anal sex with Christian and he maintained he had not; just oral sex. 'If it's anal,' said Rock, 'Christian doesn't have the virus.'

Miller went on: 'I believed him when he said that; he'd said the same thing to Dr Gottlieb. I did not believe he had had sex with Christian for four or five months and in fact, he told me in February 1984, 'I'm finished with Marc . . . I'm moving on to Ron Channell.' When I questioned him about Channell's possible exposure, Hudson replied, 'I struck out with Ron. There's no worry there.'

Back at the house, Miller and Hudson continued long conversations that day – and almost every other day – about what Hudson should do. He cried often and kept saying 'What shall I do. How do I handle this?' Miller suggested he should take a house in Mexico or Western Australia, or go to live with George Nader in their house in the desert.

Banks: 'You were talking about him dying – and how he should live out the rest of his life?'

'Yes. We talked about his moving away, but he said "I'm too famous. They will find me. I'll just stay here in my own home." '

'Did you ever tell Christian that Hudson had AIDS prior to 23 July 1985 when it was publicly announced?'

'No, I did not.'

'Why didn't you tell him?'

'Because I was asked not to.'

However, Hudson did ask Miller to arrange for Christian to have a medical check-up without telling him the reason. An appointment was made, with Miller's own physician, for a full medical. When Christian returned Miller asked him the results. He said the doctor had told him he had the body of a twenty-year-old and there was absolutely nothing wrong with him.

In July, Hudson began talking about the possibility of going to Paris for treatment. His friend Dean Dittman had called to say he had heard of a new experimental drug that was being tried out there, evidently the first in the world and he thought Hudson should try to get it. As it happened, said Miller, he had already received an invitation to attend the Deauville Film Festival that summer for a showing of George Stevens' movies which included *Giant*.

He asked Miller to make the arrangements and he called Dr Gottlieb to find out more about the drug treatment programme in Paris. Gottlieb had heard of the treatment using the new drug HPA-23 which was being administered by Dr Dominique Dormont.

125

Arrangements were made immediately for Rock to receive a consultation and subsequently, treatment in Paris. He left Los Angeles on 21 August.

While he was in Paris, Hudson and Miller spoke frequently on the telephone. But never in those conversations did Hudson ask to speak to Marc Christian. As far as he was aware, Hudson did not write to Christian either. At the end of the treatment, Rock telephoned. He sounded very happy. Dormont had told him that the AIDS virus had been removed from his blood. Miller telephoned Dormont himself the following day to enquire if he would take his friend Steve Del Re, who also had AIDS, as a patient. Dormont agreed and also confirmed to him that the treatment had removed the AIDS virus from Hudson's blood.

A new line of questioning from Andrew Banks regarding payments Miller had made to Marc Christian through Mammoth Films and on Rock Hudson's instructions, brought the trial to another halt with an objection by Harold Rhoden; counsel adjourned to the judge's chambers to discuss the relevance of the issue.

Out of the jury's hearing, Judge Geernaert said it was clear that Banks wanted to show the amount of money received by Christian by way of the $400-a-month salary and other expenses. But it was irrelevant, since a cross-complaint brought by Rock Hudson's estate to recover this money from Christian had been dismissed. If the issue was re-discussed Mr Rhoden would be free to point out to the jury that the estate had originally sought to get the money back but were no longer proceeding with that claim. It was a major ancillary issue which might help the defendants but, when fully litigated, also had the potential to help Christian.

The judge believed that the questioning of witnesses about irrelevant issues ought to stop. They had got down to who cooked the chicken as being relevant, and it was remotely connected, but the discussion of these matters was diverting the jury from the real issue of the trial. It was not about the money that Marc Christian received; that had already been ruled out even though Rhoden wanted to demonstrate how it was a 'sham and part of a conspiracy'.

Andrew Banks interjected, with respect, to point out that in his opening remarks, Christian's counsel had painted a picture of 'poor Marc Christian who was taken advantage of by these people and paid only $400 a month and some minor expenses' when in fact Miller's testimony would show that he had received a substantial amount of money after Hudson had instructed: 'Give him what he wants – give him money.'

Banks added: 'I think it is relevant . . . I have made that for the record and I won't argue with His Honour any more . . . you're the judge, I'm just a lawyer.'

The judge replied: 'On reflection, you have mentioned "the poor plaintiff". My memory of the testimony was that he never said that the only thing he got was $400 a month. He said many times, "I had a credit card. I was told to use it and I did use it." There was no effort to minimize the amounts he received by using the credit card . . . the jury should not allow their deliberations to deal with how much money he did or did not get from Rock Hudson during his life. So I am going to sustain the objection.'

When Miller's evidence resumed, Banks reverted to a different line: 'After the meeting with doctors, did Hudson ever say that he and Christian had resumed sexual relations?'

'No, he did not.'

'There was testimony by Mr Christian about a conversation with him about finding some pretties and bringing them up to the house to spice up the relationship between him and Hudson. Did you ever have such a conversation?'

'No.'

'Did you ever have a conversation about anal sex?'

'Yes. Christian said, "I have not done anal sex for ten years. I tried it one but I didn't like it; it hurt." That conversation occurred about a week after Mr Hudson told me he had AIDS.'

'Did Hudson ever say to you, "Look after the kid, I may have killed him"?'

'No, he did not.'

Miller also disputed Christian's story of how he drove him to get his passport renewed when it became necessary for him to fly to Paris during Hudson's second visit to the city. He said he obtained a new passport by contacting Rogers and Cowan, the largest publicity firm in Los Angeles, which handled Rock Hudson's publicity. They telephoned the White House in Washington. He was taken by a woman from Rogers and Cowan to the passport office, and received a new passport within twenty minutes.

Banks: 'When Hudson returned to America and was at the UCLA did he tell you whether he wanted to see Marc Christian?'

'He told me daily that he did not. I took a yellow pad to him to make a list of the people he wanted to see. Dr Gottlieb had suggested two visitors a day to keep his spirits up and I said, "So who do you want to see?"

'He replied, "I want to see Elizabeth Taylor, Juliet Prowse, Jon Epstein [producer of 'McMillan and Wife'], Ross Hunter, George Nader, James Wright, Marty Flaherty, Ron Channell, Clarence Morimoto", and then listed about twenty-five other friends.'

'Did he give names of people he did not want to see?'

'Yes. Marc Christian was among them.' [Although Christian was eventually allowed in.]

Hudson was brought home to The Castle on 30 August 1985 and apart from nurses who were to provide round-the-clock care, Tom Clark also moved back in. [It had been almost two years since Clark left The Castle and in consultation with Miller and George Nader, he decided to move back in to make Rock's last days as comfortable as possible. Additional support was needed at Hudson's house to handle the ever-present press corps gathered outside, and the avalanche of media activity that slipped past Hudson's publicist Dale Olson. Clark also took over the arrangements for visitors, of whom there were many, and initially would bring Hudson down into the garden where he would sit with his dogs and chat to his friends. Gradually, as he became weaker and disorientated, Clark could no longer manage to bring Hudson out of his bedroom and ushered the flow of callers upstairs for limited visits. Most left in tears.]

Miller's evidence-in-chief was concluded and now he faced the cross-examination of Harold Rhoden who was anxious to extend his recollection of certain aspects of events. Martin Flaherty, the twenty-nine-year-old part-time gardener, was of particular interest to Rhoden.

Was it true that he had been coming to the Hudson house since he was fourteen? No, said Miller, but probably since he was seventeen. And wasn't it true that Hudson had taken a dislike to him and banned him from the house? It was Tom Clark who banned him, not Hudson, said Miller.

And what was Miller's own relationship with Flaherty? Did Flaherty live with him at some point? Again, Miller denied this implication but said that he had been to his own home on many occasions to work, painting the house.

'How many times?'

'Three hundred.'

'He was painting the house 300 times?'

'No, he was there 300 times, working.'

Rhoden produced an income tax form of Flaherty's on which his address was given as 927 North Kings Road, Los Angeles, an apartment which Miller rented. At this point, Andrew Banks challenged the relevance of Rhoden's line of questioning and once again, the trial reverted to the judge's chambers where counsel argued their points. The judge sustained the objection, and Rhoden continued his cross-examination without further reference to Flaherty's relationship with Miller.

Once more he took Miller over his allegation that the birthday party which Christian had claimed Hudson had given him in June 1984 never in fact took place. He repeated his earlier statement that to his knowledge the party did not take place and would not alter his testimony when Rhoden produced in evidence a photograph showing Hudson, Christian, Liberty Martin and others around what appeared to be a birthday cake in a white box.

Rhoden also again challenged Miller's account of why Hudson allowed Christian to remain in the house if he was blackmailing him. It was at a time when Hudson was paying for Christian's dental work and for the repair bills to his Chevrolet.

Rhoden: 'Did you ask Hudson why he could have thrown Christian out, that blackmailer, and still continued fixing the blackmailer's teeth while he lived outside the house?'

'No.'

'Did Rock Hudson explain why he felt an obligation to this blackmailer to keep him in the house until the blackmailer's car had been repaired?'

'Because when Rock Hudson made promises, he kept them.'

Finally, Rhoden came back to the question of Ron Channell and his relationship with Hudson. The expensive Rolex watch which Miller bought for Channell while they were in Paris was bought on Hudson's instructions. He had mentioned some months before that he would like to buy Channell such a present, and though Hudson was not aware at the time it was being bought, Miller said he knew his employer would approve.

Rhoden: 'Sir, didn't you say to Ron Channell in Paris before you got the watch, "While we are here, I'm sure Rock will approve. Let's go buy you a Rolex watch." Did you say that?'

'Yes.'

'Didn't you mean: "Well, Rock hasn't approved it yet but he will when he hears about it in the future"?'
'No.'
'By the way, Ron wore the watch when he flew back from Paris on Concorde didn't he?'
'I assume so. I wasn't with him.'
'In fact, did you not say to Channell, "It's all right; it's all George's and my money now, anyway." '
'No.'
'Did you ever have a conversation with Christian indicating that you were going to get Ron Channell into bed one day?'
'Never.'
'This may refresh your memory. Did you say to Marc Christian that "Rock's money would turn Channell gay. The Movie Star's money could turn any farm boy queer and if it doesn't I don't know what would"?'
'Never.'
Rhoden now turned to question Miller on his involvement in the preparation of a book called *ROCK HUDSON: His Story* which carried the author credit of 'by Rock Hudson and Sara Davidson', and a sub-title of 'The complete, authorized and intimate story of Rock Hudson's career' and was published by Bantam in 1986.

[Hudson himself had often spoken of writing his autobiography, but had always rejected the possibility because he felt he could still not face exposing his life to the scrutiny that such a book might encourage. He wanted to be able to tell the truth but at the same time was immensely reticent about going public over his homosexuality; he was well aware that many people in the American and European newspaper and media circles knew and were generally kind to him in that respect but he remained scared that spiteful gossip and ever-eager sensation mongers would wreck him and his public image. However, in August 1985 after his collapse in Paris, Mark Miller contacted Hudson's friend and writer Lady Glenavy about the prospect of her writing a book. For various reasons she did not agree and subsequently, Sara Davidson, a journalist and author from Los Angeles was brought in.

She first met Hudson on 4 September – twenty-eight days before he died – after having previous meetings with Mark Miller and Hudson's business manager. She had a number of interviews with him though she found his attention span limited and towards the end, he was able to make few coherent recollections. Sara said that Hudson had told Mark Miller, 'You know the whole story, you'll have to do it for me' and Hudson stipulated that his share of the book's proceeds should go to AIDS research. When the book was published, it carried a copyright line attributed to the Rock Hudson AIDS Foundation and a message from Hudson dated 5 September in which he said he had asked his friends to work with Sara Davidson in telling his story. However, some of his close friends claimed after the book's publication that at the time Davidson saw him, Rock was in no state to make such a decision nor realize the extent of the book's scope.]

Rhoden, in his questioning of Miller, was interested in some of the comments in the book which were attributed to Miller who agreed that he had many discussions over a period of several months with Miss Davidson. Miller said he had not in fact read the book.

He agreed that conversations between himself and Rock Hudson would have been relayed to Miss Davidson by himself. Rhoden asked: 'Did you tell Miss Davidson that when Marc Christian learned that Ron Channell was with him in Paris, Christian said, "Why didn't you tell me? Why was this done behind my back?" and that you replied to Marc Christian, "Marc, you're not having an affair with me, you're having an affair with Rock. It's up to Rock to tell you"?' [The quote appeared on page 275 of the paperback edition.]

'What I told Miss Davidson was past tense . . . No, I did not.'

'You didn't tell her?'

'No. I did not.'

'Did you at any time tell Sara Davidson that "Dr Dormont told Rock Hudson that the virus had been inhibited but he cautioned that he still had the disease"?'

'No. He said that to Sara Davidson, not me.'

'Were you present when he said it?'

'Yes . . . I was present at the Hudson residence and heard the conversation on the speakerphone.'

'Sir, you said you never read the book, didn't you share in the profits?'

'No, I did not.'

'Didn't you have an agreement to get some of the money?'

'Never.'

Rhoden's final questioning was over Christian's alleged confession to Miller that he had received money for sex, pointing out that in his pre-trial interrogatory statement made in June 1986, he had made no mention of this confession.

Rhoden: 'Was that left out . . . because it was a trivial detail that skipped your mind or was it a lie you made up for the trial?'

'I'm very confused . . . because I did not prepare those [documents].'

'You signed this as true under penalty of perjury?'

'I'm sorry, I did not read that document.'

'You mean you signed a statement under penalty of perjury that the foregoing was true?'

'No. I gave them the information, the lawyers wrote that and I signed it.'

'Here's what it says . . . see the word "read" . . . R-E-A-D. Read?'

'Yes.'

'And you said, "I declare under penalty of perjury that this is true." Was your declaration under penalty of perjury true or not true?'

'It sounds true.'

'Then you really did read it, didn't you?'

'No. Yes. I'm sorry.'

Such exchanges had become a feature of Rhoden's questioning of Hudson's faithful servant and members of the public gallery and jurors alike sat hushed and watched intently the reaction and expressions of the witness.

Great interest would also be shown in the various questions to Miller about his expectations from the estate of Rock Hudson. At the start of his evidence Andrew Banks had asked him to detail his understanding of how he would benefit. He had known since 1974 that he and George Nader were beneficiaries in the will. At present, he was not receiving anything from the trust fund which had been set up by Hudson; the first beneficiary after certain other provisions was George Nader. Upon Nader's death, the money would revert to Miller.

Later, during questioning about his personal assets, he said he now lived with George Nader in Hawaii in a house they had bought on a joint tenancy in November 1988 for $700,000. They also owned a home in Palm Springs. His own personal assets, after tax, would be around $100,000.

Rhoden, attacking again, asked: 'Isn't it true that until the death of George Nader and until your death no other beneficiary receives one dime out of that trust?'

If he knew the answer, Miller was not going to reveal the secrets of Hudson's will, which has remained sealed in the Los Angeles Probate Office and would require a court order to have it made public. He avoided the probing assertions by saying: 'I really can't answer that because I'm not a lawyer and I didn't do the trust . . . so I can't answer.'

# CHAPTER TEN

# The Medical Evidence

When Rock Hudson was first diagnosed as suffering from AIDS, the medical profession was still in the infancy of isolating both the cause and effect of the virus and were certainly pulling in various directions with regard to its treatment. Worldwide, highly influential and exceedingly competitive medical teams were working around the clock to find the answers. At stake was a huge commercial prize for those who discovered an effective treatment and there were unseemly medical arguments over who had discovered the virus first. Their research was steeped in great complexities that were simply beyond the laymen and governmental health authorities and this in itself was one of the early causes of complacency and lack of co-ordinated effort to fight it among the international health community. Added to the vastly conflicting opinions on its origins, that made the whole question of AIDS a baffling maze of blind alleys, were the additional streams of infection which came through blood transfusion – itself a highly emotive issue – and the spread of the disease through drug users.

But in the main, the AIDS story centred initially around the homosexual community and brought with it an unprecedented wave of public resentment and persecution of male gays. Anyone who was thought to have the disease became an object of scorn, ridicule and rejection by the mass of society; even undertakers were refusing to handle the bodies as the toll began to mount. Medical teams were not alone in discovering the vastness of the problem that confronted them.

When AIDS struck the homosexual communities, social studies on the lifestyle of the typical male homosexual highlighted a

134

hornet's nest of promiscuous sexual activity that made researchers wonder why similar illness scourges had not arisen previously. After the explosion of gay activity in the sixties, it became more common to indulge in adventurous sexual acts, which perhaps could be compared with intense foreplay of heterosexual relationships involving anal reception of the penis or other objects, and oral contact with sensitive parts of the body. Studies, however, found the contrasting male-female relationships differed in two major respects: firstly, homosexuals tended to be more active and subsequently had more partners; some of those, with and without the disease, admitted in research interviews that they had as many as twenty different sexual contacts in a week, often with once-only lovers who needed to protect their anonymity.

Secondly, drugs were often a feature of sexual liaison: the most commonly used among homosexual males were seconal, dexedrine, preludin with B-12, amyl nitrate, butyl nitrate, various varieties of marijuana, and cocaine to a lesser degree. Sexual stimulation and the need to overcome the pain of intercourse and hand-insertion – known among gays as 'fist-fucking' – were the main reasons for the use of drugs but few were of an addictive nature. In fact, for a time drug use set the medical studies off on the wrong track; it was discovered that ninety per cent of AIDS patients had used 'poppers', amyl nitrate or butyl nitrate which were widely available in small phials that could be smashed and sniffed prior to orgasm. It was felt that popper use was in some way connected with AIDS and it took two years before this theory was discounted.

What did stabilize, to some degree, in the research was the percentage of homosexuals who contracted AIDS: to around seventy per cent in America, but higher in proportion to heterosexual sufferers in Europe where the figure hovered around eight-five per cent.

One of the American pioneers of AIDS research, Dr Joseph Sonnabend who examined Marc Christian at his New York clinic, made a controversial pronouncement on the reasons for the high element of homosexuals who came down with AIDS. His view was that it spread from the highly interactive, promiscuous settings where multiple sex partners were the rule, sexual interchange became contaminated with sexually transmitted organisms. There was also a widely held view, to which Sonnabend prescribed, that placed AIDS as a disease of poverty which had existed in the Third World for years yet no-one had bothered to diagnose it. It had got into the homosexual community because of the duplication of Third World conditions of lowered immunity and repeated re-infection through their activities in the bath-houses and similar establishments.

Even as late as 1985, the US Secretary of Health and Human Services, Margaret Heckley said: 'We must conquer AIDS before it infects the heterosexual population and threatens the health of the general population.' Gay community leaders were incensed; their interpretation of that statement was that so long as it was just homosexuals who were dying, it didn't matter. If everyone was threatened, only then would something be done.

It was against this background of confusing statistics and theories that the jury, twelve non-expert lay men and women, would be asked to take into account the long and laborious medical opinions when they came to make their final assessment of whether Marc Christian had proved his case for damages. If so, what should be the level of compensation?

The quest for answers would come down to a basic two-pronged argument by the defence:

(1) Christian showed no signs that he had contracted the virus.

(2) There was no evidence to suggest that he had an enhanced fear of getting it.

The jury was reminded of Christian's own statements that between the point that he learned of Hudson's illness up to March 1986, he had consulted five separate doctors: Dr Dominique Dormont in Paris, Dr Michael Roth, Dr Jeffery Rochford and Dr Moses Laufer in California, and Dr Joseph Sonnabend in New York. Christian said Sonnabend told him that he [Sonnabend] was regarded as an 'outcast' because of his cccontroversial views on AIDS and had found difficulty in attracting funding for his clinic through political pressures.

The tests taken with these doctors had concluded a negative result although he claimed that the fear of contracting it remained with him because at least three of those doctors had told him that the tests were not totally reliable and the virus might remain undetected for some years. Christian's medical statement went on: 'I would never blame Rock for exposing me to AIDS unknowingly. People contract venereal disease all the time and in many cases they pass it on without their knowledge that they had the disease. But he wilfully subjected me to that disease for eight months. I do not know whether he did it because he was *non compos* or whether he wanted to kill me or take me down with him but he wilfully withheld the information and slept with me.'

In support of its case, the defence called Dr Jeffery Laurence, an AIDS specialist whose evidence would refer to additional extensive tests which were run on Christian. First, however, the doctor was asked to outline his own involvement in the story of AIDS and provide, for the jury's benefit, an explanation of its arrival as the scourge of sexual activity in the 1980s.

Laurence himself practised at the Cornell Medical Centre in New York; he was associate professor of medicine at the Cornell University Medical College in the New York Hospital and director of the Laboratory for AIDS Virus Research. He was one of twenty people on the basic science study section of the National Institutes of Health who reviewed the grant applications of anyone seeking funding for research and study on AIDS. He was also associate editor of the advisory board of many major AIDS publications in Britain and America as well as an AIDS-targeted newsletter published in Baltimore.

He had consulted closely with Dr Jay Levy who was one of the co-discoverers of the AIDS virus, along with Dr Robert Gallo who had become a hero of the modern age in medical circles for his work in cancer and AIDS research. Laurence first became involved in AIDS studies in 1981.

To put Hudson's illness in the time-frame of AIDS discovery: he was diagnosed as a sufferer in May 1984. The new disease affecting homosexuals was first being noted by medical teams in 1981; the following year it was discussed internationally that the cause might be a virus; in late 1983, the French determined the cause as a Human Immuno Deficiency Virus (hence the term HIV), and that was confirmed by the Americans in early 1984. Their joint conclusion was that AIDS is not one single disease. It is a collection of diseases and cancers and a variety of infections which, before AIDS were more generally found in cancer patients and as far back as the war years when starving children developed poor immune systems. Certain unusual cancers, such as Kaposi's sarcoma became a feature of AIDS. Before then, it was a very rare condition found mostly among men of Mediterranean or Jewish extraction.

AIDS itself, therefore, was caused by a virus which breaks down the immune systems and the diseases which are contracted because of it are the eventual cause of death, not the virus itself.

The year of 1984 was a cornerstone in the work on AIDS when members of the French team from the Pasteur Institute collaborated with Dr Gallo's laboratory in the National Institutes of Health and Dr Levy's laboratory in San Francisco. Dr Laurence also met the French at his laboratory at the Rockefeller Institute in New York and he returned to the Pasteur Institute for further work on blood samples and to look at methods for culturing the new virus. With so many individuals dying, a free exchange of information, discovery and blood sampling was established among the international AIDS research community.

Among other specialists he regularly dealt with was Dr Michael Gottlieb, who was the first expert to see Hudson, and who became the co-chair of the American Foundation for AIDS Research. In addition, most major cities in America and Europe began setting up specialist teams for treatment and testing. By 1988, the US Government had set up thirty-nine centres called AZT-User AIDS Treatment Evaluation Units, predominantly in the areas that had a high concentration of AIDS patients, such as Los Angeles, San Francisco and New York.

In 1985, two main preliminary tests were being used for the detection of AIDS. One was the Elisa Test, the second was a confirmatory examination known as the Western Blot which was generally only used when there was some doubt over the first test. The Elisa reveals AIDS by showing antibodies of the virus which the human body develops against invading infections. The test was quick, simple and inexpensive, taking about forty-five minutes: a laboratory grows the AIDS virus, the HIV virus, in large culture dishes. A sample of the virus is taken and placed in detergent to destroy the virus's ability to affect anyone working with it and to dispose of any cell debris. That material is then placed on small plastic plates to which is added a person's blood sample. This mixture is spun and washed and allowed to incubate; a developing chemical will then reveal a colour reaction showing whether or not the person being tested has antibodies to the virus.

However, from the early stages of testing when it became clear that something drastic was happening among gay men and intravenous drug users, it was noted that some individuals did not show any antibody reaction to the virus thus rendering AIDS undetectable by the culture test. The number was small, perhaps a maximum of five out of every hundred tested, although pharmaceutical companies and blood bank screeners put it at much less. To try to eliminate any doubt, especially for the blood banks who had a duty to the recipients of their blood, the Western Blot Test was developed. It was a more complicated and more specific test and was later followed by the introduction of a battery of additional, more sophisticated and prolonged viral culture tests which all became available from the end of 1985. They included the T-Cell test which could reveal any damage to the body cells caused by the virus, and the immunofluorescence test which showed the presence of the virus in cells. These tests provided the most extensive testing base available to any patient who was concerned that he might have AIDS.

Laurence said he had reviewed the medical records of Marc Christian and had noted that: Dr Sonnabend had performed the T-Cell test on him, Dr Laufer had run the Elisa test, and Dr Levy had performed the Western Blot, the immunofluorescence test and a virus culture test. All concluded there was no virus in his blood. This brought about Robert Mills's questioning of Dr Laurence regarding the incubation period and the possibilities of latent or dormant virus laying undetected or undetectable in the body; a controversial issue which was at the heart of Christian's case.

Laurence explained that when the virus is taken into the body, the patient may at first feel nothing unusual; he appeared perfectly healthy though he could still be very infectious and extremely capable of transmitting the disease to others, while feeling completely normal. This could occur during the period of incubation which was the time it took for the AIDS victim to become ill. The time it began to show itself could vary.

Very early on, a person infected through a hypodermic needle, or blood transfusion or sexually, might begin to feel funny, with low-grade fevers and profound tiredness within a few days. The patient might think it was just a cold or flu and then it goes away. There would be no outward sign of anything being wrong. No one, including the patient, could possibly know at that time that the virus was being harboured in the body, without undergoing tests.

That condition could last for many weeks and usually for many years. A paper published by the Centre for Disease Control, at Atlanta, Georgia, stated that for the average gay man, the incubation period was between five and eight years – possibly longer - before one or more of the diseases which eventually kill the patient developed. There were recognizable symptoms, typically

139

with lymph node swelling, lymph gland swelling in the neck or under the arms, night sweats and perhaps brown or purplish blots on the skin, usually on the feet or hands, but often in the mouth. These would begin to develop towards the latter stages of incubation and until that time, a patient who has not taken any tests would perhaps have no reason to suspect he or she had AIDS. It was thought that ninety-nine per cent of the people who developed those symptoms would die and the length of time elapsing between acquiring the virus and death could be anywhere from five to fifteen years. Between the times of acquiring the virus and the appearance of symptoms, there would be two great peaks of the virus in the blood: one within the first few weeks of becoming infected, subsiding again to a low level, and peaking again when the symptoms began occurring. These were also the two periods when the patient was most infectious.

There were still areas in the testing process that did not provide a one hundred per cent guarantee of correct results; a small segment of the population, for example, could get infected with the virus yet not develop traceable antibodies. So for this percentage, the Elisa Test and the Western Blot might not reveal they were infected. For these people, a virus activator had been developed which would be as accurate as medical science could be in its results. If the activator proved negative, there was virtually no chance of that person developing AIDS in, say, ten years time.

Answering a specific question from Robert Mills, Laurence said that even in the knowledge of the sexual activity between Christian and Hudson, if Christian had the virus in his body, the tests that had been performed upon him would have shown it.

In his view, Marc Christian had not been infected.

He said that some of the tests he had described were available at major medical centres back in 1985 when Christian feared he might have AIDS. There were many people who had the same fear. Men would come to his consultancy after having been with prostitutes, or gay men whose partners had been found to have AIDS. Routinely, he would perform the Elisa Test and the Western Blot and have the patient return in six to eight months for further testing. The knowledge of the specialist AIDS centres was widespread. The Gay Men's Health Crisis for which he was medical consultant would refer people to him; there were gay men's organizations in both California and New York through which testing by himself or the likes of Dr Gallo could be achieved.

It would always be necessary to inquire of the patient's sexual history to establish the risk factor; if the person had been heavy on sex, he would always recommend going on to the virus culture test. At that time, the Elisa Test cost each patient $45, the Western Blot $75 (although there was an arrangement with the Board of Health to run the tests free). The more complicated tests were expensive: then, a standard viral culture test could cost between $600 and $1200. For the full battery, which would include the virus activator, the cost could be upwards of $4000 to a maximum of around $9000. Those fees were standardized in 1987; however, because part of the funding for his laboratory came not just from Government but from private sources, they were able to offer a free service to anyone who could show they could not afford to pay.

At this point in Dr Laurence's evidence, Mills began questioning him about Dr Joseph Sonnabend who had carried out tests on Christian. Was he aware of Sonnabend's theories with regard to the AIDS virus? Laurence said he was, but further questioning was interrupted by an objection from Harold Rhoden, claiming that it was irrelevant and called for one man's belief of another's views. The judge upheld the objection and Mills proceeded with questions about a second battery of tests on Christian's blood performed by Dr Levy and Dr Michael McGrath in San Francisco in 1988. The blood samples were separated between the two doctors and they performed every known test to discover whether the virus existed in his blood, either in an active or silent state. In Laurence's view, Christian would not come down with AIDS as a result of any sexual contact he had prior to those tests in 1988. As far as he was concerned, the tests performed would be one hundred per cent accurate.

Laurence concluded his evidence for the defence and Harold Rhoden rose to take issue with some of his assessments and to challenge others which specifically involved Christian. He agreed that he personally had never tested Christian for AIDS and had relied on his views by assessing the medical evidence of doctors who had. He argued that even back in 1985 or 1986 when Christian was in New York being tested by Dr Sonnabend, he could have been contacted for a second opinion since his was one of the best-known testing centres for AIDS; anyone who rang the telephone directory inquiries would have been given his number and that was still the case.

He said that the cost of the battery of tests run on Christian at

141

San Francisco in 1988 had cost $8000 for which the defence were paying. His own charges for standard AIDS testing to anyone who could afford to pay amounted to $1200. To clarify his earlier statement with regard to payment, Rhoden was interested in the 'free' testing service and asked: 'If someone came in and said, "I want every test you can possibly give me for AIDS and I won't be talked out of it" would you give them free? Would you give $8000 worth of tests for nothing because that person is broke?' No, said Laurence, unless there was an absolute medical necessity. He would first give a free Elisa Test and if that was positive there would be no need for the others; if they were negative, he would give the remaining tests free of charge if they were necessary. His clinic was funded to allow it to do exactly that.

Rhoden now read sections of Dr Sonnabend's deposition, made after his series of tests which he carried out on Christian, and asked Laurence to indicate whether he agreed or disagreed with the verdict. Once again, it was an exchange of views that was intended by Rhoden to lead the jury to the conclusion that everything in the field of AIDS testing was not a plain and simple issue of 'Has he or hasn't he got it?' which had been the trend so far. Indeed, Rhoden had complained to the judge on more than one occasion that Laurence was merely arguing the case for the defence.

Dr Sonnabend had made a general observation that 'the risks of getting AIDS are probably more realistically determined by the nature of the place, the timing of the exposure and the multiplicity of partners, and that has nothing to do with the virus test.' Laurence said he did not agree with that statement.

Sonnabend again: 'A negative antibody test could not – at this stage of our knowledge about human retroviruses – could not be taken in a very definite sense to mean that the virus does not exist in the body.'

Laurence agreed. There were a few people who had AIDS but who never developed antibodies in their blood as a reaction to the virus.

Sonnabend: 'We do not know enough about these human viruses . . . to say that the absence of antibodies can guarantee the absence of the virus.'

Laurence agreed.

Sonnabend: 'In other words, the reliability of the test, no test, can be one hundred per cent reliable. In this particular case, the degree of reliability has to remain a question for more research. So it would be wrong to say that a negative culture test is a guarantee of the absence of the virus.'

Laurence: 'I would agree. A standard virus culture test does not mean that the virus is not there.'

Sonnabend, on the question of the accuracy of a viral culture test: 'I wouldn't feel comfortable with it. I would feel more or less reassured but I would not take this as a guarantee that there was no virus.'

Laurence agreed. It was a standard test.

Sonnabend, on whether he told Marc Christian that he could still come down with the disease even after the tests he had run so far: 'It is possible that I might have said such a thing in the context of an explanation . . . as to how I believe one can best predict whether or not AIDS is a likelihood and that is more easily determined by [the history of] sexual contact than one's virus test. A negative antibody test could not guarantee the absence of the virus.'

Laurence agreed.

Sonnabend: 'I'm sure I indicated to Mr Christian, however, that a negative antibody test and a negative viral culture test would go fairly far to showing that there was no virus. But I believe that medical opinion would agree that antibody positive individuals may contain those in whom the virus could not be detected.' Laurence disagreed with that theory and went on to challenge one vital factor that the source of the virus went back to the type of sex practice involved. Laurence said that the vital factor was getting the virus, whether it came through sex, blood transfusion or pregnancy. However he would certainly examine the patient's sexual history in determining the type of tests.

He agreed with Harold Rhoden that there were people classed as 'sero negative', someone who shows negative on the antibody test but who has the virus, but he disagreed that the number of people who were sero negative could be as high as twenty-five per cent of all those tested; the figure only referred to a specific group of homosexual males. But further tests, using a viral activator would have recovered any latent virus and that test was virtually one hundred per cent accurate.

These figures became the subject of a long and protracted cross-examination between Rhoden and Laurence over claims that Christian had a fifteen per cent chance of being one of the twenty-five per cent who would test sero negative, thus giving Christian at the very most a 3.75 per cent chance of him having the virus while the tests did not reveal it. Wasn't that a 'statistical nonsense'? Rhoden asked. Laurence argued that the figures had been taken out of context but although he believed it was a proper figure, he now agreed that it was perhaps statistically the wrong thing to do. But the fact remained, as far as he was concerned, that the tests Christian had taken were sufficient to say fairly definitely that Christian did not have the virus anywhere in his body.

Rhoden persisted with his questioning to establish Christian's fear and asked Dr Laurence about a major AIDS conference attended by 7000 in Stockholm in June 1988. Wasn't it true that out of that conference came some alarming news that the AIDS virus could hide in cells where it was not detected by any standard AIDS test?

'Yes, that is true.'

'Doctor, consider this hypothetical case: If a man was diagnosed as having AIDS in June 1984 and continued to have alternating anal sex with his partner, would that partner have any concern that he might have contracted AIDS by July 1985? That he had the AIDS virus and it would kill him?'

'Yes.'

'As a matter of fact, isn't it true that if the sexual partner in this hypothetical case did not have a fear that he might have contracted AIDS, you'd say he was crazy?'

'Yes.'

'Now if that sexual partner then gets tests like the ones Dormont and Sonnabend gave Marc Christian, and they all test negative, would you have told that sexual partner he had nothing to worry about?'

'No, I would not.'

'Sir, have you heard of cases where someone had AIDS, tried every test which proved negative, then died, and in the post mortem they found he had AIDS?'

'I am aware of cases of people who have died of AIDS in which they had taken the antibody test and the standard viral culture test and didn't find it. I was not aware of cases where a person has had every AIDS test that I've described here in which they couldn't find it before he died.'

Now Rhoden, who had once again protested to the judge that Dr Laurence was arguing the case for the defence by the way he replied to questioning, moved to the aspect of why counsel for the

144

estate had chosen him, from New York, when there were many equally capable doctors available in Los Angeles.

'Before you came here to testify, were you paid a fee for working in this case?'

'Yes . . . $300 an hour.'

'Any other payments prior to today's hearing?'

'Yes, I was given a retainer of $5000.'

'Do you have any idea how much that is all going to amount to?'

'No, I have an administrative assistant who is calculating it for me.'

The judge (*to Harold Rhoden*): 'I would just point out you've been about an hour.'

Laurence: 'That's another $300.'

Rhoden: 'So you've got $5000. Do you know how much more is coming? Five? Ten?'

Laurence: 'I hope so but I don't know. If you keep talking, it's going to add up.' (*Laughter in court*)

Rhoden: 'Well, I don't care how much they have to pay. So we're going to take our time. Now what about expenses. You have been paid expenses for coming here have you not?'

'No. I haven't. I've had nothing paid for yet.'

'They didn't tell you to charge it on your American Express did they?'

'Yes, they did. My Gold Card is overwhelmed.'

'Would you like a lawyer?' (*More laughter*)

Robert Mills: 'No, he would like a loan.'

Rhoden: 'Now as to your fee; you're not getting any kind of a bonus are you?'

'God no. What kind of bonus?'

'I'm asking if you have any agreement to be paid a certain amount if the estate wins?'

'No, no. I do not.'

Rhoden continued for another $100 or so and then handed Dr Laurence back to Robert Mills who made a very pointed last line of defence: 'When tests included retroviral activators to the standard viral culture test, can you tell one hundred per cent of the time whether a person had been infected with the AIDS virus?'

'Yes sir. That is my testimony.'

'And that's in spite of what Mr Rhoden has asked about the antibody test showing a false positive or false negative result?'

'Yes.'

'And knowing the sexual history of Marc Christian and Rock Hudson, would you have merely run an Elisa Test?'

'I would not have merely relied upon the Elisa, or the Western Blot, nor the standard virus culture. I would have done the full battery of tests.'

'And what would you have told him?'

'I would have told him there was no virus in his body.'

Dr Laurence was also at pains to point out that he took his work very seriously, as an internationally recognized authority. The fact that he had been paid by the defence had no bearing on his conclusions, especially bearing in mind that AIDS was fatal. Nothing could, as far as medical science yet knew, alter that. Similar evidence and confirmation of the tests on Christian was given by Dr Michael McGrath.

But Harold Rhoden would certainly not let matters rest there and, as we will see, would be savage in his critical assessment of the medical evidence: that through all its proclaimed certainties, the fear factor of this dreaded disease could never be eliminated, however much Dr Laurence and Dr McGrath had tried to minimize any cause for Christian's concern.

# CHAPTER ELEVEN

# Parties and Street Urchins

The defence had completed its evidence; apart from final submissions by counsel which would come at the end of the trial
their case rested. If the jury thought that they had heard all that
could possibly be told about the private life of Rock Hudson and his
actions during those months prior to his death, they were wrong.
Nor yet were Marc Christian and his counsel finished with Mark
Miller. Still more revelations, still more allegations and still more
squabbling over who said or did what were to come.

Under the American judicial system of the Superior Court, the
plaintiff, the person who had sued in the first place and whose
evidence had already been subjected to the severest scrutiny, is
allowed an opportunity of rebuttal: that is to challenge or deny
claims made by the defence and Marc Christian would return
to the witness stand, even though it would give the opposing
side the chance to question his evidence further. In doing so,
he would manage to slip in some additional titbits of information
about the world in which he found himself through his association
with Hudson; the most sensational of his new claims would involve
young boys, street urchins he called them, who were recruited to
attend parties given by Hudson's friend, Dean Dittman. But first,
Harold Rhoden called two further witnesses to extract additional
support for evidence he had produced earlier in the trial.

Wayne Bernhard, a close friend of Christian, was there to
recall and confirm the surprising new facts which emerged during
Christian's cross-examination – that on the night of the birthday
party Hudson gave for Christian on 23 June 1984, he found them
together in a compromising situation.

It was an outdoor barbecue at which Hudson cooked the food,

chickens; the same party and the same barbecue about which so much time had been spent examining the witnesses to establish whether or not Hudson had actually given the party, three weeks after it had been confirmed that he had AIDS.

Bernhard was insistent; the party took place and at the end of it he was invited to stay the night in the Hudson home because he had a long drive to Orange County ahead of him the following morning. The party was winding down and he left Hudson and Christian on the patio to go to the playroom where he was to sleep. He stayed up for a short time to watch some television and then went back outside in search of something to drink. It was around one o'clock in the morning and everyone had gone home. He walked over to the refrigerator to get a can of tomato juice and there he saw Hudson and Christian, by the pool. They were both naked and lying on a chaise longue. They were lying down, Hudson was on top of Christian and they had their arms around each other in an embrace. He remained there only long enough to realize what was happening and quickly returned to his room.

Rhoden: 'When was the first time you told this to Marc Christian, what you had seen?'

'Maybe two weeks ago.'

'Why didn't you tell him before?'

'It was kind of embarrassing. I mean the press has already called me a voyeur. . . . '

'Well, I still have to ask you sir, and I'm not asking what the press has said so please don't volunteer that. There's a rule against that. Why didn't you say to Marc Christian the next day or so "Hey, I'm going to tell you what I saw last night"? Why didn't you tell him then?'

'Because, like I said, I was a little bit embarrassed . . . I mean it's like walking in on your parents making love.'

'Why didn't you tell him a few weeks ago?'

'Because apparently there's some disbelief about the fact that he was having an intimate relationship with Mr Hudson. And when he told me that there were no witnesses to it, I said, "That's not entirely true. . . . " '

Rhoden: 'Your witness.'

Robert Mills took up the cross-examination with the obvious intent of introducing doubt into the jury's mind over these claims. That, after all, was his function as counsel for the defence and he would pose his questions in a way that would extract the answers he wanted and at the same time, inject a note of caution.

According to Bernhard, he saw them kissing and caressing. Yes, that was right. But did he see any intercourse taking place? No, he did not see intercourse of any kind. Yes, it was true he had been a friend of Christian's since 1973, a very close friend.

Mills: 'So close that after his first day with Rock Hudson he called you up to tell you about it?'

'No, I don't remember that.'

'So close that he telephoned to read to you the letters Hudson had written to Christian from Israel?'

'Not verbatim. He told me the gist of what he was saying, about missing home and being tired of working overseas.'

Mills now read from Bernhard's pre-trial deposition in which he gave answers to various questions: he had denied having been part of any sexual acts between Hudson and Christian; he denied having been in their bedroom when sexual acts took place; he denied seeing any photographs of them having sex and he had never heard any tape recordings of them having sex. The sole basis of his knowledge had been what Marc Christian had told him.

Mills: 'Didn't you think it was important at the time to tell everything you knew about the relationship between Christian and Hudson?'

'I wasn't asked if I ever came across them personally having –'

'You were asked about the sole basis on which you made the assertion that they were continually having sex?'

'Yes.'

'And you didn't say "Because I went out to a chaise longue sometime in the summer of 1984 and saw Hudson with his arms around this man." You didn't say that did you?'

'I didn't but they weren't having sex at the time either. They asked me if I saw them having sex and I didn't.'

Wayne Bernhard stuck to his story and repeated it again under cross-examination from Andrew Banks, and re-examination from Harold Rhoden. It was strange that he had only just come forward with this piece of information; he admitted that but he restated his reasons and no amount of prodding would move him.

Now Rhoden called John Dobbs, part-time handyman at the Hudson residence and occasional Shakespearean actor. He was introduced to the jury as a hostile witness who was brought to court under subpoena; Andrew Banks challenged the assertion that

149

he was hostile to Christian and earlier in the judge's chambers the defence had questioned the calling of this witness at all because they claimed his evidence could not be considered as rebuttal. Rhoden countered that he was aligned to the defence; the judge reserved judgment on that issue until he had heard the evidence and it was an important point in view of Dobbs would say. To the trial spectators it may have appeared something of a ploy to class Dobbs as 'hostile' since his evidence was certainly of more use to Christian than it was to the defence and it opened the way for some sharp legal banter as Dobbs proceeded with his story.

His main role at the Hudson house where he had worked since 1983 was that of house cleaner. He had observed the relationship between Christian and Hudson at close hand and he thought that they were still sleeping together in May 1984. Mark Miller, he said, hated, loathed and detested Christian. He once said he never hated anyone as much as he hated Christian.

Rhoden: 'Did Mark Miller ever tell you that you and James Wright were going to be paid a percentage of the estate?'

'He told us we would receive some money.'

'Did he say a percentage?'

'I'm under oath . . . I have to be very picky about this.'

The judge: 'Just a moment; you're right to be picky. The way to be picky here is to listen to the question carefully and answer it. It called for a yes or no.'

'I can't answer it yes or no, Your Honour. I can say –'

Banks: 'Objection.'

Rhoden: 'Permission to take this witness on cross-examination. I think he's obviously a hostile witness.'

The judge: 'Hostile oversays it. Adverse is all he needs to be, so you may proceed.'

Rhoden: 'Did you ever have a conversation with Miller and George Nader in which they told you that although they did not know how much they were going to get, they would give you a percentage?'

'Yes.'

'Objection,' from both Mills and Banks.

Rhoden: 'This is not being offered as the truth; maybe they didn't intend to give him anything. Probably they didn't. I'm not offering it to show they intended to give him a piece of the estate.'

The judge: 'The point is well taken. This is not a statement that is necessarily true or false. It is a statement of an offer. The objection is overruled.'

Dobbs slowly responded to Rhoden's questioning. Miller, he said, had promised him money; he was to get it when George Nader received his share of the estate. There were others on the list who would receive the same deal: James Wright, the butler, Clarence, the gardener, Tom Clark, Dean Dittman (Rock's actor friend); and Ron Channell. Those were the only names he could remember. Miller said they would all get a percentage.

When Dobbs later saw Marc Christian in the basement of the house, there was a conversation about the money. He agreed he might have said to Christian, 'I hope you sue their asses off' and 'You should take them for everything they've got. They might have infected you.'

Rhoden: 'Did you then say, "The money is to make sure we shut up for now and then open up against you later." Did you say that?'

'I don't remember saying it . . . but I don't have access to this illegal tape of this conversation. It was taped without my knowledge.'

'Did you ever see a tape of that conversation?'

'No. But I know it was taped by Marc Christian . . . things are very carefully set up. This is a conversation he apparently remembered verbatim over a year later which I find interesting. The clever stuff is . . . that I cannot distinguish between what lines I really spoke and which he took from me and reversed.'

The to-ing and fro-ing of the alleged tape continued for some minutes, until Rhoden finally insisted: 'There is no tape, there never was one.'

'Well,' said Dobbs, 'you must have destroyed it.'

Returning to the main thrust of his questions, Rhoden pressed further about the money: Did Dobbs tell Christian during that conversation, 'They are scum, right-wing criminals. They think they can get away with murder and embezzlement. Expose them, you must'?

Dobbs laughed out loud. It was his sort of rhetoric, he said, but he did not know whether he said it or not. He could be very impetuous, very stupid at times. It was possible when Christian asked him if he would be prepared to make those statements to a lawyer, he said: 'Yes, but please, I don't want Miller to know. I need my job for as long as I can stomach them.'

Marc Christian returned to the witness stand; he looked immaculate, still, in his grey suit and carefully combed blond hair, just as he had done throughout the trial in which, daily, he had sat beside his counsel – Harold Rhoden – listening closely to the evidence, shaking his head occasionally, or smiling, or scribbling notes to Rhoden to take up a point in questioning. He strode confidently to the witness box and, as Rhoden began his rebuttal questioning, he ran straight into objections from Robert Mills for leading his witness.

Overruled.

Christian referred to his conversation with Dobbs who, he said, told him when he asked what he was to say, 'I don't know. Miller hasn't told us yet. But he's made it clear we've got to stay in line.' The conversation was not taped, said Christian.

Rhoden led him through other allegations that had been made during the presentation of the defence: he had never confessed to Mark Miller or anyone else that he had sold sex for money; that was a lie. He was never in bed with Kevin Johnson at Hudson's house; he did not even know if Johnson was a homosexual. The Brooks Street Bath issue was also re-examined and Christian maintained his story that he had met Hudson at a political fundraiser, and not as Miller stated at the baths. The first time he went to the baths was after he had met Hudson; they went together.

Rhoden wanted to clarify Christian's version of exactly what happened on the night of Dean Dittman's party that he went to with Hudson. Were there any 'straights' present? No, said Christian, they were all homosexual men. He only went to Dittman's house a couple of times and would not go back.

'Why not,' asked Rhoden, 'what kind of parties were they?'

'They were parties where Dittman would cook the food and would have street urchins dressed only in their underwear serve it.'

'What are street urchins?'

'Well, they looked under-age to me; they looked like they were fourteen or fifteen years old.'

'Boys or girls?'

'All boys.'

'And they were in their underwear serving food?'

'Yeah.'

'Was there ever a time, as has been testified here, that you went to a party at Dean Dittman's with Rock Hudson and you left and did not go back to sleep in Rock's bedroom that night?'

'No.'

'Now, you have already testified there were times after June 1984 when Hudson was diagnosed as having AIDS that Miller asked you to bring some 'pretties', referring to pretty young boys, to spice up your sex with Rock. Did Miller say this more than once?'

'Several occasions.'

Later, when Christian was once again challenged on this allegation by Andrew Banks, on Miller's behalf, Christian repeated them. This time, to Banks's annoyance, he added: 'Miller said that he and George Nader did that sort of thing . . . so why not?'

Banks responded quickly, before Christian could continue: 'That's not what I asked you –'

Rhoden sprang to the defence of his client: 'Mr Banks is asking for it. He's asking this witness to say anything along that line. He's inviting these answers. And I ask the witness be allowed, please, to answer questions put to him.'

The judge agreed: 'I think he's answered and it was an explanation. You were asking accusatory questions; you must live with the answer.'

Banks returned to the offensive: 'So during this loving relationship with Hudson, Miller tells you to go out and bring some pretties up to the house to spice up your sex life?'

'It was a suggestion, if I wanted to do it, it would make it better.'

Banks: 'That's not what you said earlier is it?'

'That's what he implied. He and Nader did that sort of thing and I should follow their example.'

The judge interrupted: 'That's volunteering, and that will be stricken.'

Harold Rhoden himself returned to the question of young boys at the Hudson house as he took Christian through the latter part of his rebuttal evidence. Christian said he had often seen boys there and when he asked Hudson about them, he was told that James Wright the butler brought them up to the house. Often they were boys off the streets. Once, in Christian's presence, Hudson told Wright he was extremely uncomfortable with him bringing in what he called 'street trash'. He was afraid of being 'ripped off' and told Wright, 'If you bring any more, you're to confine them to your own quarters and not bring them up to the house.'

Christian said there were one or two boys at a time. He also spoke to Mark Miller about Wright's activities and Miller said he could not understand why Wright was always broke; he had a salary of $2000 a month plus free room and board and other items; but he would be broke all the time and Miller surmised it was because he was always having to pay out money to the boys for favours.

The rebuttal continued. Christian repeated the allegation that he asked Ron Channell some time after Hudson's death, 'Don't you find it uncomfortable in a house where everybody is gay?' to which Channell replied, 'I'm going to hang around as long as I can to see what I can get out of it.'

He denied he had ever told Tony Rocco that he had no sexual interest in Rock Hudson nor that he had ever said 'I never loved him'. Christian painted Rocco as a lover spurned: 'He told me he had been in love with me for years. I just said "Get over it." '

Similarly, he described Susan Stafford as the one who had made a pass at him, rather than the reverse situation which she had described. On the night he took her home after decorating Hudson's Christmas tree, he said she asked him in to collect a case of wine she had for Rock. She went into another room and returned wearing only her slip. 'She asked me to spend the night but I declined and took the wine and went home,' he said.

On the day of Hudson's death, during their meeting at Butterfield's restaurant, she told him she was an emissary from Miller and Nader and that they just wanted to be his friends. Rhoden came back to the question of whether or not Miss Stafford had made the comment about making a pass at the Pope, the interlude of light relief that had taken up some minutes of her evidence from the witness stand. Christian maintained that she had said she had made a pass at the Pope at an audience in Rome; the first time he had heard the joke about the Pope and the hot tamales was when she told it to the court.

He reaffirmed his earlier claims about what Miss Stafford had said to him about going away together, or having a 'little bitty affair . . . she was sure Rock wouldn't mind'. When Christian pointed out he might have been exposed to AIDS, he said she replied that it didn't matter; many people might be walking around with it and they just had to be careful. And as for the gardener, Clarence Morimoto, his evidence of catching Christian in bed with another young man was 'an outright lie'. So it went on, as

Christian disputed adverse claims against him and continued with his assertions that Miller and Nader had inspired these allegations by offers of a share in the estate of Rock Hudson.

Finally, Rhoden turned to the medical evidence of Dr Laurence and Dr McGrath and this led him once again into the controversial area of what fear and pain Christian had suffered since he learned of Rock Hudson's affliction. He wanted to allow Christian to testify over what other well-known doctors had told him about the claims of Laurence and McGrath since their evidence had been reported. This attempt brought instant objections from Banks and Mills and yet again counsel retired to the judge's chamber for their argument out of the jury's earshot.

Rhoden said that the two doctors brought by the defence had been allowed to testify that Christian had no grounds for fear anymore. These two world-renowned experts had told him he is one hundred per cent clean. He insisted that he must allow Christian to rebut those claims; either he says, 'Oh good, I have nothing to fear anymore and so I can get damages for my fear up to this date because I believe these doctors.' Or he says, 'Oh, no. I don't believe these doctors because I've been told by others that these are a couple of quacks and I know what the facts really are.'

Rhoden said that the previous night Christian had telephoned Dr Sonnabend in New York and he said he had never heard of Laurence or McGrath, these two world-renowned experts. Sonnabend had also told him that the viral activator test that Laurence made so much of in his evidence was not available in 1985 and that even today, the test was not one hundred per cent accurate. It could only indicate a probability, never a certainty.

Next, Christian had talked to Dr Roth in Los Angeles who said it was 'bullshit' to say that activators were in use in tests throughout the US in 1985; furthermore, Roth said, Dr Michael Gottlieb, who was the first doctor on the coast to describe AIDS, was not using hormone activators in 1985. Roth said the best tests today, though greatly improved, could never approach one hundred per cent accuracy. The virus could still go undetected in its latent or dormant state by all available testing done today, in February 1989.

Christian had also telephoned Dr Sandy Levine, another AIDS specialist at the USC who had also never heard of Dr Laurence or Dr McGrath. She also maintained that the viral activator test by which Laurence and McGrath had set so much, could not be taken as totally and unfailingly accurate; there were numerous people infected with the virus who suffer the symptoms of AIDS yet go undetected in both the antibody test and the viral test, including the one with activators. She also made the valid point that the virus was still relatively unknown and medical investigators were constantly having to re-evaluate their findings.

This point was taken up by the last doctor Christian had called: Dr David Imagowa from Harbour General Hospital who said that recent studies were now showing that the virus could be introduced to the body through semen in the rectum or vagina; the virus may lodge itself in the rectal tissues and become dormant or latent, thus the virus never even enters the bloodstream where it might normally be detected with today's variety of serum testing. So even if the test was negative, Imagowa could never say with complete certainty that the patient did not have AIDS.

Rhoden made one final plea to the judge for the admission to the jury of these new facts which had great bearing on the confusing state of mind Christian might have in the light of such vastly conflicting opinions: 'It goes not for the truth, of course, but to show whether or not his mental distress, his fear of getting AIDS has been terminated by the defence doctors. That is the only reason for doing it.'

Robert Mills, for the estate, wanted his objection to the admission of this evidence recorded. He maintained it was unreliable to have a lay witness with such an interest in the outcome of the trial reciting to the jury what these doctors had told him in a telephone conversation the night before.

Judge Geernaert gave limited support to both sides and ruled that Christian may offer a brief account of these conversations in testimony, which would be offered to the jury not as the truth or fact, since it was hearsay, but to demonstrate Christian's state of mind in this case in which an issue of the claim was emotional distress. What he was told over the telephone was relevant, whether true or not and could be offered as relevant to his state of mind since he heard the opinions of the two defence doctors.

So, once more the medical opinions became the issue of the moment and after listening to Christian and the cross-examination the jury must, by the end of that day, at least have felt some sympathy with the man in the light of so much fact on this test or that, and what the results did or didn't prove. Indeed, in the corridor outside the courtroom during the afternoon recess, someone was heard to comment that merely listening to such a volume of medical matter was enough to cause anyone emotional distress . . . AIDS or no AIDS.

But the day wasn't over yet. Andrew Banks, for Miller, seemed to be looking rather pleased with himself as he rose to cross-examine Christian further. Clearly, he was about to reveal one of the surprises he had mentioned that he had up his sleeve and directed Christian's attention back to the point when he was about to fly to Paris in 1985 for an AIDS test by Dr Dormont.

He had earlier testified that he had paid for the airline tickets, on Miller's instructions, with his American Express card. The cost was $2273 for the journey to Paris and $1816 for the return to Los Angeles. Banks asked if he had ever seen an invoice from Mark Allen Travel agency for those tickets? No, he could not recall seeing one. As far as he knew, the account for the tickets had never been paid and because of that his American Express account had gone into default.

Banks asked for the recall to the stand of Mark Miller who produced for the jury's attention an account from Mark Allan Travel, showing an amount of $17,244 which was for airline tickets in the name of Ron Channell, Rock Hudson, Mark Miller and Marc Christian. It had been paid in full on 14 August 1985.

There were no further questions on this issue and the jury would be left to make up their own minds as to what, if any, was the significance of this exchange: had Christian lied in his evidence or was he merely mistaken. It was one more aspect that the counsel for both sides would doubtless reflect upon in their final submissions, which were to come next on the menu.

# CHAPTER TWELVE

## The Vital Love Letters

All witnesses had now been called and rebuttals made; the trial was entering its final phase and all that remained before the jury would be sent away to consider their verdict, were the words of advice from the lawyers and the judge himself. No counsel under-rates the importance of this last act; their analysis, as they weigh the evidence and do their best to turn it to their own advantage, is perhaps the most important of the whole trial. Theirs are the last words the jury hear before retiring and as every lawyer well knows, point scoring now can be vital.

Harold Rhoden had worked on his closing speech the previous weekend and on the morning of 7 February, he began his presentation. He would use as his basis for argument the strong relationship that existed between Hudson and Christian and no evidence spoke louder than the love letters from Hudson which he intended to read to the jury; they were poignant words expressing true feelings and nothing the defence could do, he said, would eliminate their importance in the trial.

But first he directed the jury's attention to Mark Miller. He said the law presumed that they had been listening to all this evidence without coming to any conclusions before retiring. Sometimes, as Shakespeare said, the law was an ass. Conclusions on some aspects of the case would have already been made, for example, on the question of the credibility of Mark Miller. The jury had formed their opinions: either that he was the most honest and trustworthy and thoughtful witness who had ever testified in a courtroom or that he was practically a pathological liar. In any event, opinions would have been formed.

He imagined that the jury could guess at what conclusions he, as the lawyer for Marc Christian, had heard from other lawyers, friends, relatives even before this case began: 'You can't win.' There were two basic reasons: that Christian was homosexual and, second, he did not come down with AIDS. Perhaps they were right. It was like representing a black client before a white jury in Selma, Alabama, before the days of Martin Luther King. Or representing a Jewish client before a jury in Berlin in 1939 or, today, representing an Arab terrorist before a jury in Tel Aviv.

He wanted to bring it out in the open. Was there generally bigotry against homosexuals in our society? Of course there was and society named them fairies, fags, fruits and queers. Perhaps there was no way a homosexual would make it before a typical jury. It took nine for a verdict and it could well be said that it was almost impossible to find nine jurors, picked almost at random who did not have a common bigotry against homosexuals. Everyone had their prejudices and bias, and no judge could say 'Get rid of them'. All he could ask was that they considered the fact that a male homosexual had a sexual drive for a man and a female for a woman. It was the same nature and same feelings as were experienced by heterosexuals.

The second thing against Christian was that he did not come down with AIDS. Well, he was happy he had not developed AIDS because the only thing he could look for was death. Who would care about the verdict then? It would be the beginning of the end. Could a jury award damages to someone who had, up to now, three and a half years of intense mental distress over the fear that any day he was going to come down with it – the fear of AIDS – an enhanced fear? Could a jury award damages for fear of AIDS, when, at the time of trial he did not have it?

Some would say 'No way'. If he had it, that was tangible. No one was going to pay any attention to fear of getting it. But, said Rhoden, this case was about the duty to warn. Any man or woman who had AIDS, had a duty to warn anyone whom they may infect or anyone whom they may have infected in the past. To do what Rock Hudson did and what Mark Miller did was immoral, indecent.

That duty to warn was absolute. There was no excuse for not warning Christian. Even if Hudson hated Christian in June 1984 when Hudson learned he had AIDS, he had a duty to warn him. Why?

Aside from the fact he had no right to kill him, what if Christian

159

contracted the virus, and infected somebody else, somebody Hudson didn't know; that person might infect somebody else, and on and on? Hudson had a duty to warn, a legal duty and a moral duty. Hudson would have had a duty to warn Christian even if there had been no sex between them after June 1984 because of the prior contacts, so he could give Christian a chance to go to a doctor to get some kind of cure, or at least to warn him, 'Kid, don't infect anybody else, you may have it.' Hudson did not give a damn about Christian or about the countless people who could have died because Hudson breached that duty to warn.

And Mark Miller had a duty not to conspire with Hudson. He agreed with Hudson to keep quiet about it and not to tell. Not only did these two get together and agree not to tell Christian, they lied to Christian for thirteen months. Lied. The lies began in June 1984, and they continued virtually to the time of the public announcement a year later – Rock Hudson had AIDS.

Rhoden walked back towards the jury and stood facing them: 'All right,' he said. 'There's a duty to warn, Hudson should have done it. He didn't do it. But it's all right, because by a fluke, by luck, Christian has not come down with AIDS? Even if we knew he could not have that AIDS virus lying in his body dormant – now, we don't know it – but even if we did, would it then be all right? What intent did Rock Hudson and Mark Miller have when Hudson said, "Don't tell the kid under any circumstances"? They had to know. Christian could die, he could get the AIDS virus and die. He could infect somebody else. But they also had to know that if he didn't, if Christian didn't get the virus, the time would come when Christian would find out. Sooner or later, he would find out. Why would he have to find out? Because Hudson had AIDS. And it's only a question of how soon you die from it.

'They had to know,' said Rhoden, 'that when Christian found out what it would do to him, what it would do to anybody, to suddenly realize that life was going to end; they had to know he would suffer intense emotional distress. They didn't care about that.'

Why would Rock Hudson do a thing like that? The only answer that could be gleaned from the evidence was that he liked having sexual intercourse with Marc Christian for his own pleasure; so he could keep doing what was pleasurable to him, he didn't care how many people he killed.

What about Mark's motive? He knew he was a beneficiary under a trust from the estate of Rock Hudson; Miller and his companion, George Nader. This would be no time to displease your boss, would it? No time to say: 'Rock, we can't do this to this kid. We can't do it to countless other people whom he could infect. If he doesn't know he's got it, we can't do it.'

No. That was not the time to displease the boss. That was the time to obey him.

The defence would say that Hudson had no duty to warn Christian because there was no sexual activity with Christian after Hudson found out he had AIDS in June 1984. There was no sex.

They would also argue that because Hudson believed that when he left Dr Dormont in Paris in September he was 'free of AIDS', he had no duty back in June 1984 to tell Christian that he had AIDS.

Rhoden said: 'Now, this may seem to you to be rather strange reasoning. Does something Hudson learned in September relate back to June? This is the type of theory, I tell you, that only lawyers can dream up. It doesn't make any sense. But you're going to hear it argued just the way I told you. Aside from the fact that it's illogical, it's an absurdity, just as surely as you know that you're in a courtroom. You know what everybody knows about AIDS: it's fatal; when you've got it, you die. And the only question is when.

'Now, they are going to try to sell this one to you: Dr Dormont informed Rock Hudson that, "Voilà, a miracle has occurred, and it's happened to nobody else, but it happened to Rock Hudson, he's free of AIDS now, he got cured." And Rock Hudson, of course, believed this, although he's dying of these symptoms. Can you imagine Dr Dormont saying anything like that? This is Dr Dormont, an authority in the field of AIDS. Can you picture for one moment anything as idiotic as that, telling this man he's cured? That didn't happen.'

He said Mark Miller wanted the jury to believe there was no duty to warn Christian. He had a reason for that.

Rhoden said he was not going to say Christian had AIDS. But that did not mean the virus was not lying in his body dormant. He was not going to say it was there, because that would be a lie. But what if then – a week, a month, two months after the verdict – Christian woke one morning and the sheets were soaked with sweat, or there was the rash, and there were the sores and a doctor tells him, 'Better get your affairs in order.'

The judge (*interrupting*): 'Well, Mr Rhoden, I want to interrupt you, and I apologize for doing this but this argument suggests that the jury should consider the possibility of Mr Christian coming down with AIDS and deciding whether or not the plaintiff should prevail, and if so, how much should be awarded. I know you don't intend to argue that because what you are seeking on behalf of the plaintiff here is limited to the increased emotional distress suffered by reason of the fear of these things happening. So I think that you need to mention that the only relevance of this possibility is not the award of damages for that possibility, because the jury will be instructed that it is inappropriate to award damages based on speculation about something that might possibly happen in the future.'

Rhoden: 'Yes, Your Honour. The concern for this is part of the mental distress that Marc Christian feels, that anybody in his shoes would feel; part of that mental distress, the concern would be this: when and if it does happen to him, there is nothing he can do, no place he can go, no one he can turn to, except find a hole somewhere, crawl into it and wait to die. That is the kind of mental distress anybody would be under who went through what he did.'

Rhoden said the jury should remember that his kind of sexual activity with Rock Hudson was the highest risk imaginable for anybody, though he didn't know it at the time. Hudson was guilty of outrageous conduct which went beyond all possible bounds of decency, so as to be regarded as atrocious and utterly intolerable in a civilized community. Hudson knew he had AIDS.

The relevance of the continued questioning over the birthday party then became apparent in Rhoden's submission. About two weeks after he was told he had AIDS, Hudson gave a birthday party for Marc Christian. There were several photographs of it that the jury could look at in the jury room. He was very nice to Marc. Very nice to his friends. Hudson cooked dinner for them; had a cake, gifts for his friend, Marc Christian. That night he makes love to Marc Christian.

Opposing Counsel Mills (*interjecting*): 'Well, Your Honour, I hate to object to that characterization, but there's been no evidence, no testimony he made love to him.'

The judge: 'This is the kind of thing that you're going to have to rely upon the jury for and take up in your rebuttal argument. The characterization is, I think you'll have to agree, somewhat uncertain as to just what that would cover in any circumstance.'

Rhoden: 'All right. All right. When I said "make love" I meant have sex with. I suppose you can have sex with somebody and not love them. All right. It's a euphemism for having sex. That night at the party – and you've heard the testimony of Wayne Bernhard – Mr Mills is going to tell you that doesn't mean they were making love, and he has a right to that argument; how he can do it with a straight face is beyond me, but he has a right to make it. The scene was described to you. Both of them were on the chaise lounge, both naked, Hudson on top facing Christian, their arms around each other in a long . . . in a kiss. And Bernhard didn't watch anymore; he got out of there, the way almost anybody would when they open the wrong door and "whoops". And Bernhard, since the objection was made, what are we going to say about him? He's a perjurer, he came in here and he lied? Ladies and gentlemen, if he wanted to lie, he could have made up a little better story. And he could have given Mr Mills what Mr Mills has been asking for. All Bernhard had to do – all he had to do if he were going to lie is say the position was a little different, and he could describe an insertion to you, couldn't he? He didn't do that. He just told you what he saw.'

Rhoden returns to his theme: 'Any time in the month of June after Hudson knew he had AIDS, he had this young boy living with him; having sex with the young boy because he liked it. Imagine, not just because of what it would do to Christian, but of what that could do to countless other people.'

Christian, of course, was bisexual. Suppose he got married, he left Hudson, met a girl, got married. He could have infected her and their children could be born with AIDS because the great movie star didn't want to comply with the decency of the duty to warn. If anything, it was even worse with Mark Miller. Rhoden painted a graphic picture of Thanksgiving 1984 inside the Hudson house: 'Christian was walking around doing something, Miller was in his office, the door was open. He saw Christian walking around. He knew about their relationship. Miller knew that Hudson had AIDS and knew that Christian did not know it. Maybe, as of this minute by luck, by some fluke of luck, Christian did not contract the AIDS virus, but he might.

'And Miller saw Christian walking around, one word could

163

have saved Christian's life and the lives of – pick your number of people – and he keeps –'
Banks: 'I will object to that.'
Rhoden: '– and he keeps his mouth shut.'
The judge: 'Just a moment.'
Banks: 'I object to all of these "countless numbers of people". This case is about increased emotional distress of the plaintiff and nothing more, and it's improper argument, and it should be stricken and the jury admonished to disregard it.'
The judge: 'At this stage, that's certainly true, ladies and gentlemen. What is before you is what amount, in any compensatory damages, for the loss by this plaintiff suffered by reason of the conduct of the defendants or either of them. And, therefore, the reference to wrongful conduct exposing other people is beyond at least this phase of the case.'
Rhoden: 'Oh. Oh. I'm not referring to what Your Honour has in mind at all. I'm talking only about liability by the definition of outrageous conduct, defined for the tort of infliction of emotional distress. I'm not talking about anything like – and I won't even mention the words – I am not, Your Honour, and I know better than to do that.'
The judge: 'All right. Well, then, there is one aspect of the case that I guess this would be related to.'
Rhoden: 'On liability alone.'
The judge: 'At least arguably. So you may proceed.'
Rhoden: 'Thank you. All right. His Honour is going to tell you what emotional distress is, His Honour is going to use certain words, and you're going to hear the words I've mentioned. And that's my only purpose in mentioning them. Nothing else.'
Resuming his argument, Rhoden ridiculed the defence that Miller was only following orders of his boss, Rock Hudson. Suppose Hudson had said to Miller: 'There's a bottle of poison wine in the cellar. Don't tell Marc Christian that it's poison, because I think he's going to drink it and I don't want you to tell him.'
Later in the cellar Christian took a drink of the poison wine, he did not know it's poison, and Miller says simply, 'Have another drink'. Christian drinks the poison and dies. Could Miller then claim he was 'only following orders'?
In July 1985 when Christian learned that Hudson had AIDS, it might be asked: 'Well, wasn't he concerned about the sex he had had with Hudson long before Hudson had a duty to

warn him?' In fact, Christian had no right to complain about that. Tough luck! He was only concerned about the time after July 1984 and for the next eight months when he had sex with Hudson, because that is when Hudson knew he had the disease.

Christian could recover in this case if the jury decided there was a duty to warn and if there was mental distress over the acts which occurred after June 1984. Only then. That was what was meant by enhanced fear.

This was explained in evidence very well by Dr Laurence, about whom Rhoden would have some unkind comments later. Laurence pointed out that the virus could lie dormant and inactive in the body for years, during which time it is undetectable.

So that was the meaning of enhanced fear.

Rhoden now turned to what he termed 'the basic facts': that Rock Hudson and Marc Christian met in 1982; the defence team would undoubtedly try to argue that this was a sordid, ugly affair, that they met in a gay bath-house. That was not true; they did not meet in a bath-house, gay, straight, or any other kind of bath-house.

They met at a political fundraiser. It would be so easy to discuss all of this if they were talking about heterosexuals; that would be no problem at all: man meets a lady, they date and later they have an affair. There would be no problem. But because they were dealing with homosexuals, 'you have no idea how tough it makes it, even to talk about it'.

They dated for many, many months before there was any sex between them; that was the kind of relationship it was – it was a good one. Here was Rock Hudson, very friendly with Liberty Martin, the lady Christian had been living with. It was warm and the two fell in love. Who said so? Well Marc Christian said so. But Rhoden didn't expect the jury to take his word. There had to be some back-up proof, something else.

Who said that there was really love between the two of them? Rock Hudson did, said Rhoden, in the letters he wrote to Christian which said more about the affection between these two men than anything he as a lawyer could say. Nothing spoke louder than these letters.

First there was a letter from Christian to Hudson, very short.

165

*Thank you for being you and having the patience to understand me the way you do. I love you more than my tongue can tell. We have a lot to do when you get back. I love you, Marc.*

The letters were written more than one year after they met, not in the first month or two, but more than a year later. And there was Rock Hudson writing to Marc Christian:

*Hi, babe, I went to the window and looked at the sun setting and thinking about how you would be feeling all of the day to come and thinking about the sun coming up on you, and then I shed a tear or two. Were you by any chance looking at the sunrise? I tried mental telepathy and concentrated as far as I could and then proceeded to get smashed and went to bed without eating, which is hardly the thing to do.*

This is December of 1983 to January 1984, that period when Hudson was in Israel making the movie. Another sentence:

*I love you so much, baby. The countdown is now twenty more days to go and they are dragging like you can't believe. I love you, love you, love you.*

Rhoden continued reading from the next letter from Hudson:

*Hi babe. Every scene I keep thinking, how would HE like it if I did the scene this way, or would it be better if I did it this other way? Learning something new in my life, trying to adjust to something new, trying to throw out all the old habits, trying to be fresh, trying not to judge anything by previous habits, trying to learn. You'll really have to help me, babe. It's not easy. It's not easy for you either, I know, but just be patient for a while. Okay? We have a lot to do. You know that. You know, even though I'm half way around the world, I feel so full, so complete, so warm. Knowing I am so much in love, so completely, and when it's returned, it is the only real thing in the world for me. Nothing else matters. To say I miss you terribly is true. I have comfort in knowing it's temporary, and fairly soon I will be able to hold you in my arms forever. I love you with all of my heart.*

Rhoden pointed to the defence evidence that Hudson had also met Ron Channell in August of 1983. They were going to try to tell the jury that Rock Hudson was really in love with Ron Channell. Did these letters sound like Hudson was in love with the man who had been his work-out instructor for about eight months before the letters were written?

'Listen to this,' said Rhoden, reading from another letter:

*Hi, honey. I just heard 'Islands in the Stream' on the radio. I love it almost as much as I love you. Finally, I got your note yesterday, so it took ten days to get here. It was marked on the 10th. Have you mailed the tape yet and is it all music or are you talking, too? I hope. Yesterday afternoon I went all through the old city looking for something to either send you or bring it home with me, but there is nothing you'd want . . . Babe, I miss you so much. I think about you all the time. It's almost strange. I've been in love before, or at least I thought I was a few times, but nothing like the way I feel now. I'm consumed and obsessed by you, but in a very warm and wonderful way. Perhaps I mean in a very healthy way. My heart feels like it's going to explode with joy. When I get home, I'm going to hug you and never let you go. We're both going to starve to death because I will not let you go long enough to even eat. To say I love you is the understatement of all times. I love you.*

The last one, from Hudson to Christian:

*Hi, babe. Enclosed are the stills I told you about on the phone last night. It was so good talking to you last night. I was really depressed, despair really, and I didn't usually get that way. However, I kept thinking about how we just got started together and all of a sudden I'm all the way over here banging my head against the wall. That is why I had to call, just to hear your voice. I love you so much. Still no tape from you. I think it's a communist plot. Anything to keep us away, including hearing a tape you made. I love you, my baby.*

Rhoden, smiling, faced the jury: 'So Hudson was really in love with Ron Channell, was he? Do you know that it wouldn't make any difference if he were? What difference would it make? This business of bringing Ron Channell here, who is also going to get – oh, never mind. They brought Ron Channell here, and the object was to show he was really Rock Hudson's love. Just for the moment, let's suppose that it's true. So what? This is not a lawsuit for alienation of affection. The question is: *Did* Hudson get AIDS? Yes. Did he know of it? Yes. Did he have a duty to warn Christian? Yes. Did he warn Christian? No. Did he continue to have sex with Christian? Yes. Who cares about who Hudson loved?'

But truly, said Rhoden, Hudson was in love with Marc Christian; you could see it in the letters. Nothing could make it clearer than that. And if Christian had known in June of 1984 that Hudson had AIDS, Christian – and he told the jury – would not have left Hudson, because he loved him. He would have stayed with Hudson and tried to care for him and make his last days as happy as possible. But Marc Christian would not have had an act of sexual intercourse with Rock Hudson again. This boy was not bent on committing suicide. Nobody would knowingly have sexual intercourse with someone who at that time has symptoms of AIDS. Nobody would.

And why did Miller admit: 'Look kid, I'm sorry, I know it doesn't seem fair.' What was Miller sorry about? The truth was that Miller was sorry because he exposed Marc Christian to death. And he did it for money.

Throughout June of 1984, Miller made statements like: 'Why don't you bring some pretties in here to spice things up between you and Rock', apparently referring to homosexual boys. Mark Miller would say to Christian: 'Is The Movie Star making you happy? Are you making The Movie Star happy? How are things in the love-making department? We like a happy house, the house is singing, that's the way I like it.' Then Miller walked into the courtroom and said they had no sex after June 1984. Of course he says there was no sex going way back to about February 1984. Looking directly at the jury, Rhoden asked: 'You believe Miller?'

One thing was for sure. Somebody in the courtroom had lied. Because sex continued. Along came July 1985, and Marc Christian suffered the chilling, sweating fear that he, too, would die the same way Hudson was soon to die. Within days he tried to get medical help and the jury should be concerned with his mental state at the time.

Rhoden declared: 'Consider this for a minute – suppose when he went to see Dr Dormont, Dormont took a test and said, "Monsieur, everything is okay. Not only do you not have AIDS, you couldn't possibly have it. Our tests are one hundred per cent accurate. You are okay. You're clean. Relax." He would have relaxed. It would have been all over. There would have been no problem. There would have been no lawsuit. And if he went to a second doctor and found that out, just to double-check, and they said, "Listen if the test shows negative, it's negative. What are you worried about?" That isn't what happened is it? I wish it were. Dr Dormont said, "Here's the result of the test, it shows you are negative for AIDS, negative. It doesn't show that there are antibodies here or that the virus is here. You are negative. But it doesn't mean you don't have it. You have to come back for tests indefinitely. The tests are not reliable. We don't know, we can't be sure. We know you are not positive, but the negative doesn't mean you are really negative." Then Dr Dormont explained to Marc Christian that this is exactly what happened to Rock Hudson when Hudson was diagnosed as having AIDS. And could anyone imagine the mental distress he went through then?'

The defence, said Rhoden, had tried to diminish Christian's fear by attempting to prove there had been no sex between them after February 1984. They had concocted a scenario in which Hudson says: 'I'm being blackmailed by this guy, but I'll let him stay in my house until I can get my blackmailer's teeth fixed.' Did that make any sense? It was an absurdity. Hudson would have said, if anything, 'I'll knock the teeth out of your mouth.' As to Christian's car, Hudson would have said, 'I would like to run you over with it.'

But instead Hudson said: 'This blackmailer, it's terrible, but I'm going to get his teeth fixed, and until I complete the dental work, I'm going to let him continue living in my bedroom.'

Then the defence had tried to convince the court there was no sex because the plaintiff had sex with others. Even if it were true, and it was not, Christian could still have had sex with Rock Hudson. They brought in the butler, Mr Wright, who testified, among other things: 'I saw Christian in bed with a brunette.' But in his (pre-trial) deposition what he said was, 'I never saw Marc in bed with anybody.'

Rhoden returned his gaze towards the jury: 'You see, Wright told the truth in his deposition; he never saw Marc in bed with anybody. But he comes here in the court, brought in here by the defence team, and he testifies: "I saw Marc in bed with somebody". Why do you suppose he did that? Any idea? He was promised a percentage of what Mark Miller and George

169

Nader are going to get when this is over. And so that man came in here, and, for his percentage, he lied. And that isn't all he lied about. He said he also received $50,000 in severance pay right about the time Hudson died. Severance pay is when your employment is severed. But Wright's employment was not severed, he continued to work for the next year and a half, so got severance pay that wasn't severance pay, and he got a promise of a piece of the action.'

'Mr Morimoto was also promised a percentage of the estate. Mr Morimoto testified not quite as badly as Wright – that goes for Miller too – he saw somebody, he wasn't positive, but the implication was he certainly did see a boy with Marc Christian. But Morimoto, of course, was promised a percentage. And an interesting thing about that percentage: I want to remind you of something about that percentage. Do you remember a fellow who took the witness stand called Tony Rocco? He was the only one coming into the courtroom wearing a vest, and even the lawyers here don't wear vests. He came in, looked like somebody who was out to play the part of a diplomat. He was asked if somebody representing the estate tried to bribe him and if he agreed to take a bribe, he was going to get money for a car; to do a little lying about something about which he knew nothing. And he said he didn't do it. And what's interesting is the words that were used are: "Rocco was promised not a set amount, but a percentage of what Miller was going to get".'

Conversely, the defence, he said, would try to convince the jury that the witnesses for Christian had all lied; that Liberty Martin was the blackmailer's assistant and the others committed perjury by their claims. But even if the jury accepted their evidence, the defence would then try to rely on another mitigating factor: that after Hudson's death Christian showed no outward sign of fear; fear that he had AIDS.

But their own Dr Laurence said: 'In view of the type of conduct Rock Hudson and Marc Christian had engaged in, when Marc Christian heard that Hudson had AIDS, if Marc Christian didn't become – if he didn't suffer extreme fear, he'd have to be crazy.' What was the fear from? It was based upon two factors: his knowledge of what he had been doing, high-risk sex, combined with what the doctors told him. They would argue that there was no fear, because about six months or so later Marc Christian went on this talk-show tour.

Rhoden said: 'Now, it's common knowledge there are some lawyers, not all lawyers, but some lawyers that are press happy, who like to see themselves on television, and they like to talk a lot and they like press conferences. That gets them more clients and higher fees. They get a thrill of seeing themselves in the newspaper or on television. Unfortunately, Marvin Mitchelson – nobody is perfect now – is one of these. So he drags Christian on this talk-show tour and on the programmes. Christian didn't seem to be in any fear; he was answering questions the same way you saw him answering questions up here.

'The argument is going to be if he had any fear of his life, he wouldn't have gone on a tour to those different cities with his lawyer Mitchelson. But is a man who is in fear someone who's going to whimper every minute of the day? If he doesn't whimper, if he doesn't cry, if he doesn't shake, does that mean he doesn't have a constant nagging fear of death? Marc Christian has had this fear now for three and a half years and on this witness stand he did not put on any act for you. He didn't give you a demonstration of what it's like to be scared. And he would not. And I wouldn't have him do it. What is that kind of fear? That kind of fear that he has had for three and a half years is the kind of fear you're going to have when you wake up in the morning and you check to be sure there are no symptoms. If you lose a couple of pounds, you sweat it out, because: Is that the beginning of a weight loss? And you check it every day. And all you can do is hope that you're not told by the doctor "You better get your affairs in order".'

The defence was going to say that he didn't mitigate his fear. The analogy was a typical automobile accident case, and the innocent victim gets a broken leg. But because he would not go to a doctor to have it fixed, the leg didn't heal; the bones grew crooked, infection set in, and there are $100,000 of medical bills. The defence could rightly claim that was not fair; the victim did not mitigate the damages and was entitled only to an award for a single broken leg.

In this case the defence was that Christian should have lessened the fear by going to a psychotherapist to have cured him of the fear and he should have gone to an AIDS expert in New York whom they hired in 1987, Dr Laurence, because he would have received a different opinion then. True psychotherapists could work wonders but psychotherapy is not for everybody in every situation. Also, Christian did not have the money. He could not have afforded it. He did try. He floundered so badly, he did not know where to turn. What to do? He tried some psychologist or psychiatrist, and the moment they realized this could involve litigation, they did not want to be called in as witnesses, and they declined to see him again until after the case.

One said: 'I would see you for $150 an hour.' He didn't have the money. When they threw him out of the house, he was flat broke. He went back to see Liberty Martin, to live with her, because he had no other place to go and no money to get there. His mother could not help. She lived on social security but Robert Mills had the gall to suggest more than once, that Marc Christian did not properly mitigate damages because he did not go to his mother.

The other part of the mitigation was that he did not go to the right doctors. If Christian had gone to Dr Laurence in New York in 1984, then Dr Laurence would have told him: 'No problem at all, everything is okay, no reason for any fear', and they would not have to be annoyed with this little troublesome lawsuit. But what of Dr Laurence? He was first retained by the defence in 1987, two years after the fear began.

'What kind of sense does this make?' asked Rhoden. 'How in the world could Marc Christian have anticipated in 1985 that two years later the defence would hire an expensive $300-an-hour expert in New York and anticipating that, Christian should have gone to him in 1985?'

In fact Christian saw Dr Sonnabend in New York who told him, 'If because of your sexual activities you're in a high-risk group, you're in danger of getting AIDS, and that's it. And the test that is negative isn't going to tell you anything, because too many of those tests that are negative are not reliable.' Dr Dormont in Paris had told him the same thing. So should he have solicited a third opinion in New York from Laurence?

And what would Laurence have told him? Would Laurence have told him about the test that showed that there can be as high as twenty-five per cent of the cases that test negative for the virus on people who have got it? Would that have put an end to the plaintiff's fear? Even Dr Laurence had to admit that Christian's conduct with Rock Hudson put him in an extremely high-risk category and that for years after the initial stages, when the virus is in the body it could be undetectable.

Rhoden asked: 'Now let's take a little look at this. Why Dr Laurence? What's he doing here? Think a minute. This is Los

Angeles, it is the great UCLA medical centre here where they do a great deal of work in AIDS. And one of the great pioneers in this field is a Dr Gottlieb. He's right here in town. He happens to work in the same office with Dr Roth, another doctor whose testimony is involved in this case, a doctor who talked to Marc Christian. Competent people. This is Los Angeles, it isn't Crooked Elbow, North Dakota. Why didn't they get a doctor, one of the great experts here, to just come in and say: "tests are perfectly good, no problem with them, they are perfectly good in 1985 and, if this guy had gone to the right doctor, he had mitigated damages, he wouldn't have had any fear"? No doctor came in to say that. Why do you suppose? You know why. They couldn't get a doctor in Los Angeles to say that or they would have done so.

'What do they do? They go all the way to New York. They find a guy who's going to say what they want him to say, what the defence wants the doctor to say, he says it for them for $300 an hour. And they bring him here. If they had gone to Chicago and found an expert there, they would have said: "Plaintiff should have gone to Chicago". They have another fellow, McGrath from San Francisco. Now let's take a little look at the second doctor, Dr McGrath from San Francisco. You may remember him. He was the pleasant-looking fellow with the brown curly hair and the brown moustache. We have the same utter nonsense. Why should plaintiff have gone to see McGrath in 1985? These are their two experts.

'Of course, I have to, in fairness, point out to you McGrath is getting only $250 an hour. You know, the thing about Laurence, it's funny, he was given a $5000 retainer. He doesn't know how much he's going to get; $10,000 or more, he hopes it's more. He has so many hours in the case, he can't compute them; he has an administrative assistant working on it. She doesn't take ten minutes to just run them off on an adding machine. Do a little multiplying, add up the hours and multiply. She's got to sit down and go to work on it. Boy, are these guys going to get a bill.'

Rhoden pressed home his point: 'There's a wrinkle in the defence. Not only did their two doctors testify: "If he had come to me in '85, what I would have told him would have cured him of any fear", but somebody had had a bright idea: "Let's cure the plaintiff right in the court room, in front of the jury, right on the spot". Let's have these doctors testify as though Christian were a patient: "Mr Christian, nothing to worry about. You're free of it."

173

But what were the true facts? Christian knew from Dr Roth of a case where a man had AIDS and finally died of it, but they could not test him positive. Dr Laurence also knew of a case like that. Christian had heard what Dr Dormont in Paris said, "We just can't tell". He knows what Dr Sonnabend said, "We just can't tell". He went to a third doctor. He did not stop with two opinions. He agreed, "It's true, the tests are not reliable if you are negative. You can't tell." So Christian was now being asked to put all of his faith in these two defence experts, one at $300 an hour and one at $250 an hour, believe them, and "Hallelujah, I'm cured". That guy deserves a special award,' said Rhoden.

'Yet Dr Laurence put in an affidavit: "There's only a fifteen per cent chance that Mr Christian is one of twenty-five per cent who are antibody negative and may still have live virus in their blood. Thus, theoretically, there is at most a 3.75 per cent probability that Mr Christian falsely tested negative for the AIDS virus." This is Dr Laurence. This is their expert you are supposed to believe. You know what this is – this 3.75 per cent figure? It's a fake. It's a sham. It's a lie. It's utter nonsense. A kid in high school taking statistics would laugh at it. There was and never would be any statistical basis for that kind of multiplying. That was Dr Laurence. And my client, they are going to argue, should believe him and discount everything all of the other doctors told him. And notice now that he has no fear; you see, they've mitigated it. They've now ended it.

'Look, he's doing a noble work. Anybody who's in the field of AIDS trying to save lives is doing a good thing; it's only that their expert has a little problem with integrity; he lacks it. Maybe after this they'll talk Dr Laurence into cutting down his fee a little bit; they really should try.'

In the end, it came down to reliability and who the jury believed. If Christian were just out for money, he could simply tell a lie: 'Rock Hudson promised me that when he died he was going to leave half of his estate to me in his will; when we talked, nobody else was present.' There would be no one to contradict him and he could sue to get half of Hudson's estate. He would probably get it.

There was another important aspect, commonly known as 'building up the medical'. Some lawyers, some law firms in the typical automobile accident case build up the medical; they had the injured party go out and see a lot of doctors and sustain a lot of medical advice and a lot of medical bills. A lot of it was exaggerated so that if medical bills turned out to be, say $5000, the man might settle his case for $15,000, three times the medicals. It was called building up the medical. It was unethical, rotten and ought to be stopped. And if Christian did not have the credibility and integrity he had, all he would have to do would be to start going to doctor after doctor, several doctors, to be cured of his fear. A doctor would have come to court and say: 'Oh, yeah, I treated him three days a week, and I gave him this medication and that medication, and I had sessions with him.' Whatever the doctor's going to say, he did: 'because we had to cure his fear'.

Yet still the defence claimed that Christian was a gigolo, a man who sold sex for money, hustler, whore, and that was going to haunt him the rest of his life. He would never get a job in Hollywood not even at McDonalds because they were afraid that he could spread AIDS.

In conclusion, Rhoden again thumped home the crux of his action: Rock Hudson had a duty to warn Christian that he had AIDS. Rock Hudson did not comply with that duty. Miller conspired with Hudson to help Hudson breach that duty. The damage was that Christian suffered intense emotional distress because of what Miller did after Hudson knew he had AIDS. The tests that showed he did not have it were simply not reliable and that was what caused a problem. The truth was that there was no way he could say he was going to spend the next twenty years or thirty years suffering. Because they may have a cure for AIDS tomorrow, or they may come out with a test tomorrow that was absolutely certain. The jury could only account for his suffering from the time in July 1985 when the public announcement was made, up until the time when his fears were put to rest.

One thing was certain. It had affected Christian's life in many ways: he could not have sex with anybody. He would not do what Rock Hudson did; he'd have to warn anybody and no one would want to come near him.

If any woman or man did, for example, say: 'I love you so much, I'll take the chance', he still would not do it because he might kill that person. No one could tell you how long that would go on. Perhaps it would be for the rest of his life.

# CHAPTER THIRTEEN

# The Empty Chair

Rock Hudson had been on trial. Of that there could be no doubt and it was a point to be made instantly as the defence lawyers began their own attack on Christian's evidence. As Robert Mills, counsel for the Hudson estate rose to begin his final submission, he made reference to the 'empty chair' at his table, where Rock Hudson would have sat if the action had been brought during his lifetime. The estate, he said, was only liable for the actions of Hudson and since 'his client' was not there, it put him in a difficult spot. Because Rock Hudson could not get up and say what did or did not happen, what was or was not said, the jury was being asked to rely on what other people contended Hudson did or did not do, said or did not say. But they had to look at the evidence: Christian hired Mitchelson in August of 1985 – on the advice of Howard Weissman who used to be the attorney for John de Lorean – to settle the dispute as to whether he should be in the house at that time. He continued to draw his pay. He never told Hudson he was going to sue him. So Hudson died: an estate was opened, a claim was filed, and a lawsuit was filed. It was easy to cast aspersions on people when they were not here to defend themselves and because of that the jury would have to look at it with the utmost scrutiny.

Mills spoke of a quote from a picture of Clarence Darrow hanging in his office. Darrow was a lawyer he admired who, in the 1930s started out basically defending the railroads against the unions, then switched sides. Eventually he was involved in a number of famous cases, such as the Scopes Monkey Trial. They made a movie about it, *Inherit the Wind* with Fredric March and Spencer Tracy. The quotation from Darrow said: 'A courtroom is not a place where truth and innocence inevitably prevail; rather, it's an arena where competing lawyers fight not for justice but to win.'

Mills said: 'I don't buy that. We are not here to win. We are here to ask you ladies and gentlemen to exercise your reason, your logic, and come to some justice in this case. One little other story about Clarence Darrow – it does lend to what "smoke and mirrors" are. It's a magicians' term. It's someone getting you to think about something so you don't see the obvious. Magicians use them all the time; they use mirrors and smoke. They get you to look over here but over here is where the real issue is.'

During closing arguments, Clarence Darrow – when Surgeon-General Koop and others had not come to a conclusion that smoking is hazardous to your health and while the other attorney was getting up and waxing and waning – would be smoking on his cigar as the other guy was pounding away his points. All of a sudden the jury began looking over at Clarence Darrow and at that cigar. Clarence Darrow was a shrewd operator; he put a reed in the cigar and the ash never fell off. So, as the opposing lawyer was up there arguing away, the jury kept looking at this ash and it was not falling off. Soon that was all they were looking at.

The smoke and the mirrors: similarly this case was not about homosexuality. Mr Rhoden had asked them to be concerned that: 'Gee, you can't be prejudiced because Mr Christian here is homosexual or bisexual'. They should disregard that implication. This was not a case of homosexuality. It could have been a man versus a woman. It made no difference. They should feel that they could be accused of bias against homosexuals. It was also not a case where the defence was trying to challenge the seriousness of AIDS but neither was this a case of AIDS. Nor was it a case about an attempt to kill somebody. It was not even a case about somebody dying. And, more important, it was not necessarily a case of duty to warn. It was about liability, about damages, and about the burden of proof and that fell into three categories:

1) Did Rock Hudson or Mark Miller emotionally misrepresent the state of Rock Hudson's health between 8 June 1984 and the end of February of 1985 to induce Marc Christian to continue to have high-risk sex with Rock Hudson? Did they intentionally misrepresent the state of his health?

177

2) Did Rock Hudson and Mark Miller intentionally conceal the state of Rock Hudson's health between 8 June and the end of February of 1985 to induce Marc Christian to continue to have high-risk sex with Rock Hudson?

3) Did Rock Hudson or Mark Miller intentionally engage in outrageous conduct in misrepresenting or concealing the state of Rock Hudson's health between 8 June and the end of February of '85 to induce Marc Christian to continue to have high-risk sex with Rock Hudson causing severe and emotional distress to Marc Christian?

The burden of proving those three causes of action or theories in this case fell upon Christian and if he did not prove any one of them, he had failed.

Mills said that those three questions would interplay in most of his argument, which was still: If there was such a close relationship, why wasn't Christian in the will? If he does not have AIDS, why was he suing? And if it was not Rock Hudson or a figure of that stature, would he still be filing the lawsuit? Rhoden, he said, had used the 'bait and switch' tactic where, first of all, he tried to tear down the defendant's case [that is the bait], and the switch is in trying to get the defendants to spend their entire time trying to rebut everything that was said about their case.

Mills said he was not falling for that one. But nonetheless, some of Rhoden's claims could be challenged. He failed to mention for example a statement made by Christian to Dr Rochford three days after the public announcement when Rochford asked him: 'Do you believe you have AIDS?' Mr Christian said: 'No, I don't believe so.' What was good for the goose is good for the gander. That was under oath in his deposition but he could not accept that from the witness stand, because he said: 'Oh, I wouldn't have said that; I don't believe I would have said that.' So much for his fear.

Rhoden tried to indicate that two doctors with their reputation on the line came on to the witness stand and lied for $300 an hour, $250 an hour. Who was he kidding?

They said what they said because they believed it.

But Christian had produced no medical evidence but he wanted the jury to believe, 'Well, gee, my state of mind is such that I believe what these doctors told me, all this stuff, and I'm scared.' But where were these doctors? He had not called any. And when a man came in and asked for $10 million, a jury would want more than his word on it. Perhaps there was a reason he did not call them. Maybe they did not say what Christian believed he heard or they did not say what he wanted them to say.

Mills said he had been practicing about eighteen years and it was the first case in which every witness called by the defendants were called liars. They had not been offered money and they were not lying: 'Well, heck, they propositioned the plaintiff. Susan Stafford did; Richard Lovell did. . . . '

When it came to something Mr Christian did not like, they were lying.

Yet persistently, Christian had changed his own stories: 'I don't remember necessarily saying it that way. I mean, I don't really know if I believed I was in the will or that Mr Hudson was going to put me in the will. No, no, no, I didn't tell . . . I didn't mean it when I said I told . . . No, I couldn't have said that, I couldn't have told Dr Rochford three days after this, that, no, I don't believe I have AIDS.' Why could he not recollect that now? Perhaps it was that any man who claimed he had 160 sexual acts with Mr Hudson during this eight-month period better have a fear.

He was lying when he said: 'Well, I paid for all these airline tickets going to Paris.' What are the facts? They were not paid for by Christian. They were paid either through Mammoth Films or by the estate when he went there. Then he said: 'No, no, after the public announcement I was never paid.' But the estate produced the cancelled cheques. But, 'No, no, they must be phony dates on there.'

Mills said he himself came from Missouri and there were certain things that he learned while growing up, perhaps because they were part of the Westward frontier movement, or had too many flim-flam men coming through in the 1800s. Mills said the only evidence of fear was from Christian himself. There had been no evidence from a psychiatrist; no psychometric testing; there had been nothing other than his word. It was interesting that the last time that Christian cared enough about his own health and his own health and his own fear, alleged fear, to ever check the problem out, was 1986.

The only person that really cared about trying to convince Christian to get on with his life was Mills himself because he wanted those tests in 1988. Wasn't it unusual that in two years he had not cared to find out anything about his health? He did not go to see another doctor until 1988 when the defence put him through 'every test you can think of'. They were all normal.

These two doctors from the witness stand said with one hundred per cent certainty: 'You have not been infected with the AIDS virus.' If these people weren't convinced, they would not have said it. They have too much at stake in their own reputations.

And looking at his own actions, one must also challenge Christian's words. For instance, there were the letters: 'If I understood the testimony, apparently these letters were sent by Hudson to Christian, and after Hudson came home, he put them into his desk drawer where they remained forever until some time after he died, when Mr Christian found them again. If you believe that, I've got a bridge I would like to sell you. When a person gets a letter, first of all he discards the envelope, unless he's a stamp collector and saves the envelope? I've – I don't know, maybe it's something with me – I submit that maybe those letters were never given back to Hudson, maybe they were not found later on in his desk drawer after he died. Maybe Mr Christian kept them all along, from the very beginning. It is kind of curious, because I don't have an answer to this, but it is consistent with the fact that maybe Mr Hudson was somewhat concerned about his reputation because, you know, maybe he made a mistake in judgment. He's been with an individual for ten years. His reputation was important, his career was important.'

And, said Mills, if Hudson was trying to kill, injure, maim, intending to harm Christian, why was he telling him in August 'I'm going to put you in the will?' Perhaps that was why Christian stayed on at the house, to control him. Christian claimed that they had this continued sexual relationship, but others testified that they were of the belief, from what they saw, that Christian was no longer staying in Hudson's room after February of 1984.

There was testimony about evidence of sexual activity on the sheets in the Red Room. James Wright had testified to that but Christian said he washed all of the sheets in his room. The butler did every other set of sheets in the entire house. Did he just decide not to do those?

The issue was: Was there high-risk sexual activity between June of 1984 and February of 1985 when Christian says that that all occurred? And did that cause an increase in fear from what he would have had with regard to any sexual activity he says he had before that? The only evidence, apart from Christian's, was the testimony from Wayne Bernhard that he allegedly saw these people, saw two naked bodies in front of God and everybody, naked, embracing one another, kissing one another. Yet Bernhard also testified under oath, that the only basis for his knowledge that they were having continued sexual activity was because Marc Christian told him so.

Then, lo and behold, out of nowhere, this friend of his for thirteen years who knew about this litigation, knew what the allegations were, said: 'Hey, I got to tell you something.' But there was no credible evidence that there was ever any sexual activity after June of 1984, unless the jury wanted to believe Marc Christian.

'In light of all of the other evidence, including the medical evidence, which in my belief is irrefutable, there's no way in the world that I can think of that you can have sex, anal intercourse, 160 times from June of 1984 until February of 1985 and not have the AIDS virus if the person is infected with AIDS and is in the process of dying of AIDS. It just ain't so,' said Mills.

More likely to be the truth was what Hudson told Miller when he asked: 'Do you do any anal intercourse with Marc Christian?' Hudson said: 'No'.

Miller said he asked the same question of Christian when they got home or the next day. Christian said: 'No'. He had not done that in ten years.

So there was no evidence that there was sex after February of 1984, other than Christian's word. Neither was there evidence of sexual activity with Christian between June and when Hudson went to see Dr Dormont. When he came back from Dormont, he said, 'Hey, I don't have the virus in my blood.'

But what of Hudson's actions? What was his belief, his state of mind at that point? Did Rock Hudson act consistently with the manner that he did not believe he had the AIDS virus in his blood when he came back from Dormont? Were they the actions of a man who believed he had AIDS and was going to die? No one knows what he believed; but he seemed to think that he did not have the AIDS virus in his blood any more. No witness had said: 'Rock Hudson told me that "I'm not going to tell this kid, and I'm going to have sex with him in the knowledge that I'm going to expose this person to a deadly disease"?'

The true test of the matter was that Rock Hudson told the

entire world on 23 July 1985, the first celebrity to do so, that he had the AIDS virus. If he believed he had it before, why wouldn't he have said it back in October? He said it in July. Why? Because it was then he was told that it was still there and that he had it. And what did he do? He told the entire world.

Mills went on: 'I can't impress upon you strongly enough; my belief based upon the medical evidence, is that he did not have high-risk sex with Marc Christian after June of 1984. He did not have high-risk sex of an anal nature before June of 1984. Otherwise, a man from April of 1983 until February of 1985, with sex three to five times a week, would surely have contracted this disease and not tested negative on every test that has been run on him. Show me where the intent was to misrepresent something between June and February. Show where the intent was to act outrageously.'

If Hudson did not have sex, he did not expose him. If he didn't expose him, there was no liability. Finally, it came down to credibility; and an example of Christian's credibility came when he was asked: 'What motel did you first sleep in?' He replied, 'I don't remember.'

'Name one motel.'

'I can't name you one motel.'

Credibility? Who would believe this man? Anyone with a lover of the stature of Rock Hudson would sure as heck remember the place where he had his first relationship with him. Christian could not remember.

The motivation? Here was a man who did not have any evidence that he has the AIDS virus, claiming he has an outrageously intense relationship with Hudson and suing for $10 million for not revealing he had AIDS. So far, he did not appear infected, the inference being they didn't have high-risk anal sex. So, the only possible, plausible motivation was the publicity. The empty chair there (*pointing to the one next to his own*) would have been Rock Hudson sitting there.

Mills stood in front of the jury: 'That chair over there, that's a sixty-year career but Rock is not here to defend himself. He could not say, "Whoa, this isn't right. This didn't happen." '

Christian hired a lawyer before Rock Hudson died; he filed a lawsuit after the will was probated, after he wasn't in it. He went on every talk show even after the lawsuit was filed, as a public announcement. Mills said he could have done the same: 'I could have paraded on a bunch of celebrities and a bunch of stars and we could have had a dog and pony show in this case.

I didn't want to do that. Instead, I brought in Ron Channell. He talked about Rock Hudson. He talked about what he did for his family; what he did for his sister. I think that is the real Rock Hudson.

'It's unfortunate that we have to hear some other story, when the man is not here to defend himself. I've thought about it. I'm not talking about $10 million, I'm not talking about $1 million. How can you give something with the evidence in this case? That would be outrageous conduct, there's no evidence. Christian has nothing; there's no evidence by any of his actions that he has got any increased fear of anything. You could say: "Well, yeah, okay. Maybe there should have been some telling or something more, even though maybe that's not intentional, but maybe there should have been something more done to inform him." Okay. So we give him some token amount of money, however small it may be, to say "Okay, maybe somebody should have done something a little bit more than they did even", but that's assuming you believe they had that kind of sexual activity of a high-risk nature, of any kind. If not, don't give him anything.'


Next it was Andrew Banks's turn to summarize the defence of Mark Miller and with a patronizing approach, he said the jury had sat for seven difficult weeks; they had taken an enormous amount of notes and now had to do some hard thinking, weighing issues, and deciding on credibility and believability. Anybody could come to court and sue anybody for anything. But the key was: Could they win? The key gets turned by ordinary people, a jury, who must subject the claims to an acid test, twelve acid tests, one for each member of the jury.

Regardless of how the trial worked out, it was because of the commitment of those ordinary people that the system worked. The first thing he wanted to talk about was the first words that came out of Mr Rhoden's mouth. He said his client could not get a fair trial because he was a homosexual, that there was bigotry in this country; there was no way Christian could get a fair trial. That was bunk, said Banks. Homosexuality and Christian's lifestyle as a homosexual was not the thing in issue. So the jury should forget about that.

And another thing that Rhoden said several times in his initial remarks was his reference to Christian as 'this boy'. This was not a boy. Christian was a thirty-six-year-old man. In 1983 when he says he started having sex with Rock Hudson, he was a thirty-year-old man. He did what he did and he acted the way he has acted – the testimony has shown – as a man, not as a boy. No one should be thinking about this 'poor little boy' that Rhoden was trying to portray. He and Rhoden agreed on one thing, however, that Mark Miller did have a duty to tell Christian that Rock Hudson had AIDS. The evidence in this case as it related to Miller showed him as a good and loyal friend.

However, when Rock Hudson learned he had AIDS and when Rock Hudson was crying that he had AIDS and when Rock Hudson was depressed about the fact, he turned to Mark Miller, not to Marc Christian, not to somebody else. He turned to Mark Miller. He poured out that secret that he had that disease and he talked about his fears. And he looked to Mark Miller for comfort, for help, for solace – and for secrecy.

That showed the depth of the friendship between these two people, that the person he turned to was Mark Miller. It also said something about his relationship with Marc Christian, because if the relationship was as wonderful as Marc Christian claimed, Rock would have turned to him. Christian testified that when he saw Rock Hudson in the hospital at UCLA he said: 'Why didn't you tell me?' and Rock Hudson responded: 'When you have this disease, you're all alone.'

Banks said: 'Kind of a great line, isn't it? The only problem is that Hudson's actions didn't sound like the actions of a man who thought he was all alone. He told Mark Miller. He shared that secret with Miller. George Nader, we now know was told. James Wright was told, and so was Hudson's friend, Dean Dittman. Again, Marc Christian was not told, and you have to wonder why Rock Hudson didn't tell him and I submit the reason he didn't tell him – he knew that was not the person to tell. He knew the reason he was not going to find comfort and understanding is because the relationship was over.'

Christian had to prove otherwise. He had to prove that Rock Hudson and he were having sex after June of 1984. That was the jury's first question and the verdict deals with the claims against Rock Hudson. Then they had to ask: Did Miller know if they were having sex? Miller was being sued for fraud and conspiracy and basically the jury had to ask: Did Mark Miller conspire with Rock Hudson to conceal that he had AIDS for the purpose of getting Mr

Christian to continue to have sex with Rock Hudson? The answer was no, and nor did he deliberately cause emotional distress. There was no evidence that Miller knew that Hudson was having sex with Christian after June of 1984. He didn't live in the house. He didn't spend the night there. He went to work. The fact that Miller had kept the secret of his best friend who turned to him in a time of great need, the fact that he gave his best friend comfort, solace, support, and understanding, was that not atrocious conduct? Was that beyond all bounds of decency? Was that what they were going to tell the citizens of the State of California?

The jury had to view Mark Miller separately from Rock Hudson and always make those separate determinations. What Mark Miller did was keep a confidence, he gave his word he would keep it. He did not do it because he was trying to get Christian to keep having sex with Rock Hudson. He did it because he was a friend; there never was any reckless disregard of the probability of causing emotional distress to plaintiff or reckless disregard of the probability that could cause Marc Christian emotional distress.

Mark Miller was told this secret from Rock Hudson and there was no doubt Christian would have been suffering some emotional distress if he was having sex with Rock Hudson had Miller told him in June 1984, or any month, during this time that they were having sex. The law did not put upon Miller the duty to tell. Miller did not have the duty under law to tell Marc Christian that Rock Hudson had AIDS.

If he told, he would have betrayed the trust of a man with whom he had a confidential relationship. Mr Rhoden would argue that there was a confidential relationship between Christian and Hudson, but there was no such relationship between Christian and Miller. That was important, because Miller followed his conscience. He did what he thought was right. He did not do anything with the intent to hurt Christian, to cause him emotional distress, or to induce him to have sex with Rock Hudson.

Christian had testified that his daily activities were the same now as they used to be. He got up in the morning; he had breakfast; he watched the news on TV or read the paper; went to work, if he was working; if not, he worked on 'Decades'. He had dinner with Liberty Martin in the evening four or five times; and he went out to see his friends. His life is just as it was before he met Rock Hudson. He had not told of any inability

185

to work because he was so emotionally distraught that he could not function.

He said that he did not have any psychiatric or psychological counselling and no doctor told him that he should seek psychological or psychiatric care. None of his friends had recommended that he sought help and the best acid test was his mother. She never said a word that she felt her son needed to get psychiatric or psychological care, that he was so distraught that he could not function, that he couldn't go to work.

If he had any of those pieces of evidence, they would have been brought forth, because he had the burden of proof.

Christian was so comfortable with the knowledge that all the tests were negative that he never again sought a test to find out what his status was. Almost three years later and he still had not gone to find out. He knew he didn't have the virus, he knew he was not in exposure and he didn't go out and find any other tests until asked to do so by the defence. The fact that Christian never sought out a medical test after 1986, within a year of the time he learned Rock Hudson had AIDS, was evidence that he never thought he was at risk.

And that was why he did not have any psychiatric or psychological care, either. He had provided no proof of any emotional distress that impacted itself on his life in one way. He was like Chicken Little who ran around telling all his friends: 'The sky is falling, the sky is falling', and he got all his friends worked up. 'The sky is falling'.

Just a Chicken Little. It was more fun for Christian, instead of going for testing and getting a complete set of tests at UCLA, instead of going to a psychiatrist for this fear – or a psychologist or a free clinic or a mental health centre or to a priest, a rabbi, anyone for some counselling – it was more fun to go on the 'Larry King Show' in November of 1985, the same month he filed his lawsuit. And it was more fun to go on the 'Phil Donahue' and '20/20' shows, 'Good Morning San Francisco' and 'P.M. Magazine' and 'Good Morning Australia' and be interviewed by people from *Penthouse*, *New York Native*, the *New York Post*, and the various Philadelphia magazines, than it was to seek help for this great emotional distress.

The talk about not being able to afford treatment was just not true. He testified that he had received from his mother – and she confirmed she gave him – $5000 for Christmas in 1985. No strings attached. He could have mitigated his damages. He never did. He didn't even try. He chose throughout the whole course of this litigation not to go to seek any psychiatric or psychological care for this fear. He chose to stop getting tests within a year of the time of Rock Hudson's announcement. He was a man with a brain, with two lawyers, Harold Rhoden and Marvin Mitchelson. If there was a fear, the tests would have been done, a complete set. Then after being questioned by defence counsel, the court is told he has suddenly found the name of one psychiatrist, one person that he had attempted to get care from.

Said Banks: 'Give me a break. After being shown the weakness in his case on his direct examination . . . he goes to all this trouble to find somebody, and he can't remember whether this guy is a psychiatrist or a psychologist? It just doesn't ring true to me. His case is like Swiss cheese; it's got so many holes in it, it's hard to believe.'

Christian had chosen to give the medical evidence himself by way of: 'this is what they told me', instead of bringing them into the courtroom. It was evidence the jury should distrust. If he did not have the intestinal fortitude to bring them here and let them give their opinions, it was because he was afraid that they were not going to say what he had said they said.

First Christian testified that he met Rock Hudson in 1982 at the bottle initiative. But he said on the 'Phil Donahue Show', in December of 1985 and the 'Larry King Show' in November of 1985 that he met Rock Hudson at the Gore Vidal Campaign. He said he gave Rock Hudson his phone number at that bottle fundraiser and Rock called him, but on the 'Phil Donahue Show' he was asked: 'What did you do, give Rock your phone number and he called you a few days later?' And he says: 'No, no, no, I didn't give him my phone number. Rock called me a week later when he went to a friend of mine, got my number, and called me.'

He testified that from April of 1983 to November of 1983 he and Rock Hudson had sex three to five times a week; but he did not move in until November of 1983, so during those seven months, they were not in Rock Hudson's house.

He had also testified, in deposition, Mr Mills brought this out, that they only had sex outside of Rock Hudson's house in the entirety of their relationship six times – one of which was at, he claimed, George Nader and Mark Miller's house in February of 1984. And if he was having sex three to five times a week from April to November and he never goes up to Hudson's house and he only has sex outside of the house a total of six times, where did he have this sex?

When he was caught in that, he said: 'Oh we went to motels. We went to motels and had it.' He didn't say that in his pre-trial deposition. There were other discrepancies in his story. He had claimed that in November of 1984 Hudson had asked him if he should do 'Dynasty'. But Hudson had signed the contracts in October of 1984 and had filmed several episodes in November. So he could not have had this conversation in November.

Then he denied that on the medical form he filled in at Dr Rochford's office, he had admitted having had venereal disease. He claimed it was the doctor who wrote that but the handwriting looked suspiciously like his own. And then he said to his knowledge no one had seen him having sex with Hudson until Mr Mills started his cross-examination and it came out that Mr Christian had just that weekend discovered someone who saw Christian and Hudson have sex; his name was Wayne Bernhard. Eventually Mr Bernhard gave evidence. Even then they managed to contradict each other. Christian said it was in the jacuzzi; Bernhard said it was on a chaise lounge.

Finally there was the 'heart-rending story' of how the American Express bill wasn't paid for the flight to Paris. He got a bad credit report. Yet in evidence is an invoice showing the cancelled cheque from Mammoth Films dated 14 August for the exact amount of the invoice.

Banks said: 'My question to you now is – After hearing all of this, are you, the jury, going to give the plaintiff credibility on these issues where he's the only person testifying? You know, Mr Rhoden made a point in his opening argument that it's fair game to attack the lawyer's theories and tactics, but, ladies and gentlemen, the tactics used in this case are very questionable. Also it is the law that evidence offered when there is the opportunity to produce stronger or more satisfactory evidence should be distrusted. The examples I have taken out of this case to show you about the credibility you should give Mr Christian's testimony warrant your not believing him. You have to wrestle with that problem. But isn't it interesting that there are no trips between Rock Hudson and Mr Christian going anywhere in the world, he doesn't take him to Paris or Hawaii or Florida or New York or to Disneyworld. Isn't it interesting that nowhere in all of these wonderful pictures we have seen is there a picture of Rock Hudson with a loving inscription to Marc Christian?'

But there was no evidence that what Miller did was to harm Mr Christian. What he did was keep his friend's secret . . . and if the jury found against him they were saying no one could keep in confidence a secret unless they were willing to be sued for millions of dollars. Banks concluded: 'On the evidence of this case, there is no proof of anything Christian has claimed.'

Under the American Superior Court system, counsel for the plaintiff is able to make a closing address to the jury to refute any points made by the opposition in their final summary.

Harold Rhoden rose again and approached the jury with an apology: 'I know you are tired of hearing of me – from me, but there are a lot of points that have been made in two very impressive closing arguments, and I would like now to answer them.'

Mr Mills, he said, had laboured the points that Marc Christian did not tell Rock Hudson before Hudson died: 'I'm going to sue you.' In the first place, Christian did not know he was going to sue Rock Hudson before Rock Hudson died. That came later. Secondly, there was a document in evidence dated 9 August 1985, containing the signature of Rock Hudson. 'I ask you, when you go into the jury room, to compare the signature with the signature of Rock Hudson when he was normal. You can see from the signature itself the man could not have been in his right mind at all. He was dying of AIDS. Can you imagine anybody, no matter what Rock Hudson had done, to go to this man while he's dying in bed and say 'I'm going to sue you'? Christian did not do that. And that is one of Mr Mills's earliest points as to why you ought to find against Christian. That is one of many. It gets better.

'Mr Mills then said: "This is not a case of an attempt to kill somebody". He was right, it was not a case of someone's attempt to kill somebody. Rock Hudson did not decide, "I am going to kill Marc Christian and here's how I'm going to do it." Miller never said, "I'm going to kill Marc Christian and here's the way." Neither of them deliberately wanted to kill Marc Christian; that was absurd. But it was done with the reckless disregard of that probability. They just did not care. Hudson did not care after he knew he had AIDS. He cared about himself, but after he knew that, he did not care whether Christian got it or not. He did not care if he passed it on to anybody else, and the same was true of Miller. It was a case of reckless disregard of the probability of hurting somebody.

'Mills also said: "This is not about a case of AIDS." Oh, yes, it was,' said Rhoden. It was about two cases. One was Rock Hudson's case of AIDS. The other one was a big question mark. Had Marc Christian got it? No evidence said that he had, but there was no reliable evidence that he does not have the virus lying dormant, causing no harm at all, somewhere in his body, lying in wait.

'Mills said: "This is not a case about the duty to warn." Oh, yes it is,' said Rhoden. It was a case about three things, liability, damages, and the burden of proof. What kind of nonsense was that? Every single lawsuit was always about three things: liability, damages and the burden of proof. Did Mr Mills really mean that every case was about the same thing? Of course not.

Mr Mills gave an example of Clarence Darrow. By the way, said Rhoden, it wasn't Darrow. The story about the lawyer who sat at the counsel table with a cigar – and he let the ashes come practically up to his lips, this very long, thin ash that everybody was looking at, and not listening to the other lawyer – was an old, old story, told a million times. It must have begun ten decades ago. No judge today would allow such trials. But that did not keep Mills from saying that this case was about 'subterfuge and trickery'. The fact there was no evidence of it, though, did not seem to bother him. Christian, he said, had been criticized for failing to produce medical evidence of his fear of AIDS. In fact he did all that was possible within his resources. He could not afford more. He had to give up a job he had in order to come to the trial every day. He was living in a small apartment and on borrowed money. Where was he going to get the money to call these doctors or pay $8000 for a battery of tests?

It was not within his power to produce stronger medical evidence because it took a lot of money to bring doctors to court, even local doctors. The defence, meanwhile, had it within their power to produce stronger and more satisfactory evidence. Why didn't they bring Dr Dormont from Paris? Why did they not bring Doctor Sonnabend from New York to contradict Christian and blow him right out of the courtroom? Why? Because the testimony would have slaughtered them. They knew what he said in deposition: 'A negative antibody test could not guarantee the absence of the virus.'

190

Rhoden slammed home his point: 'I don't know which of the two dreamed that one up, but like a lot of the other things, the dreamer didn't start to reason it out. It wouldn't make any sense, because in 1986 Christian got a very expensive AIDS test given by and paid for by the defence. In 1988, we again let the defence pay for thousands of dollars, $8000 to one lab, to give him AIDS tests because we couldn't afford it. We co-operated fully. What sense would it make for me to say, "Don't go get another one because it will only prove what they want to prove"? It would make no sense for him to want another AIDS test. It would have made no sense for me to tell him, "Don't get one." We know what the tests show. They show negative for the virus and negative for antibodies. It would have made no sense for me to say that.'

There had been a lot of silly talk, too, that Dr Dormont had told Hudson he was cured of AIDS after the first treatment. Hudson knew that his lover could have been exposed at some time but did not tell him about the cure. A lie was made up, but those advancing it just did not stop to think it out.

Rhoden stood before the jury and pleaded: 'Can you imagine for a second Dr Dormont telling something as nonsensical as that to a patient like Rock Hudson, "You've been cured. We're going to keep it a secret from the world"? Wouldn't they say, "We're not going to use your name, but just say 'we did cure a patient' "? Wouldn't they have done that? Think a minute. Can you imagine how the world would have applauded if they had found a cure for AIDS? They could do it without mentioning the name of the patient. But no, no. They want you to believe that Hudson believed he did not have AIDS, that Miller believed he did not have AIDS in September. Therefore, there was no duty thereafter to tell Christian.'

Turning to Mr Banks submissions, Rhoden gazed intently at members of the jury, his eyes seeking first one and then another as he said: 'Banks claimed there was no evidence that there was sex after 1984. He said there was no evidence of it. Do you hear this? No evidence of it. Where has Mr Banks been? How many admissions did we get out of Marc Christian? Out of Mark Miller? How many of them? Miller admitted saying things like: "Look, I'm sorry, kid, I know it doesn't seem fair" or, "I stayed up late last night or all night trying to figure out a way to tell you." Would Mark Miller have said those things to Christian if Miller didn't know that Christian had been having sex with Rock Hudson? He would have said, instead, if he believed there was no sex, "What do you mean why didn't I tell you? Who are you? Why should I tell you? I didn't tell the milkman either. Get lost." It was Miller who said in 1984, around September, to Marc Christian, "You're not having an affair with me, you're having an affair with Rock Hudson. Go ask him." Lies and more lies. Why did Miller do it? He did it because he didn't want to displease his boss . . . because his boss was dying, and Miller knew that he was going to take a portion of that estate, and he didn't want to be fired and cut out.'

Mr Banks had said: 'I don't believe Miller did it for money.' But nobody cared what Mr Banks believed or did not believe. It was evidence that mattered.

Further, said Rhoden, Mr Banks had tried to divert the jury by saying that if they found against Miller they would be sending a message to the world that a man could never keep a secret for a friend. Wrong, said Rhoden, a verdict against Miller would send out this message: 'If you think someone has AIDS and has a lover, not only do you not dare agree to conceal that fact from the lover, but you must not lie to the lover and say it's anorexia.' Why? Because that could mean the lover will then go ahead, keep making love and die as a result. The message they were sending out would be: 'There's no duty to warn. It's okay to agree to not tell the lover that the other one has AIDS. It's okay to lie to him. It's okay.'

Rhoden ended on an earnest note: 'You are not going to bring in a verdict that's going to send that message. I don't believe you people will.'

# CHAPTER FOURTEEN

## *The Verdict is Yours*

Even disregarding the bias and passion of the rival counsel's speeches, what had undoubtedly been established in the to-ing and fro-ing of the trial evidence was that Rock Hudson had lied about the true cause of his illness for thirteen months from the very moment it was diagnosed to the point when Yanou Collart gave her dramatic press conference in Paris. Mark Miller – along with George Nader, the butler James Wright and Rock's close friend Dean Dittman – had kept his secret. Apart from his doctors whose confidentiality could be assured, no one else knew for certain that Hudson was dying of AIDS. He lied about it to his staff, colleague actors and actresses, and his closest friends. He even tried to delude himself as to the severity of his suffering. So what was it that drove him to imagine that he could continue to keep it hidden? What inspired him towards what was perhaps the greatest acting performance of his life, to give the appearance to the world that nothing was wrong when he knew his days were very numbered?

These questions had not become a feature of the trial because Rock Hudson's state of mind was not an issue; undoubtedly the jury must have given it a passing thought. They might have considered, for example, that the one thing he cared about most, his career, was the root cause of his actions and quest for secrecy. Perhaps he still thought that even in death, he could protect that image he had worked all of his adult life to create and build, and that seemed to be borne out by the smokescreen of excuses he had offered for his weight-loss. At the point he learned the news, he was still in control of his mental faculties so the blame could not be placed on diminished level of reasoning. Just one month after he had received the awful news he flew down to Las Vegas for the filming of a television movie called *Las Vegas Strip Wars* and talked about the future with confidence. Was it self-delusion? Did he consider himself to invincible that he could laugh it off and say: 'It'll never happen', despite Gottlieb's warning that he should put his affairs in order? Or did he decide with cold and calculated disregard for others that he would try to keep his secret as long as he could, and try to continue to have sexual pleasures wherever he could find them until it was no longer physically possible?

Only Rock Hudson could have answered those questions and he died before anyone could ask him. But what seems more likely, and this is borne out by other case histories, is that he took no single decision on how he would live out the last days of his life. He passed through the progressive stages of AIDS: first, the total rejection in his mind that he could be dying; then, he was gripped by the fear and realization which is when irrational behaviour takes hold; and third, he moved into the stage of acceptance when he knew that the end was in sight and the battle calmed. The emotional trauma that any ordinary AIDS patient feels as those stages are reached is beyond imagination; the fact that Hudson also had to contend with his great public image of The Movie Star must have made it all so much worse. But could that barrage of incredible emotional strain excuse what he did? And even if the answer to that was an unlikely yes, there was still the question of the suffering which he might or might not have caused Marc Christian. This was the issue.

So the spotlight turned to the jury. On the afternoon of 9 February, when Harold Rhoden completed his final submissions, an air of tension had enveloped the twelve men and women who would soon be asked to bring in their verdict. As Rhoden had pointed out in his closing speech, they faced an awesome responsibility at the end of what had been a long, tough and loud trial which had seen sparks fly and passions roused.

The speech-making was all but done. They had sat through evidence which, in transcript form, ran to well over 3000 foolscap pages. They had listened to allegation and counter-allegation, claim and denial, from the principals and their witnesses. They had heard important and graphic stories and they had endured endless trivia and conversely, complex and contradictory medical evidence. They had watched the faces, they had seen a gamut of emotions: fear, nervousness, nonchalance, hostility and anger.

They had occasionally observed hate, and sometimes deceit. They would have seen through devious attempts to mislead them; and they had witnessed the legal ploys, the tricks of the trade, aimed at diverting their attention or attracting it.

They had seen it all and they knew that, somewhere along the line, one or more of the witnesses had been economical with the truth.

What would they make of it?

Judge Geernaert wanted to make their position clear as he gave them final instructions. Despite the pleadings of counsel Banks, it was not the duty of the jury at that time to send any 'messages' to the world in reaching a verdict. Their sole job was to adjudicate on whether or not Marc Christian had proved his case for compensatory damages. That was the first phase of their task and if they agreed that he had, they may also face a second phase to discuss punitive and exemplary damages.

It was their duty, said the judge, to weigh the evidence received in the trial; they could not consider material they may have read or heard from any other source. They were the sole and exclusive judges of the believability of witnesses and in doing so they should take account of a witness's demeanour while testifying and of any bias or motive that might have influenced his evidence. A witness false in one part of his testimony was to be mistrusted in others yet they had to bear in mind the distinction of innocent misrecollection, which was not uncommon.

Judge Geernaert made a point of guiding the jury on the expert evidence which had been called in the case. With witnesses who had a special skill or training, they should consider not only their qualifications for giving evidence but also the reasons for their opinions. They should not be bound by any opinion yet they should not disregard medical evidence unless it had been contradicted. They should consider this evidence in conjunction with Christian's state of mind and the emotions and physical sensations he experienced.

For it was Christian's burden to prove that the defendants had conspired to make false statements, that they knew them to be false and that they were made with intent to defraud. He had to prove they concealed material facts from him that they had a duty to disclose and had acted outrageously and recklessly in their intentional concealment through which he had suffered increased emotional distress. The defence would have to prove that he had failed to mitigate that distress.

Judge Geernaert spoke also of the confidential relationship of Mark Miller's role as Hudson's secretary. Failure to disclose facts obtained through a confidential relationship was not an actionable fraud. However, intentional concealment arose when a person under no obligation to speak, did so but did not speak honestly or made misleading statements or suppressed information. Similarly, a conspiracy was when two or more people take concerted action which might damage another.

Christian was entitled to recover damages for severe emotional distress if it was caused by the outrageous conduct of the defendants or by their reckless disregard of the possibility of causing distress. Extreme and outrageous conduct, said the judge, occurred if in the jury's view the defendants' actions had been beyond all possible bounds of decency so as to be regarded as atrocious and utterly intolerable in a civilized community. It was not merely insults, indignities, threats, annoyance or petty trivialities. It was conduct that would cause an average member of the community to feel outrage.

Intent to cause distress would be established by deciding whether the defendants would have known with substantial certainty that distress was likely to be caused by their actions and in determining the severity of emotional distress, the jury had to consider its intensity, duration and whether any reasonable person could be expected to endure it. If the jury decided that Christian had proved his case, then they should award him damages which reasonably compensated him for the increased emotional distress he claimed he had suffered. The amount of the award should include compensation for pain, discomfort, fear, anxiety and similar suffering that was reasonably certain to be experienced in the future.

The judge steered the jury further on this point: he said they could only award damages for emotional distress resulting from homosexual relations with Hudson after he learned he had AIDS. They were not allowed to take into account any sexual activity before that time, nor could they award speculative damages based upon any future development which was conjectural and uncertain. They must, in considering the amount of the award, consider also whether Marc Christian had used reasonable diligence in preventing and limiting any suffering to himself.

And now to the jury themselves; it was rarely helpful, said Judge Geernaert, for a juror to express an emphatic opinion upon entering the jury room nor announce any determination to stand for a certain verdict. Positions were then quickly taken which through pride, a juror might not change though he knew he wanted to. They were not partisans or advocates; simply impartial judges of the facts. If they came into difficulties, the law forbade them to decide the issue by flipping a coin or drawing lots but as soon as nine of them were in agreement, they could return to the court to announce their verdict.

To assist the juror in reaching that verdict, a questionnaire had been drawn up by the defence and agreed by Judge Geernaert and by Harold Rhoden who went on record as saying he would have preferred not to have submitted the document. The system adopted was that after their lengthy discussions on all aspects of the trial, each member of the jury was to give his or her answer to each of a list of thirty-seven questions. It is known as a special verdict form which has proved helpful in concentrating the minds of jurors involved in a long and complicated trial. The form is designed to take the jury through the process of considering each major point and arriving at their verdict with the final question. The same rules of a majority vote applied to each separate question, so that when any nine jurors had answered a collective yes or no to any single question, they could move to the next.

The jury retired on the afternoon of 9 February and returned to court on the morning of 14 February with a query for the judge. They wanted to hear his definition of certain words, such as 'intent' and 'fear' as they applied to this case.

At lunchtime on Wednesday, 15 February whispers around the court building suggested the jury was reaching its conclusions. Everyone was placed on alert. The judge returned to his chambers in readiness; counsel took a shorter lunch and then hurried back to the courtroom to wait. Reporters and photographers held themselves in readiness; television crews checked their wiring and sound equipment and their tripods.

At 3.45 p.m. that afternoon, the jury returned.

Judge Geernaert: 'Have you reached your verdict?'

Juror Foreman Garelick: 'Yes we have Your Honour.'

197

He handed the sheaf of papers to the judge upon which the jury had answered their questions. The judge read them to the court and in response to a defence counsel request, each individual member of the jury was polled to discover how he or she voted on each question, thus to establish the level of agreement among the jurors themselves. In the following list, which shows how the jury voted, figures in brackets show the actual votes cast.

[Part One of the questionnaire regarding plaintiff's claim against the estate of Rock Hudson for fraud, intentional misrepresentation.]

*Question No. 1:* At any time after Rock Hudson knew that he had AIDS, did plaintiff (Christian) and Rock Hudson have sexual relations of a type that put plaintiff at risk of acquiring AIDS (which is referred to as high-risk sex)?
*Answer:* Yes. (Unanimous verdict)

*Question No. 2:* Did Rock Hudson make a representation to plaintiff that he, Rock Hudson, did not have AIDS at any time between 8 June 1984 and the end of February 1985?
*Answer:* Yes. (Unanimous)

*Question No. 3:* Was the representation false?
*Answer:* Yes. (Unanimous)

*Question No. 4:* Did Rock Hudson know that the representation was false when he made it?
*Answer:* Yes. (Unanimous)

*Question No. 5:* Did Rock Hudson make that representation with an intent to induce plaintiff to have high-risk sexual relations with him?
*Answer:* Yes. (9 votes to 3)

*Question No. 6:* Was the plaintiff unaware of the falsity of the representation?
*Answer:* Yes. (Unanimous)

*Question No. 7:* Did plaintiff have high-risk sex with Rock Hudson in reliance on Rock Hudson's representation that he did not have AIDS?
*Answer:* Yes. (9-3)

*Question No. 8:* Was plaintiff reasonably justified in relying upon the representation made by Rock Hudson?
*Answer:* Yes. (11-1)

*Question No. 9:* Did the plaintiff suffer increased emotional distress because of an increased fear of AIDS as a proximate result of his reliance upon the truth of Rock Hudson's representation that he did not have AIDS?
*Answer:* Yes. (9-3)

[Part Two regarding plaintiff's claim against the estate of Rock Hudson for fraud, concealment]

*Question No. 10:* Did Rock Hudson conceal from the plaintiff the fact that he had AIDS?
*Answer:* Yes. (Unanimous)

*Question No. 11:* Was Rock Hudson under a duty to disclose that he had AIDS to plaintiff?
*Answer:* Yes. (Unanimous)

*Question No. 12:* Did Rock Hudson intentionally conceal the fact that he had AIDS with the intent to induce plaintiff to have high-risk sex with him?
*Answer:* Yes. (9-3)

*Question No. 13:* Between 8 June 1984 and the end of February 1985, was the plaintiff unaware of the concealment?
*Answer:* Yes. (Unanimous)

*Question No. 14:* Did plaintiff have high-risk sex with Rock Hudson at any time between 8 June 1984 and the end of February 1985 by reason of the concealment?
*Answer:* Yes. (Unanimous)

*Question No. 15:* Did the plaintiff suffer increased emotional distress because of an increased fear of AIDS as a proximate result of the concealment by Rock Hudson?
*Answer:* Yes. (Unanimous)

[Part Three regarding plaintiff's claim against the estate of Rock Hudson for infliction of emotional distress]

*Question No. 16:* Did Rock Hudson engage in outrageous conduct?
*Answer:* Yes. (Unanimous)

*Question No. 17:* Was such outrageous conduct done with either the intent to cause emotional distress or with reckless disregard of the probability of causing emotional distress to plaintiff?
*Answer:* Yes. (Unanimous)

*Question No. 18:* Did the plaintiff suffer severe increased emotional distress?
*Answer:* Yes. (Unanimous)

*Question No. 19:* Was the outrageous conduct of Rock Hudson the proximate cause of the increased emotional distress suffered by the plaintiff?
*Answer:* Yes. (11-1)

[Part Four regarding plaintiff's claim against Mark Miller for fraud, intentional misrepresentation]

*Question No. 20:* After Mark Miller knew that Rock Hudson had AIDS, did Mark Miller know that plaintiff and Rock Hudson were having sexual relations of a type that put plaintiff at risk of acquiring AIDS?
*Answer:* Yes. (Unanimous)

*Question No. 21:* Did Mark Miller make a representation to plaintiff that Rock Hudson did not have AIDS at any time between 8 June 1984 and the end of February 1985?
*Answer:* Yes. (Unanimous)

*Question No. 22:* Was the representation false?
*Answer:* Yes. (Unanimous)

*Question No. 23:* Did Mark Miller know that the representation was false when he made it?
*Answer:* Yes. (Unanimous)

*Question No. 24:* Did Mark Miller make the representation with an intent to induce plaintiff to have high-risk relations with Rock Hudson?
*Answer:* Yes. (11-1)

*Question No. 25:* Was the plaintiff unaware of the falsity of the representation?
*Answer:* Yes. (Unanimous)

*Question No. 26:* Did plaintiff have high-risk sex with Rock Hudson in reliance on Mark Miller's representation that Rock Hudson did not have AIDS?
*Answer:* Yes. (11-1)

*Question No. 27:* Was plaintiff reasonably justified in relying upon the representations made by Mark Miller?
*Answer:* Yes. (11-1)

*Question No. 28:* Did the plaintiff suffer increased emotional distress because of an increased fear of AIDS as a proximate result of his reliance upon the truth of Mark Miller's representation that Rock Hudson did not have AIDS?
*Answer:* Yes. (10-2)

[Part Five regarding plaintiff's claim that Mark Miller conspired to commit fraud, concealment]

*Question No. 29:* Did Mark Miller conspire with Rock Hudson to conceal from plaintiff the fact that Rock Hudson had AIDS with the intent to induce plaintiff to have high-risk sex with Rock Hudson?
*Answer:* Yes. (11-1)

*Question No. 30:* Between 8 June 1984 and the end of February 1985, was the plaintiff unaware of the concealment?
*Answer:* Yes. (Unanimous)

*Question No. 31:* Did plaintiff have high-risk sex with Rock Hudson at any time between 8 June 1984 and the end of February 1985 which he would not have had except for the concealment?
*Answer:* Yes. (11-1)

*Question No. 32:* Did the plaintiff suffer increased emotional distress because of an increased fear of AIDS as a proximate result of that concealment by Mark Miller?
*Answer:* Yes. (10-2)

[Part Six regarding plaintiff's claim against Mark Miller for infliction of emotional distress]

*Question No. 33:* Did Mark Miller engage in outrageous conduct?
*Answer:* Yes. (Unanimous)

*Question No. 34:* Was such outrageous conduct done with either the intent to cause emotional distress or with reckless disregard of the probability of causing emotional distress to plaintiff?
*Answer:* Yes. (Unanimous)

*Question No. 35:* Did the plaintiff suffer severe increased emotional distress?
*Answer:* Yes. (Unanimous)

*Question No. 36:* Was the outrageous conduct of Mark Miller the proximate cause of the increased emotional distress suffered by the plaintiff?
*Answer:* Yes. (Unanimous)

*Question No. 37:* What is the total amount of damages suffered by the plaintiff for increased emotional distress proximately caused by the conduct of Rock Hudson or Mark Miller?
*Answer:* $14,500. (9-12)

The Foreman (Juror Garelick): 'That's not right.'
The judge: 'May I have that?'
The judge: 'I'm going to ask you – then, is it stipulated that
the general murmur from the jury indicates that they want to
correct the figure? It is $14,500 as written. I suggest that we
stipulate that they retire to the jury room, and complete the
question as nine of the twelve agree. If you will kindly do
that, then.'
(*The jury retired briefly and returned with their amended form.*)
The judge: 'All right, Mr Foreman, may I please have
the verdict form again.'
*Question No. 37:* What is the total amount of damages
suffered by the plaintiff for increased emotional distress
proximately caused by the conduct of Rock Hudson or
Mark Miller?
*Answer:* $14,500,000. (10-2)
*Dated:* 15 February 1989.
*Signed:* Charles Garelick, Foreperson


Marc Christian and Harold Rhoden shook hands in elation.
Fourteen and a half million dollars was beyond their wildest
dreams. Of that there was no question. Friends would rush to
congratulate him; newsmen and television cameras would crowd
around to get his comments. The scenes for Christian were jubilant;
never had he imagined such an outcome, though he would never
say as much.
The defence and Mark Miller were left desolate and dejected.
And their misery had not yet ended. After the jury deliverance,
Judge Geernaert reminded them that they had adjudicated upon
only the first phase of the trial, to establish Christian's claim for
compensatory damages. They now had to consider whether an
award for punitive damages should also be made . . . and for that,
they were asked to re-assemble the following day to hear counsel's
pleadings.

# CHAPTER FIFTEEN

# The Jury's Message

It would be understandable if Mark Miller was now facing the remainder of the trial with his own fear and apprehension because the question of punitive and exemplary damages was going to be a vital one to him personally. He alone would have to face the final outcome. As Judge Geernaert reminded the jury as the second phase of the trial began on 16 February, the law did not allow for damages of this nature to be awarded against the estate of a deceased person. Therefore, Miller himself would become the sole bearer of the burden.

He was called once more before the jury to answer questions on his assets. He told of his joint ownership of his homes in Palm Springs and Hawaii with George Nader and reckoned that his net assets were in the region of $100,000. He had not received any money from Hudson's estate nor did he know when this was likely to be disbursed. He could not give any information about Hudson's will or how he would eventually benefit from it because it had been sealed in probate.

As in the first part of the trial, counsel were given the opportunity of making their arguments and submissions to the jury. Harold Rhoden came first, clearly as pleased as punch and going as far as he was able to express his thanks. He told them: 'That magnificent verdict that you brought in yesterday was for compensatory damages only. The law does not allow a lawyer standing here in this situation to do any thanking of any jury for a previous verdict. Therefore, I shall not make any comment of any kind now.'

He said the jury's decision had decided two vital issues:

1) that there was a duty to warn. The jury had made that clear and they could be sure the world had heard it.

2) They said, by that decision, that in breaching that duty to warn – even if the lover of the partner who had AIDS did not get or hadn't got it yet – the fear of getting it was compensable.

There was another thing they had established, though it was not mentioned on the verdict form. It was that a homosexual could get a fair trial. 'Whoever said he can't is all wet,' said Rhoden (seemingly unconcerned that it was he who had raised the issue of bigotry against homosexuals in the first place). 'He did get a fair trial here and in doing that you did a great deal.'

Now there was something else to be done. In bringing this action, Marc Christian sought compensation for what was done to him. The jury had settled that; now the hearing concerned something which was radically different; punitive and exemplary damages and that was a question of law. Christian was not important in this argument. It was for the lawyers to make their case. Of course, Christian was involved in it; so was Mark Miller but it concerned others, too, and this was an aspect, Rhoden submitted, the jury may not have thought about.

He told them: 'There are countless millions of people who are involved, people who might benefit from your verdict if it makes an example of Mark Miller. I say millions because I can't know the number. It would be other people in the world in Marc Christian's position.' From that standpoint, the decision the jury was now being called upon to make was more important than the first.

He likened the punitive and exemplary damages to the two sides of a coin. On the one side was punitive damages which were awarded to punish someone who had done a grave wrong, such as the conduct of Miller whom the jury had decided was guilty of outrageous conduct not to be tolerated in a civilized society. The other side of the coin was exemplary damages – which meant setting an example – for which Rhoden chose to remind the jury of Andrew Banks's submission when he said: 'If you bring in a verdict against Mr Miller, that would be a message to the whole community that nobody must ever dare to keep a secret for a friend because they could be sued.'

That, said Rhoden, was an untrue statement. He gave his own example of a man who had AIDS telling his sister that he had it, but asked her not to tell their parents. She promised not to tell; there was nothing wrong with that. It was honourable and decent. That was not the message a verdict against Miller would give. The ones to be protected were those who could be infected.

They were the people entitled to be warned and the jury's message could only be this: 'There is a duty to warn on the part of anybody who has got AIDS; a duty to warn anyone he may infect or whom he may already have infected. Because the chain could be endless, involving homosexuals, heterosexuals, men, women and even unborn babies. Anyone with that knowledge has a duty to warn. You, the jury has said so.'

The jury had it within its power to say this kind of conduct of withholding such vital information ought to stop and they could help stop it. It was a violation of rights that was at issue and once again he gave an example: A man discovered he had AIDS but did not want to tell his girlfriend because he wanted to continue to enjoy sex with her. So he tells his doctor whom he has put in his will that he does not want the girlfriend to find out that he has AIDS. The doctor agrees to keep his secret and they continue having sex. She gets the virus and spreads it to others; they get it and spread it further.

The jury might say: 'Now, come on, nobody is going to do a thing like that.' No? Well for argument's sake, said Rhoden, call the doctor Mark Miller and the woman Marc Christian and there was the case. It was despicable conduct on Miller's part tinged with malice, said Rhoden. But how could that affect the future?

It was a simple transference of example to others that the jury was able to initiate. If the case of the doctor and the man with a girlfriend had happened *after* Marc Christian won $14.5 million from the estate of Rock Hudson, the doctor would have said: 'Hold on, I can't do that. I can't keep that secret.' The girlfriend had got to be told. That, said Rhoden, was how the example worked. That was how other people would benefit from it.

Rhoden: 'You, the jury, are the message senders and if you bring in a verdict that is just a slap on the wrist for Miller, the message isn't going to get anywhere. But if you bring in a verdict, like yesterday's, you can know that the whole world is going to take notice of it. This is a verdict to help others, by making an example of Mark Miller. Who are the others. Thousands? Hundreds of thousands? Millions? I can't tell you the number. I don't know how many people could now or will be in Marc Christian's position. But obviously, it could be millions of people all over the world, not just today or tomorrow but in the future. These are the people whom you have the opportunity to do more than just help.'

Rhoden's plea became more emotional as he went on with a

statement that some court observers felt was over the top, even for him: 'Let's face it. We all have only a limited time on this earth. If some people have the opportunity to help others, they're lucky at any time in their lives. If some people have the opportunity to save lives, or even the life of just one person, they must be among a fortunate few. But if by accident, by having your name drawn out of a box somewhere and you find you have the opportunity of bringing in a verdict that could save lives of untold millions, surely you must be blessed. These people whom you've saved are people who will never thank you. They'll never know your names. They may never know you did this, that you set this example. But you will know. Frankly, I wish I could sit where you are and have that opportunity.'

Now Rhoden came to the crux of his speech: how far that message would travel depended upon how effective it was. The amount. That's what mattered. Miller had shown he did not care what happened to Marc Christian. His conduct was reprehensible and the jury had demonstrated that by awarding Christian $14.5 million. It was a figure they had placed on his claim for compensation and now they had to work out the deterrent for others.

In Rhoden's view, the jury should at least bring in a verdict equal to the first. At least $14.5 million. Not just to punish Miller . . . but to send from the courtroom a message that would benefit other people by the example they set. 'I suggested to you that the verdict you brought in was magnificent. It was. I now suggest that the verdict you're about to consider could well be sublime. Thank you.'

Clearly, the jury was impressed. Rhoden was a difficult act to follow and Andrew Banks rose to make his final speech on behalf of Mark Miller: 'I remember the words of my father when I was a young boy: "You don't tug on Superman's cape and you don't spit in the wind." It's in a song. And quite frankly, I feel like I am standing here before Superman and I'm being asked to tug on Superman's cape and I'm not going to take my father's advice. I'm going to tug a little bit.'

There was, said Banks, an empty chair, still between where he had been sitting and Marc Christian. He had put it there not because he did not like Christian but because he wanted it to symbolize something: the person who was not in court, the man who did have sex with Marc Christian; the man who could not be present, Rock Hudson.

The jury had made their decision; they had been heard. Fourteen and a half million dollars was a very loud message that had been sent and there was no doubt in his mind that it had been heard. But message sending was not the purpose of this portion of the trial.

It was to consider Mark Miller as an individual. Rock Hudson and his estate were out of it. They had heard Miller testify that he had a net worth of less than $100,000, and he has a verdict against him of $14.5 million. That was one heck of a deep hole to be into. He now had a negative worth; he was not a wealthy man nor a person who could start life over again. He was sixty-two years old and faced this enormous judgment against him. There was no need to harm him further with any punitive damages because they had already taken everything he had. The jury had taken his entire net worth assets. Their purpose was not to be mean-spirited or evil and if they wanted to send a message, as Harold Rhoden suggested, they had already done that.

Miller, he said, had not acted out of malice and it was he who had instigated the first medical examination of Christian and it was he who went in to bat for him to make sure he retained kitchen privileges at the Hudson house. Miller had made some decisions with which perhaps the jury did not agree. But he was in the firing line; he did the best job he could. There was no real use or purpose in trying now to say what he should or should not have done back in 1984. It was easy to be a Monday morning quarterback, but there was a higher standard on which the jury now had to make its judgment. There were many mitigating factors which should be taken into account.

Banks insisted: 'You are going to hear [from the judge] that the purpose [of your verdict] is to have a deterrent effect on the defendant in the light of the defendant's financial condition. But [bear in mind] he is not the man who's dead, he's not the one who had an estate, he's not the man who had sex with Marc Christian. He's one step removed from all this and in a very difficult position.'

Banks concluded his submissions and as with the first phase of the trial, Harold Rhoden was entitled to come back to answer any points that had been raised. He began on that course, and immediately brought the trial to a halt with heavy objections from Banks.

Rhoden, speaking directly to the jury, said: 'Mr Banks told you that Miller has nothing left. He told you that yesterday's verdict wiped him out. He told you that Miller now has a negative worth of $14.5 million. There is not only no evidence of this, it is simply not true. I cannot here – I don't have the right because it's not in evidence – argue the consequences of that verdict. But the idea that he is going to pay is simply false. . . . '

Banks: 'Your Honour. I object.'

The judge: 'Just a moment – Okay, I'm going to have to talk to counsel for a moment.'

They retired to the judge's chambers again, out of jury hearing. There, the judge pointed out that they had a problem. Firstly, Mr Banks had gone beyond the evidence by suggesting his client had been wiped out financially. There was no evidence of that at all. It was a joint and several judgment which the jury knew nothing about; the question of who paid the $14.5 million had probably not been sorted out and Banks had created a situation which needed to be clarified. Mr Rhoden, he said, had obviously been referring to insurance cover when he intimated that Miller would not have to pay the first judgment.

Rhoden: 'Yes, Your Honour. I don't want to mention insurance, I can't. But the truth is, there is a carrier on the estate that will pay this judgment.'

Banks: 'A carrier won't pay punitive damages.'

Rhoden: 'Miller isn't going to pay a dime of it.'

John Schroeder, co-counsel with Banks: 'That's not true.'

Banks: 'The law is quite clear. Punitive damages are never covered by insurance. The law is also quite clear that either defendant may get up and argue his net worth. He has $100,000. Mr Rhoden kept the value of the estate out of the trial when His Honour upheld an objection to that evidence and so the jury were never able to be told that the value of the estate is worth between $7.5 and $8 million.'

The judge: 'All sorts of things can happen between now and collection of the judgment. . . . '

Banks: 'But you can't get into that. You have to say [in court] what you have done. . . . '

The judge: 'You got into it.

'Let's clarify. There's certainly nothing wrong with pointing out the $100,000 net worth. That is one of the factors that the jury will be instructed they should consider. And if you had limited it to that there would be no cause for argument . . . but what you did is open up a subject that is not in evidence. To fully inform the jury of this we would have to tell them all the legal procedures . . . it opens up a lot of ancilliary things that are not in evidence. It is certainly not proper – and I am going to have to strike it – for them to consider any insurance coverage. I am going to have to strike the comment that Mr Rhoden made that he will never have to pay . . . .'

Banks: 'He raised the entire issue of who pays . . . I move for a mis-trial on the grounds of improper argument of counsel.'

The judge: 'The problem is that he [Mr Rhoden] was responding to Mr Banks's statement on negative net worth.'

Banks: 'Which is an obvious inference from a verdict of $14.5 million and a net worth of under $100,000.'

The judge: 'It isn't that at all. Not even close to an overall analysis . . . this does not warrant the granting of a mis-trial. But what I am going to do is strike the comments by Mr Rhoden and Mr Banks as to the effect of this net worth on the judgment.'

Andrew Banks was not satisfied. He reiterated his objections and warned that it was a fraught situation that might have repercussions on appeal.

Judge Geernaert noted his objections and moved to return to open court where he proceeded to instruct the jury to disregard all comments about Miller's negative net worth.

Harold Rhoden continued with his attempt to demolish the submissions of his rivals and insisted that Miller had by his very actions deprived Christian of the right to know that Hudson had AIDS. It could have caused quite an injury. Death. Which it might still cause. He concluded, 'I ask you to bring in a verdict that will make an example of Miller for the people you'll never know. And I ask you that you cause a headline: 'Rock Hudson Jury Does It Again'. You do that and boy oh boy, you will send a message.'

Judge Geernaert added his own instructions and ended with a simple assessment of the task that the jury had to perform without passion or prejudice: 'You must consider the reprehensibility of the defendant's conduct, the amount of punitive damages which have a deterrent effect in the light of his financial condition and thus arrive at the amount of actual damages.'

Once again, members of the jury were provided with a special verdict form to help them arrive at their decision. They retired at mid-day on 16 February and returned at 9 a.m. the following morning to announce they had reached their verdict.

*Question No. 1:* Do you find by clear and convincing evidence that the defendant Miller did intend to cause injury to the plaintiff by his conduct?
*Answer:* Yes. (11-1)

*Question No. 2:* Do you find by clear and convincing evidence that the defendant Miller acted with a wilful and conscious disregard for the rights or safety of the plaintiff?
*Answer:* Yes. (Unanimous)

*Question No. 3:* Do you find by clear and convincing evidence that defendant Miller's fraudulent conduct was done by defendant Miller with the intention on the part of defendant Miller of thereby depriving plaintiff of a legal right or otherwise causing injury to plaintiff?
*Answer:* Yes. (Unanimous)

*Question No. 4:* What is the amount of punitive or exemplary damages, if any, which you assess against defendant Miller?
*Answer:* $7,250,000. (10-2)
*Dated:* 17 February 1989
*Signed:* Charles Garelick, Jury Foreperson.

The trial had reached a sensational climax; a huge cash award beyond anyone's expectations. The judge thanked the jury and told them that the court and society was indebted to them. Marc Christian's smile had grown by several inches. They had awarded him, by way of these two verdicts, a total of $21.75 million.

But as they walked from the courtroom at 10.30 a.m. that Friday, 17 February Harold Rhoden struck a note of caution: 'Don't spend it, yet!'

# Epilogue

The furore burst in headlines around the world. The mere extent of the damages awarded to Marc Christian was in itself sufficient to secure fever-pitch press and television coverage. If, as Harold Rhoden suggested, the jury wanted to send a message, they had certainly achieved that. But with it came outrage, especially from gay community leaders who were ferocious in their attacks on the verdict and seemed to be at one in the view that once again, AIDS sufferers were being pilloried.

They said the trial had inspired a new wave of hostile public reaction to an already distraught group of people; the verdict would merely bring them further unwarranted persecution and heartache at the very time when they needed care, sympathy and support. To be gay was not a crime; to be infected by AIDS was the dreadful and accidental result of liaisons which, in their view, were as natural as any heterosexual relationship. The gay community had cleaned up its act and had reacted more responsibly than most to the public campaigns for safer sex.

For one thing, they had been universally terrified by the prospect of picking up the virus and precautionary measures were widespread. There could be few gays left in 1989 who had not put into practice the guidelines for safe sex issued by the American Surgeon-General, the British Government's Health Department and similar governmental and health organizations the world over. But the gay community would continue to be the greatest sufferers and the high-risk members of society because the virus implanted in their midst, as everyone now knows, can take five or ten years to materialize and world health experts are fearfully anticipating another explosion of sufferers in the early 1990s.

212

If Mark Miller and the estate of Rock Hudson were to be made an example in the adjudication of damages, then it seemed to follow that homosexuals in general, and those with AIDS in particular, would be similarly treated at a time when the virus had long since crossed the boundaries of the gay community and was engulfing huge sections of the community, gay and otherwise. The verdict had also established untold implications for AIDS sufferers – homosexual or not – and perhaps for those with other serious diseases. Though many conceded that such a drastic example of 'the right to know' would be difficult to imagine again, public awareness and appreciation of the disease and its dormancy problems had moved on substantially since the early days when Hudson was first told.

But the stigma was still there and the reactions to the award granted to Marc Christian indicated once more the intense emotions of those at the heart of the AIDS problem, whether they were partners or sufferers, AIDS counsellors, or those devoted people who spend their lives caring for an ever-increasing group of desolate souls. What happened in the Hudson trial could be just the start of it.

Gay rights leaders believe that AIDS is set to become one of the great human rights issues of the next decade. There is already substantial evidence of world-wide police harassment of gays and gay clubs and bars; almost thirty countries have already introduced travel restrictions on known HIV positive cases.

The evidence emerging from the trial of Marc Christian's lawsuit, though tame compared with some stories, was music to the ears of the anti-gay lobby, even though it was a double-edged sword which vilified one homosexual and gave the other $21.75 million.

Harold Rhoden was man enough to admit to the author soon after the trial that he personally thought the award was excessive. He was still 'thinking in terms of millions' and he knew he still had a fight on his hands. As Marc Christian came from court on that day in February, Rhoden told him the battle was not won yet. The defence immediately lodged an appeal for a mis-trial and a knock-down of the damages.

In the meantime, Christian had become something of a media star and the television talk-show producers and magazine interviewers went quickly to their telephones to book him. The following week, on 27 February, he and Rhoden appeared on the coast-to-coast television current affairs talk-show, 'Donahue', one of the pro-grammes that Marvin Mitchelson had taken him on soon after launching his lawsuit.

Phil Donahue, a brusque and tough host whose style and very direct approach has made his show one of the top-rated talk shows in America, summed up the mood of the moment and the implications as he asked his audience: 'Anguish? If your husband had Herpes and he never told you, you'd kill him. But you don't have it . . . and Marc Christian does not have AIDS but the jury has given him more money than he ever thought of asking for. And this is Harold Rhoden, Mr Christian's attorney. Boy, are you hot. Wow! The phone must be ringing at your office. No kidding.'

Donahue, like a courtroom lawyer cross-examining the witness, fires the questions his audience wants to hear: 'Tell us the story – this is more than a passing interest to Americans. I mean, was there a guy in the whole white world with more sex appeal than Rock Hudson. And Holy Cow! He's gay. So now we know, and while we are trying to recover from that, we discover he had AIDS. And he never even came out of the closet did he?'

Christian's answers were brief, because Donahue is the star of the show. He tells the audience that by the time Rock collapsed in Paris, he had no short-term memory; so he never knew that the world knew he had AIDS. He died still believing that only a handful of people knew. As a matter of fact, said Marc, when Sara Davidson, the author, was doing her book with Hudson, he had inquired of Christian: 'Who is she? Is she one of the nurses?' That was an illustration of the state he was in, and no, he never did come out of the closet.

Christian is off and running again and picks up the story of Rock's love for him and agrees with Donahue's explanation for his audience that Hudson's love was not the kind the voyeurs describe in relation to the gay world; it was a love that was very like that of a man and a woman, only the plumbing was different.

Then Donahue turns to the legal implications about which there had been so much controversy and posed the question of a drunk driver whose perilous actions bring terror to his passengers, though no one was killed. Could the passengers sue for the fear that they had endured? No, said Rhoden. That was not an acceptable metaphor because the people who got into the car must have known he'd had a few drinks; it couldn't have been concealed from them as Hudson concealed his illness.

And what about the wife whose husband had Herpes and didn't tell her? No, again. Syphilis, gonorrhea, any of those diseases did not kill; they could be cured with a shot. AIDS was different. It kills and people were entitled to know if they risked a death sentence. What about doctors? Did they have a duty to tell? Yes, said Rhoden, and he had even thought of filing a suit against a certain doctor who told Hudson: 'You'd better not tell your lover because it might upset him.' The only reason he did not sue was because the information came only from Mark Miller, in his testimony, and since Rhoden could not believe Miller, he could not in good conscience serve the doctor with a writ.

The discussion goes on; someone says it was the same as a lawyer whose client tells him he is going to murder someone. The lawyer had a duty to warn the victim or the police, or someone. 'Wow,' said Donahue. 'We're really in wa-wa land now. What happened to confidentiality.' It was a question of balancing obligation, Rhoden replied.

There were many irate phone-in callers to the Donahue show that day, some supportive, some castigating Christian; others followed the line of recent protest that at the end of the day, the only people who would suffer as a result of the verdict was the gay community. It seemed to be a typical cross-section reaction that displayed, in the main, an underlying lack of acceptance by the masses towards gay activity; and thus, presumably, it will always be.

Christian did not help their cause when he told the questioners that he was fed up with men. 'Just ask any woman out there . . . they'll know what I'm talking about.' He said he had never been with anyone since Hudson and he didn't know when he would feel able to have sex again. He never waivered. The cool manner he had displayed in the previous seven weeks remained.

Privately, the facade slipped a few days later when he learned from Harold Rhoden that the defence had come up with some damaging new evidence and they were pressing hard for a new trial. There were also rumours that the defence would be claiming misconduct among certain members of the jury. So now, there were doubts that Christian would ever see his $21.75 million.

Indeed, they were all called back to the Los Angeles Superior Court before Judge Geernaert on 7 April 1989. The defence team of Robert Mills and Andrew Banks had been working hard; they presented a three-pronged attack, claiming the jury's original

215

award had been excessive, that they had since obtained evidence that Christian had sex with another man in 1985 and that two members of the jury might have adversely affected the majority decision.

The defence produced in support of these claims a sworn statement from Gunther Albert Fraulob, a physical-training instructor from Orange County who claimed he had been intimate with Christian soon after Hudson's death. This proved, said the defence, that Christian could not have been concerned even then about the possibility of having AIDS.

Further, their misconduct claim alleged that one juror had a friend who had died of AIDS and had shared her knowledge of that case with other members of the jury and another juror had confided to the rest that she was 'prejudiced' against rich people. The judge commented that he felt these matters had undoubtedly been influenced by the 'almost hysterical response in the media immediately after the jury's verdict.'

It was a fact that after the trial ended, several members of the jury were approached by the press for interviews and it became clear that the $14.5 million decision had been a compromise decision; some members of the jury had voted for $20 million in compensation, others suggested $10 million. One had even gone as low as $3 million. Lawyers in the case also spoke to some of them, and Christian himself admitted having had conversation with five members of the jury. None of that held sway with Judge Geernaert, though he did say he was contemplating reducing the amount of the damages which he agreed were too high.

He reserved his final judgment for further consideration and on 21 April, the case and its protagonists returned to the courtroom to hear his verdict: Motion for a mis-trial was denied; the sworn statement of Gunther Fraulob presented by the defence would not have affected the outcome of the trial. And he ruled as 'not credible' the claim of juror misconduct.

As to damages, he had decided to reduce the compensatory award from $14.5 million to $5 million and the punitive award from $7.25 million to $500,000, the latter reflecting Miller's financial condition which was an element that should be taken into account when setting the amount of damages.

The beaming smile which displayed the gleaming white teeth that Rock Hudson paid to have fixed, had slipped from Christian's now sombre face. He was still a rich man of course, but somehow

$5.5 million didn't have the same kind of ring to it. That night, the author spoke to Harold Rhoden about the reduction. He was not dispirited: 'Naturally, I would have liked more. Ten, maybe. But it's still a good result. Before we went in today, I told Marc the judge would knock it down. We knew that. It was too high. But my view was that so long as it remained in the millions, it would be a fair outcome. It remains a very loud message. And that's what we wanted, so that no one in Rock Hudson's position will ever do this kind of thing again.'

Rhoden himself had so far received no recompense for his two years of work on the case; he will be paid his percentage when the money finally comes through and there could still be a long wait if the defence proceeds to the higher courts of appeal. The donation from Hudson's trust fund to actors' charities would not be affected by the award. Rhoden explained that Hudson was well covered by liability insurance and it was the insurers who had forced the case to go to court. They would have to pick up the expense of costs and compensatory damages while Miller himself will have to pay the punitive damages.

Meanwhile, the dreaded virus which was at the root of this sensational case marches on, leaving more scavenged bodies in its wake. The projections for the future are frightening and they are perhaps best demonstrated by these simple statistics: during the weeks of the trial of Marc Christian versus the estate of Rock Hudson and Mark Miller, 1061 people in America died of AIDS, 4443 new cases were reported and as of 20 February 1989, 87,188 Americans were known to be suffering from it. One million four hundred thousand are thought to have it but don't know they've got it, yet.

Marc Christian does not have AIDS. But he does have five and a half million dollars.

# Select Bibliography

Brode, Douglas. *The Films of the Fifties*; Citadel Press, New Jersey, 1976.

Davis, Professor Ronald L. 'Rock Hudson interview'; taped and transcribed for Southern Methodist University, Dallas, Texas, 1983. And with Paul F. Boller Jr, Hollywood Anecdotes; Macmillan, London, 1988.

Day, Doris, with A.E. Hotchner. *Doris Day, Her Own Story*; Star Books edition, London, 1988.

Friedrich, Otto. *City of Nets*; Headline Books edition, London, 1987.

Gates, Phyllis, and Bob Thomas. *My Husband, Rock Hudson*; Angus and Robertson, London, 1987.

Hudson, Rock and Sara Davidson. *Rock Hudson: His Story*; Batam edition, London, 1986.

Oppenheimer, Jerry and Jack Vitek. *Idol: The Unauthorised Biography of Rock Hudson*; Villard Books, New York, 1986.

Parker, John. *Five For Hollywood*; Macmillan, London, 1989.

Peary, Danny. *Close-up: The Movie Star Book*; Simon and Schuster, New York, 1988.

Sheppard, Dick, *Elizabeth: The Life and Career of Elizabeth Taylor*; Doubleday, New York, 1974.

# INDEX